WILD FRANCE

EDITED BY

DOUGLAS BOTTING

SIERRA CLUB BOOKS

SAN FRANCISCO

Published in the United States by Sierra Club Books,
San Francisco, 1994

Designed and produced by
Sheldrake Press,
188 Cavendish Road,
London SW12 0DA

Copyright © 1992 Sheldrake Publishing Ltd

Wild France / edited by Douglas Botting.
    224p. 21.0 x 14.9cm.
    Includes bibliographical references and index.
    ISBN 0-87156-476-9
    1. Natural history—France—Guidebooks.
    2. France—Guidebooks.
    I. Botting, Douglas.
    QH147.W55   1994
    508.44—dc20   93-28771
                                                  CIP

Printed in Spain by Imago

EDITOR-IN-CHIEF: Simon Rigge
Managing Editor: Malcolm Day
Editor: Lisa Cussans
Picture Editor: Karin B. Hills
Art Direction and Book Design: Bob Hook, Ivor
Claydon
Consultant: David Stubbs
Assistant Editors: Roger Boulanger, Sean Connolly,
Judith Harte, Anita Peltonen, Chris Schüler, Caroline
Smith
Editorial Assistants: Tracey Stead, Sarah Tudge
Picture Researchers: Eleanor Lines, Elizabeth Loving
Production Manager: Hugh Allan
Production Controller: Rebecca Bone
Maps: Swanston Graphics Ltd, Donna Dailey
Index: Indexing Specialists

THE GENERAL EDITOR

DOUGLAS BOTTING was born in London
and educated at Oxford. He has travelled to
the Amazon, South Yemen, the Sahara,
Arctic Siberia, to many parts of Africa and to
many European wild places.

Douglas Botting's travel books include *One
Chilly Siberian Morning, Wilderness Europe*
and *Rio de Janeiro*. He has also written a
biography of the great naturalist and explorer
Alexander von Humboldt, entitled *Humboldt
and the Cosmos*. He has recently returned
from a second expedition to the rarely-visited
Arabian island of Socotra.

CONTRIBUTORS

MICK HAMER wrote the chapters on
Brittany and Normandy, the Alps, Central
France, and the Loire and Burgundy. He is a
journalist, writer and environmentalist and,
in addition to contributing to many national
newspapers and magazines, has worked for
several years for Friends of the Earth.

ROBIN NEILLANDS, who wrote the chapter
on the Pyrenees, is a journalist, travel writer
and author of over 40 books. In his travels he
has canoed down the Zambezi, cycled from
Turkey to Jerusalem and walked across France
from the Channel to the Mediterranean. He
has a home in Spain.

ANDREW SANGER wrote the chapter on the
Western Mediterranean. He studied at the
French Lycée in London and went on to travel
world-wide, returning to live for a number of
years in Languedoc. He is the author of several
travel books and a frequent contributor to the
travel pages of many national newspapers.

KEITH SPENCE wrote the chapter on the
Atlantic Coast, and specializes in travel, the
environment and conservation. A regular
contributor to major national newspapers and
magazines, he is particularly concerned with
increasing public interest in the environment
through local museums and project work.

DAVID STUBBS wrote the chapter on the
Eastern Mediterranean and Corsica. He is an
ecologist who has been involved in a wide
variety of wildlife projects throughout Europe,
particularly in France. He now works as a
consultant specializing in ecological surveys,
wildlife habitat assessments and conservation.
He is the author of several scientific papers
and magazine articles and has broadcast on
TV and radio in Britain and France. He was
the overall consultant for *Wild France*.

GILLIAN THOMAS wrote the chapter on
Northeastern France. She is a travel writer
and a regular contributor to national
newspapers and magazines in Britain. Having
studied languages at university, she worked
for the BBC in its Paris news office. She has
long been concerned about environmental
issues about which she writes regularly for
The Times Educational Supplement.

CONTENTS

ABOUT THE SERIES

What would the world be, once bereft
Of wet and of wilderness? Let them be
  left,
O let them be left, wildness and wet;
Long live the weeds and the wilderness
  yet.

Gerard Manley Hopkins: Inversnaid

These books are about those embattled
refuges of wildness and wet: the wild
places of Europe. But where, in this most
densely populated sub-continent, do we
find a truly wild place?

Ever since our Cro-Magnon ancestors
began their forays into the virgin forests of
Europe 40,000 years ago, the land and its
creatures have been in retreat before
Homo sapiens. Forests have been cleared,
marshes drained and rivers straightened:
even some of those landscapes that appear
primordial are in fact the result of human
activity. Heather-covered moorland in
North Yorkshire and parched Andalucian
desert have this in common: both were
once covered by great forests which
ancient settlers knocked flat.

What then remains that can be called
wild? There are still a few areas in Europe
that are untouched by man – places
generally so unwelcoming either in terrain
or in climate that man has not wanted to
touch them at all. These are indisputably
wild.

For some people, wildness suggests
conflict with nature: a wild place is a part
of the planet so savage and desolate that
you risk your life whenever you venture
into it. This is in part true but would limit
the eligible places to the most
impenetrable bog or highest mountain
tops in the worst winter weather – a rather
restricted view. Another much broader
definition considers a wild place to be a
part of the planet where living things can
find a natural refuge from the influence of
modern industrial society. By this
definition a wild place is for wildlife as
well as that portmanteau figure referred to
in these pages as the wild travellers: the

hill walker, backpacker, birdwatcher,
nature lover, explorer, nomad, loner,
mystic, masochist, afficionado of the great
outdoors, or permutations of all these
things.

This is the definition we have observed
in selecting the wild places described in
these books. Choosing them has not been
easy. Even so, we hope the criterion has
proved rigid enough to exclude purely
pretty (though popular) countryside, and
flexible enough to include the greener,
gentler wild places, of great natural
historical interest perhaps, as well as the
starker, more savage ones where the wild
explorers come into their own.

These are not guide books in the
conventional sense, for to decribe every
neck of the woods and twist of the trail
throughout Europe would require a
library of volumes. Nor are these books
addressed to the technical specialst – the
caver, diver, rock climber or cross-country
skier, the orchid-hunter, lepidopterist or
beetlemaniac – for such experts will have
reference data of their own. They are
books intended for the general outdoor
traveller – including the expert outside his
field of expertise (the orchid-hunter in a
cave, the diver on a mountain top) – who
wishes to scrutinize the range of wild
places on offer in Europe, to learn a little
more about them and to set about
exploring them off the beaten track.

One of the great consolations in the
preparation of these books has been to
find that after 40,000 years of hunting,
clearing, draining and ploughing, Cro-
Magnon and their descendants have left so
much of Europe that can still be defined
as wild.

Douglas Botting

WILD FRANCE: AN INTRODUCTION

France is a country that has the best of both worlds—sophisticated civilisation and vast expanses of wild terrain. In spite of being a thoroughly modern nation, it has preserved much of its traditional rural landscape. Like everywhere in Europe, nature is continually retreating in the face of development, but in a country over twice as large as the United Kingdom, supporting roughly the same number of people, France still provides welcome respite for those in search of timeless countryside and relatively untouched wild places. Fast, efficient communications take us from one bustling centre to another, but in between lies the rural charm of a much quieter existence—and a great reservoir of much of Europe's precious wildlife.

This mixture of old and new, wild and developed, makes France a very accessible country, well laid out for the traveller's convenience. However, the very accessibility of the countryside renders it at times alarmingly vulnerable in the mind of the conservationist. One of the great joys of France is the freedom to wander off into the wild places, to 'take to the maquis' and forget about mankind. To walk for hours through stately forests or across Provençal hills cloaked in thorny *garrigue*, is to experience an environment that has existed for centuries. Wild places, be they mountain tops or marshes, are the lungs of a nation. They provide space and respite. They offer a sense of balance and perspective, and the satisfaction of knowing that, for all the centuries of human activity, nature still thrives as abundantly as ever.

In France, as elsewhere in Europe, however, there are few places that are totally natural or free of any history of human influence. All the great forests have been managed, for timber or hunting or even for browsing livestock. Wetlands are controlled, grasslands cut or grazed, crops are grown, but all in a sustainable, small-scale manner. The French farmers have retained their ancestral landscape of small fields, thick hedges, wooded hills and meandering rivers. Indeed, the French landscape is one of tradition, of harmonious co-existence. From the *bocage* country of Normandy, across sparsely populated central France to the Mediterranean hills of cork oak forests and olive groves, one still gets the impression that nature reigns and man simply harvests.

Elsewhere, however, are to be found huge prairie fields, the intensive farmland of the latter 20th century. Here it is man who dominates and nature that is reduced to a mere fragment of its former glory. But even in the industrial north-east or in the heavily cultivated Paris and Aquitaine basins, there are still green oases where wildlife flourishes in exuberant defiance of the surrounding monocultures.

Sometimes the old and new lie side by side. On one occasion I stopped at a motorway rest area, somewhere between Auxerre and Beaune. At the edge of the parking area I climbed over a fence and immediately found myself in an ancient flower meadow. A pale blue carpet of pasque flowers spread before me and Duke of Burgundy fritillary butterflies were everywhere on the wing. Yellowhammers and lesser whitethroat sang from nearby bushes and the patchwork countryside stretched out across the valley as far as one could see.

Nature should not be hurried. All one needs is a map, binoculars and a willingness to use one's full range of senses. Wilderness is not an empty view. Everywhere the landscape is a mixture of innumerable sights, sounds and smells. In the intense heat of the Provençal summer, the scenery fades into a hazy blur, but all around is the incessant rasping call of the cigale, and the air is full of the heady aromas of myrtle, lavender and thyme. In the great high forests further north, the rich leaf litter gives off a distinctive musty smell and on calm days the tall columns of mature trees seem to exude a silent force. One is completely dominated by the living forest, yet there may be no active sign of life. You can walk for ages without

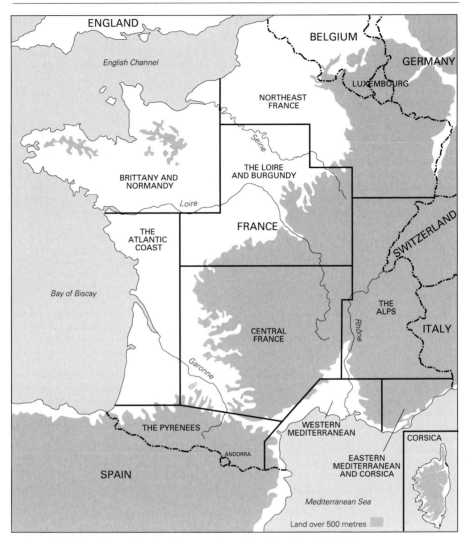

seeing a bird. But listen closely—far away a woodpecker may be tapping at some dead bough, and a thin, almost inaudible high-pitched note tells you a goldcrest or a tree-creeper is nearby.

From the subtle charms of lowland rural areas, to the Atlantic coast lashed by the elements, or the high mountains fashioned from millennia of glacial activity or volcanic eruptions, France is a land of contrasts. But every region has its special character and notable features. Each has its devotees, hence the number of authors for this book.

We are not offering you an encyclopaedic coverage of all France's wild areas. There are simply too many for any reasonable volume to do justice to them all. Moreover, despite the ravages of modern life, there are still vast areas for the enquiring country-lover to discover afresh. What we want is to give you a taste of the natural ambience of our chosen regions and, we hope, a desire to explore them for yourself.

6

THE KEY TO FRANCE'S WILD PLACES

WILD HABITATS

An appreciation of habitats is essential for anyone interested in experiencing a whole range of wild species in their natural environment. In turn, to understand the nature and distribution of the various major wildlife habitats of France, it is necessary to look at the major influencing factors of climate and geology.

France is a superbly rich country for the naturalist and general country-lover alike, and it would take a multi-volumed book to do full justice to its wide spectrum of natural environments. In brief, though, a simplified look at its geology shows a country composed of ancient rocks, usually forming mountain chains and, in the case of the Massif Central, topped with volcanoes. Younger rocks make up the Alps, Jura and Pyrenees and, between all these, lie the great sedimentary basins and transition zones such as Languedoc and Burgundy.

Contrasts in vegetation cover can be traced to differences in substrate, or underlying rock type. In some areas this substrate is composed of sedimentary rocks which were formed under the sea. These chalk and limestone areas support a typically calcium-loving vegetation such as ash, wych elm and field maple, dogwood, privet, wayfaring tree and spindle. In other areas silicious soils, formed from crystalline and metamorphic rocks, favour a calcium-avoiding flora, such as the ericaceous heaths in the north and cork oak and maritime pine forests in the south.

Over this picture lies a network of riverine or glacial river valleys, the latter group including some of the great names of Europe—Seine, Loire, Rhône and part of the Rhine. Further variation has been created over the millennia by the actions of volcanoes and glaciers in the mountain regions and by sea and wind erosion around France's 5,500km (3,500-mile) length of coastline.

France lies at the crossroads of four principal European climatic belts. The west and north are influenced by the moist and cooler Atlantic climate, which can extend up to 150km (90 miles) from the coast. In the south and extending up the Rhône valley into central France is the Mediterranean climatic belt, characterized by hot dry summers and plenty of sunshine throughout the year. In the northeast of the country continental climatic influences take over, producing a huge temperature range between summer and winter, with all seasons being predominantly dry.

Mountains and uplands: The different altitudinal levels in mountain regions support vegetation characteristic of different climatic types, depending on the aspect, often providing thereby an isolated refuge for rare Arctic–Alpine species such as marmot, ibex, chamois, alpine accentor and snow finch. In the Cévennes and in some of the pre-Alps, or Alpine foothills in Haute-Provence, the southern slopes endure hot Mediterranean conditions with evergreen oak and pine forests, while the shaded northern slopes are more typical of cooler temperate conditions with beech and deciduous oak forests.

Forest and Shrubland: France is one of Europe's most wooded countries, with a tree cover of some 27% of the total land area. Beech and oak dominate across vast areas of the country, while in the northeast hornbeam is very common. The Jura and Alps support some of the finest fir forests, while the low-lying Landes de Gascogne are the home of the stone pine. In the Mediterranean south there are still some fine evergreen oak and cork oak forests. Cork oaks do not provide a dense canopy, so plenty of light is able to penetrate through to the ground, allowing for a vigorous field and shrub layer, known as *maquis*. These areas are becoming increasingly ravaged by extensive, fierce fires, with the result that a more dry, scrub vegetation known as *garrigue* has become established. Forest of one kind or another shelters much of France's rich mammal fauna, from the rare Pyrenean brown bear to the widespread and universally hunted wild boar. The forest is home to innumerable birds, including birds of prey, such as goshawk and honey buzzard.

Wetlands: The wetlands, including lakes, swamps, marshes and rivers are of great interest for the richness of their plant and bird life. The Camargue with its marvellous flocks of flamingos is surely the most famous, but the natural parks of Brotonne, Normandie-Maine and Armorique offer the possibility of great discoveries.

7

Coastland and islands: The French coast with its sea shores, estuaries, cliffs and sand dunes offers a spectacular variety of wild places, some of them—such as the Baie du Mont St-Michel—being internationally renowned. In addition its wild coast includes islands such as the Sept Iles and the Iles d'Ouessant with their impressive colonies of breeding birds including choughs and puffins in addition to migratory species such as ring ouzel and wheatear.

PROTECTED AREAS AND NATURE CONSERVATION

Nature conservation has a long history in France and indeed the French claim to have created the first 'reserve' in the world. As early as 1861 a decree was passed confirming the protected status of approximately 125 hectares (308 acres) of the Forêt de Fontainebleau. Nowadays large parts of the French countryside are categorized under different forms of protected area status and it is useful to have a rough idea of the meaning of each.

Parcs Nationaux: These are by far the largest protected areas in the country, usually covering several tens of thousands of acres. There have been six created to date, and with the exception of the smallest, Port-Cros island off Hyères, they are all located in remote mountain areas with few inhabitants. The National Parks are simply areas put under the protection of the state for use by all the population.

Parcs Naturels Régionaux: More numerous than National Parks and offering less strict wildlife protection (hunting and fishing are generally allowed), these parks afford some control over development. They are generally formed at the initiative of local communities and interested conservation groups.

Réserves naturelles: In common with National Parks, these official nature reserves are decreed by the state and are generally small areas notified for their particular biological or geological interest. Some are private reserves belonging to a particular commune or individual landowner. Most of these reserves can be visited, and several have

especially marked nature trails.

Arrêté de biotope Sites which provide critically important habitat conditions for protected species can be notified as 'Arrêté de Biotope'. The initiative usually comes from local conservation groups. Such sites are characteristically small, well defined areas and the regulations do not provide for supervision and management.

Sites naturels classés: This is an old form of protection for sites of great natural beauty which can range in magnitude from Mont Blanc to a single specimen tree. It is unusual for this form of protection to be accorded for a site's ecological value and it is principally used as a landscape preserving measure. There are some 3000 classified natural sites in France.

Le Conservatoire du littoral: In 1975 the Conservatoire was established to protect the remaining unspoilt areas of coastline and inland lakes for the public benefit. The programme, relying on public funds and voluntary contributions, has acquired relatively small areas, selected for their ecological significance and natural beauty.

Species protection: On paper much of the naturally occurring flora and fauna of France is protected. This includes all 31 species of bat, most of the larger mammals such as ibex, lynx, beaver and wild cat, 244 species of birds and their eggs, notably all birds of prey, and many larger marsh and sea birds. Many of the 33 reptile and 29 amphibian species are also protected, and the laws which were passed in 1976 also cover several insects, mostly butterflies. Even molluscs are theoretically protected. Over 400 of France's rich flora, which numbers some 4,762 species in total, are protected. The effectiveness of such laws is unfortunately less impressive since there is no statutory authority charged with nature conservation and the enforcement of protection measures. The success of conservation in France rests on the vigilance of voluntary organisations and support from the international conservation community.

Information on the many voluntary conservation bodies in the country can be obtained via their umbrella group the Fédération Française des Sociétés de Protection de la Nature, 57 rue Cuvier, 75231 Paris, Cedex 05.

EXPLORING WILD FRANCE

France is a very accessible country and there are innumerable tracks and paths which criss-cross the countryside, even in remote areas. Many of these are simple access routes to isolated cultivations, while others just trail off into the forest or *maquis* for no obvious reason. For the most part these paths need to be searched out, as they are not marked as official public footpaths.

For the serious walker France has an excellent network of marked long-distance paths, the 'sentiers de grande randonnée' or GRs. They enable one to explore all parts of the country without hindrance and they provide one of the best ways to penetrate the soul of rural France. In Paris the Comité National des Sentiers de Grande Randonnée (CNSGR, 8 av Marceau, 75008, Paris) publishes a whole range of topographic guides, full of practical information about the GRs. There are also several rambling associations who organise group excursions along the GRs.

Walking is not the only means of experiencing wild France at close quarters and there are associations which promote randonnées for cyclists, horse-riders, cross-country skiers, canoeists and, for the less energetic, canal and river tours by barge. There are also three exciting sailing itineraries along the French coast—Brittany, the Iles d'Hyères along the Provençal coast from Saint-Tropez to Saint-Mandrier and a tour of Corsica's magnificent coastline.

THE RULES OF THE WILD

The Mountain Code: Learn the use of map and compass. Know the weather signs and local forecast. Plan a route within your capabilities and leave time to get down before dark. Know simple first aid and the symptoms of exposure. Never go alone. Leave written word of your route and estimated time of return, and report when you get back. Take warm weatherproof clothing and survival bag. Take map and compass, torch and food. Wear climbing boots. Keep alert all day. Be prepared to turn back if the weather becomes bad or if any member of your party is becoming slow or exhausted. *If there is snow on the hills*—always have an ice-axe for each person. Carry a climbing rope. Know the correct use of ropes and ice-axe. Learn to recognize dangerous snow slopes. Lack of space precludes a detailed description of equipment and techniques recommended for travellers in wild places. If in doubt refer to one of the many manuals on this subject.

The Country Code: While you are in the countryside there is an internationally recognized code of behaviour that should be observed at all times.

Enjoy the countryside and respect its life and work. Fasten all gates. Keep your dogs under close control. Keep to public footpaths across farmland. Use gates and stiles to cross fences, hedges and walls. Leave livestock, crops and machinery alone. Take your litter home. Help to keep all water clean. Protect wildlife, plants and trees. Take special care on country roads. Make no unnecessary noise. Guard against all risk of fire. In France fires become a major risk under dry conditions and each year hundreds of thousands of acres are burned with devastating destruction of plant, animal and even human life. Such fires are almost always the result of human carelessness.

TO THE READER

Eagle symbols: The eagle symbols used at the head of some entries in this book indicate the wildness quality of the place to which they refer. This is based on a number of factors, including remoteness, ruggedness, spaciousness, uniqueness, wildlife interest and the author's subjective reactions. Three eagles is the highest rating, no eagles the lowest.

Updating: while everything possible has been done to ensure the accuracy of the facts in this book, information does gradually become outdated in the ever-changing countryside. For this reason we would welcome readers' updates, corrections and comments for incorporation in subsequent revised editions. Please write to Douglas Botting, Sheldrake Press, 188 Cavendish Road, London SW12 0DA.

Non-liability: both the author and publishers have gone to great pains to point out the hazards that may confront the traveller in certain places described in WILD FRANCE. We cannot under any circumstances accept any liability for any mishap, loss or injury sustained by any person venturing into any of the wild places listed in this book.

CHAPTER 1

Brittany and Normandy

L eaving Paris and travelling west through Normandy to Brittany, I was struck by the number of times the landscape changed. The cultural links between England's West Country and Brittany and Normandy are well known, but I was surprised by the physical similarities of their coasts and hinterlands.

First come the chalky hills of Normandy and, meandering through them, the Seine, which emerges into the Channel at Le Havre. On a chalk plateau, enclosed on three sides by one of the great bends in the river, is the Forêt de Brotonne, a *parc régional* that provides a rare glimpse of how the area must have looked in its pristine state. Despite the oil refineries that line the estuary of the Seine, its marshes still shelter a wealth of aquatic wildlife.

As you progress westward, you come to the *bocage* (copse) country, reminiscent of Hampshire and Dorset although less affected by mechanized farming than its English counterpart. Inland, Normandy is given over to dairy farming and orchards. Around Alençon, the rocks change from chalk to granite, a transition that in Britain occurs around Somerset and Devon. Once part of a great mountain range, these ancient granite rocks have been eroded over millions of years into gently rolling hills. They are the source of the Caen stone from which many English cathedrals were built from after the Norman Conquest. South of

The Parc Naturel Régional de Brotonne was created in 1974 to protect the lower reaches of the Seine from the menace of industrial pollution. The 12,000 hectares are dominated by Atlantic beech woodland.

Caen itself, around Thury-Harcourt, the hilly landscape has been dubbed Suisse Normande; its rugged outcrops offer an exciting challenge to rock-climbers. Just west of Alençon is the Parc Naturel Régional Normandie-Maine, with its upland woods and timeless pastoral beauty.

To experience really wild countryside, however, you must continue into Brittany. This is the western extremity of France, a jagged finger of rock pointing, like Cornwall, far out into the Atlantic.

The outstanding historic human contributions to the landscape in both Normandy and Brittany are the megaliths. Brittany has the lion's share; there are more than 3,000 standing stones in the Carnac region alone.

Roman Armorica was divided into two zones: Armor and Argoat, the coastal and inland regions, respectively. Numerous rivers cut valleys through the granite plateau of Argoat on their way down to the sea, and closer to the sea these rivers meet deep estuaries. The rise in water levels since the last Ice Age has flooded the lower valleys and the inlets, known as *abers*, provide safe harbours for many fishing fleets. Nevertheless the Brittany coast has the largest tidal variations in Europe, and its waters are extremely dangerous for many days of the year.

A century ago, a tract of the Argoat woods still covered the territory between Rennes in the east and Carhaix in the west. Most of the forest has since been felled and its wildlife population has dissipated or died out. Brittany's last wolf was killed in 1891. Two swaths of the ancient oak and beech forest of Argoat remain, however: the Paimpont (southwest of Rennes) and the Huelgoat, in the Monts d'Arrée south of Morlaix. Brittany's waterways are relatively free of pollution; it is one of the last regions of France where salmon still swim in most of the rivers.

Brittany and Normandy both depend on their agricultural productivity, however, and there are worse evils than tilled land. A proliferation of new suburbs around older villages and towns now infringe very noticeably on the countryside, and they overwhelm the older settlements as well. As a result of the extra traffic, the animal life has dwindled, and it now takes far longer to get out of the settled areas into more remote walking country.

Still, Brittany and Normandy provide some superb wild areas for walking and cycling in, and the sense of history here, from remote events in centuries long gone to the still-fresh memories of World War II, is vivid.

The Atlantic salmon is still found in unpolluted rivers.

GETTING THERE

By air: the main regional airports are at Brest, Caen, Le Havre, Nantes, Quimper, Rennes and Rouen.

By sea: there is an enormous choice of crossings from ports on the southern coast of England to Normandy and Brittany, in addition to the ferries and hovercraft plying the Straits of Dover. The shortest crossing (4½hr) is from Newhaven to Dieppe. Sealink runs up to 8 crossings a day in summer on this route, with less frequent services from Portsmouth and Weymouth to Cherbourg. P&O operates services out of Portsmouth to Cherbourg and Le Havre, while Brittany Ferries has a service from Portsmouth to St-Malo or Ouistreham (near Caen) and from Plymouth to Roscoff.

By car: most areas of interest are within easy driving distance from the Channel ports. From Paris, motorists have a hefty drive up A11 to Rennes, A13 to Rouen and Caen or N12 towards Alençon.

By rail: daily trains from London-Victoria link up with sailings from Newhaven and from Waterloo with sailings from Portsmouth. From Paris, main-line trains serve Brittany from the Gare Montparnasse; the line runs to Rennes and on to Brest and Quimper. Paris's Gare St-Lazare links with the Normandy towns of Caen, Cherbourg, Le Havre and Rouen. For further information call SNCF in Paris, T:45 82 50 50 (T:45 82 08 41 for information in English).

By bus: it is far easier to get around rural France by bus than you might think. The buses often connect with trains, although they rarely run on Sun. One useful daily service runs to Caen from its ferry port at Ouistreham. For further information, T:35 90 13 38 (Normandy); or T:99 30 13 34 (Brittany).

WHEN TO GO

Brittany and Normandy are for the most part summer destinations, being fairly cold, damp and overcast much of the rest of the year. Birdwatchers, however, will enjoy the profusion of wintering wildfowl around the coast.

WHERE TO STAY

There are many hotels in the area, mainly concentrated around the coast; local tourist offices have lists. Advance bookings are recommended in summer.

ACTIVITIES

Walking: the area is good walking country, bisected by numerous footpaths (long-distance or otherwise). The only special equipment needed is waterproof clothing.

Climbing: there are climbing opportunities around Thury-Harcourt in Suisse Normande, south of Caen. Further information from the Caen tourist office, 14 pl St-Pierre, T:31 86 27 65.

Cycling: the Fédération Française de Cyclotourisme (8 rue Jean-Marie Jego, Paris, T:45 80 30 21) publishes a book, *La France à Bicyclette*, listing tours in Brittany; it also has English-language booklets on tours in upper Normandy, and around the Brittany coast.

Adventure holidays: the Union Nationale des Centres Sportifs de Plein Air (UCPA) offers cycling, riding and watersports holidays at more than half a dozen centres in Brittany and Normandy; information from UCPA, 62 rue de la Glacière, Paris, T:45 87 45 87.

Riding: The Fédération Française d'Equitation publishes a free comprehensive booklet, *Tourisme Equestre en France*, listing stables; contact them at 15 rue de Bruxelles, Paris, T:42 81 42 82.

Fishing: salmon, trout and pike are just some of the fish found in Brittany's rivers. Information on restrictions and licences from Le Conseil Supérieur de la Pêche, 135 av Malakoff, Paris, T:45 01 20 20.

FURTHER INFORMATION

Tourist information: for regional information, contact Délégation Régionale du Tourisme, 3 rue d'Espagne, Rennes, T:99 50 11 15 (Brittany); or 46 av Foch, Evreux, T:32 31 03 03 (Normandy). Local tourist offices are listed under individual exploring zones.

FURTHER READING

In the series *Guides Naturalistes des Côtes de France*, by Marcel Bourne-Rias (Editions Delachaux et Neistle) 2 cover the northern coast: *La Bretagne du Mont St-Michel à la Pointe du Raz* and *La Manche du Havre à Avranches*.

Parc Naturel Régional de Brotonne

A mixture of woodland and marsh lying northeast of Caen

I first saw the Forêt de Brotonne when I was a schoolboy, back in 1962.

13

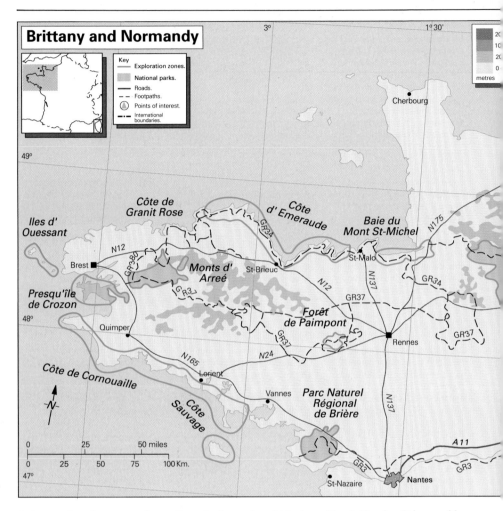

Brittany and Normandy

Key
— Exploration zones.
▨ National parks.
— Roads.
-- Footpaths.
🅐 Points of interest.
-··- International boundaries.

Cherbourg

49°

Côte de Granit Rose

Côte d' Emeraude

Baie du Mont St-Michel

Iles d' Ouessant

N12

Brest

GR380

Monts d' Arreé

St-Brieuc

St-Malo

N175

Presqu'île de Crozon

GR37

N12

GR37

GR34

48°

Quimper

Forêt de Paimpont

GR37

GR37

Rennes

Côte de Cornouaille

N165

Lorient

N24

-N-

Côte Sauvage

Vannes

Parc Naturel Régional de Brière

N137

0   25   50 miles
0   25   50   75   100 Km.

A 11

47°

St-Nazaire

GR3

Nantes

GR3

Spring was late that year and the trees were not fully in leaf. The family I was staying with thought I would be disappointed. I can't now say whether I was or not, but my memory of the forest—of the young trees sprouting their first milk-green leaves—is still vivid.

Twenty-seven years later I went back. This time spring was early, the foliage more advanced. Of the mature trees, the chestnuts and silver birches were the first to come into leaf. Climbing a small hill

above the forest, I could look back down over the treetops and pick out the silver birches, showing green among the leafless oaks and beeches.

The forest is a home for a variety of wildlife, including foxes and deer. Even before the trees are fully in leaf it is difficult to see any sign of these mammals, however, possibly due to hunts that regularly beat the thicket.

The forest lies enclosed on three sides by the meandering Seine. The river's next bend encircles the horsehoe-shaped

Marais Vernier. It is a world apart from its surroundings: 2,000ha (4,900 acres) of marshland criss-crossed by drainage channels and dykes. These are lined throughout by alders and willows and a variety of herbaceous plants, such as marsh valerian and flowering rush. The shady copses provide ideal conditions for the spectacular royal fern.

Among this botanical paradise lurks a wealth of wild animals. Common frogs are abundant, as are viperine

14

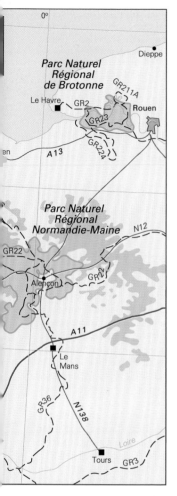

Before you go *Maps:* IGN 1:100,000 Nos. 7 and 8; IGN 1:25,000 Nos. 1811 (east) and 1911 (west).
Getting there *By car:* the A13 *autoroute* skirts the southern bank of the Seine, D982 the northern; if you arrive on D982 take D490, which crosses the Pont de Brotonne and continues into the forest, itself crossed by D913, D131 and D40. For Marais Vernier, take N182 off A13 or out of Pont-Audemer, and turn left on D103, which cuts straight through the marsh.

By rail: the nearest station is Bourgthéroulde, too far away (10km/6 miles) to be much use unless you take a bicycle on the train.

By bus: buses run every hour from Rouen to Le Havre by way of Caudebec, but you must then cross the Pont de Brotonne on foot, a fearsome expedition. A better bet is the bus from Rouen to Pont-Audemer.

Where to stay: Rouen is the best of the larger towns; despite its industrial outskirts it has an interesting old centre. Other options are Caudebec-en-Caux, Duclair and La Mailleraye-sur-Seine, or the pleasant old town of Pont-Audemer, about 10km (6 miles) from the forest.

Activities *Walking: grande randonneé* routes traverse the forest (GR2, GR211-A, GR23 and GR23-A), while GR23 skirts the Marais Vernier. The tourist office in Rouen has guides to a series of more modest walks, ranging from 2–16km (1–10 miles).

Riding: the Centre Hippique, Poney Club du Bois du Parc (Notre-Dame-de-Gravenchon, T:35 38 67 96) offers a variety of equestrian activities. The Centre Equestre du Parc (Le Fief du Wuy, La Mailleraye-sur-Seine, T:35 37 34 46)

organizes riding weekends.
Further information *Tourist information:* Caudebec-en-Caux, quai Guilbaud, T:35 96 62 65; Pont-Audemer, pl Maubert, T:32 41 08 21; Rouen, pl de la Cathédrale, T:35 71 41 77.

The park office is at 2 rond-pont Marbec, Le Trait, T:35 91 83 16.

Parc Naturel Régional Normandie-Maine

Rural park of orchards and forest

The regional nature park of Normandie-Maine begins where the chalk of the Parisian basin ends, close to the towns of Alençon and Argentan. The park's landscape is varied, a mixture of hilltops and ridges crowned with forests. The valleys between are the realm of agriculture, and the source of the district's famous butter and cheese. The rolling countryside has a timeless pastoral feel. This part of Normandy is also known for its hedges—and its orchards.

The important forests of Normandie-Maine are the Ecouves, between Alençon and Argentan, and the narrow connecting forests of Andaines and Monaye. About a fifth of the park is upland woods; the deciduous woods are mostly oak and beech, with some coppicing of trees like the hazel. On poorer soils pines have been planted. These woods are mostly private property, however, and the realm of the huntsman.

snakes, a close relative of the harmless grass snake. The common viper, or adder, is also numerous, frequently inhabiting the tussocky mounds of rushes. One bird which readily feeds on snakes is the stork, regularly seen here on migration. Another star bird of the marshy grasslands is the corncrake, now very rare in Normandy though only a few decades ago its persistent rasping call was one of the traditional night-time sounds of the *bocage*.

15

Before you go *Maps:* IGN 1:100,000 Nos. 17–19; IGN 1:25,000 Nos. 1515–16, 1615–16 and 1715–16 (east and west).
Getting there *By car:* the direct route is via N12 from Paris to Alençon.
By rail: 6 daily main-line trains link Paris's Gare Montparnasse to Argentan, Briouze and Flers-de-l'Orne.
Where to stay: the spa town of Bagnoles-de-l'Orne lies in the centre of this sprawling park, but it's on the expensive side. Other convenient bases are Alençon, Sées, Carrouges, La Ferté-Macé or Domfront.
Activities *Walking:* 2 long-distance footpaths cut through the park: GR22 from Paris to St-Michel and GR36 from the Channel to the Pyrenees. Details from Fédération Ornaise pour le Tourisme de Randonnée, 60 rue St-Blaise, Alençon, T:33 26 18 71.
Cycling: Rent bicycles at railway stations of Alençon, Argentan, Bagnoles, Flers and Sées.
Canoeing: the park's 2 rivers, the Mayenne and Varenne, are good for canoeing. Contact Direction Départementale du Temps Libre, Jeunesse et Sport de l'Orne, Alençon, T:33 26 66 80.
Further information *Tourist information:* Alençon, pl La Magdelaine, T:33 26 11 36.

Baie du Mont St-Michel

Tidal bay enclosing a wetland environment of international importance

The bay of Mont St-Michel is situated at the bottom of the Cotentin Peninsula. The tidal variation here is tremendous (15 metres/50 feet), and the picturesque abbey, perched on its rocky outcrop, can be reached only at low tide. This beautiful complex of Romanesque and Gothic buildings, in its stunning natural setting, attracts hordes of tourists, especially in summer; but those in search of wild places and wildlife can easily avoid the crowds by withdrawing to the landlocked cliffs on the edge of the bay, or to the intervening wetlands.

The turnstone is a common migrant wader on the rocky shores of the Atlantic coast.

For within sight of the Mount lies a wide expanse of salt marshes, part of a protected bird reserve. The marshes are bisected by an old sea wall. On the landward side of the wall is the reclaimed marshland known as *les polders*, an area of flat fields crossed by roads that soon peter out into mere tracks. From here, the best way forward is on foot.

Beyond the sea wall you encounter a landscape of grass and sea lavender. Farther out are mud flats. Here, in spring you'll notice busy colonies of oystercatchers, shelduck and curlew.

The best time to visit, though, is winter, before the wading birds migrate to their summer breeding grounds. There are reckoned to be up to 150,000 birds here in winter, around half of them migrants. Huge flocks of waders, especially lapwing, golden plover, gulls and ducks make the bay their home, and in hard winters rare visitors such as whooper swans can be seen. The relative winter warmth also attracts the white-fronted goose, which the French know as the *oie rieuse*, or laughing goose. The bay is also a major breeding ground for shelduck, while the island of Landes, at the western end of the bay, is Brittany's only nesting place for cormorants.

This wealth of birdlife naturally attracts predators, including buzzards and peregrine falcons. The best time to see many of these birds is when the tide comes in, for it does so with such terrific force they take to the air *en masse*.

BEFORE YOU GO

Maps: IGN 1:100,000 No. 16; IGN 1:25,000 No. 1215 (east and west).

Guidebook: Marcel Bourne-Rias, *La Bretagne du Mont St-Michel à la Pointe du Raz* (*Guides Naturalistes des Côtes de France*, Editions Delachaux et Neistle).

GETTING THERE

By sea: the most convenient crossing is from Portsmouth to St-Malo on Brittany Ferries, who also run the service to Caen.

By car: N12/N176 lead to the bay from Paris.

By rail: there are about 6 daily main-line trains from Paris (Gare Montparnasse) to Granville; change at Folligny for local trains to Avranches, Pontorson and Dol. A connecting bus runs from Pontorson to Mont St-Michel.

By bus: buses are infrequent, and most do not run on Sun.

WHERE TO STAY

The choice is limited, but the most convenient towns are Pontorson and Dol; Hôtel du Chalet in Pontorson (T:33 60 00 16) is good value for money. Farther afield are St-Malo, Avranches, St-Jean-le-Thomas; further inland Fougères, Coutances and St-Lô.

ACTIVITIES

Walking: GR22, GR34 and GR39 pass through the area, the first 2 along the sea wall.

Cycling: this flat marshy area is ideal for cycling; rent bicycles at the railway stations in Pontorson and Dol.

Riding: treks are organized by La Gourmette du Mont St-Michel (T:33 60 27 73) and La Ferme de Chenedet, Fougères (T:99 97 35 46).

FURTHER INFORMATION

Tourist information: Avranches, 2 rue Général-de-Gaulle, T:33 58 00 22; Dol, Grande Rue des Stuarts, T:99 48 15 37; Mont St-Michel, Corps de Garde des Bourgeois, T:33 60 14 30; Pontorson, pl Eglise, T:33 60 20 65; St-Lô, 2 rue Havin, T:33 05 02 09; St-Malo, esplanade St-Vincent, T:99 56 64 48.

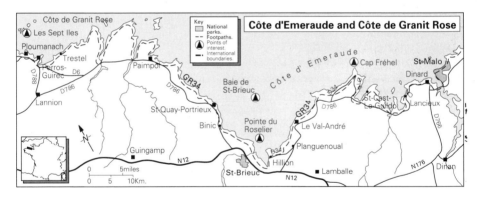

Côte d'Emeraude and Côte de Granit Rose

Côte d'Emeraude and Côte de Granit Rose

Brittany's dramatic northern stretch of coast

The port town of St-Brieuc lies between two of the best-known ranges of cliffs in Brittany. To the east, the Côte d'Emeraude (Emerald Coast) runs towards Dinard and St-Malo. Its most northerly point is Cap Fréhel, a headland jutting out into the English Channel. The view from here is spectacular—on clear days you can see the Channel Islands. The cliffs provide a home to gulls, cormorants, razorbills, guillemots and fulmars, and are an officially designated bird reserve. To the west, the Côte de Granit Rose (Pink Granite Coast) stretches beyond the Pointe du Roselier and up to Perros-Guirec. The glister of the pink granite is mesmeric, especially when a slight haze reddens the setting sun.

Off this dramatic coastline, near Perros-Guirec, is the bird reserve of Les Sept Iles. Only the largest of the islands, the Ile aux

17

Moines, is open to the public, but it affords distant views of the colonies of gulls, guillemots, cormorants, puffins and the only gannet colony in France. Don't expect to see the penguins optimistically mentioned in the English edition of the Michelin Green Guide—though you might glimpse a razorbill (*petit pingouin* in French) or, on the slabs of rock, a few grey seals at rest.

The coastal paths of northern Brittany are home to many other birds, including skylarks, stonechats, whinchats and, in summer, swallows. Along the clifftops, the trees are covered in remarkable encrustations of lichen; at least half a dozen different species can be found. The interior of the Cap Fréhel reserve comprises a diverse heathland. Through the seasons the vegetation displays ever-changing masses of colour, which reach a peak in late summer. These heaths are home to all the small mammals known in Brittany and among the birds is that characteristic denizen of heaths, the Dartford warbler.

The walk out of St-Brieuc west to the coastal footpath is scarcely the most prepossessing. You start by following a long line of suburban villas. The first hint of an improvement comes as the road narrows; you then begin a steepish descent between two hedges, and there is your first *grande randonnée* (GR) signpost. At the bottom of the hills lies Gouet estuary, a stretch of river dominated by light industry. Overriding this valley is a huge motorway viaduct.

Things improve when the path begins to sidle downstream, alongside the river. It then ascends to the coastal cliffs, and at last, maritime Brittany opens up before you. There are good views from up here across the Baie de St-Brieuc. If you come past when the tide is out, you can walk down onto the beach, which you'll find covered with an extraordinary array of shells—cockles, clams, scallops, whelks and oysters—as well as sea lettuce and wrack.

The well-trodden coastal path picks its way among the seaside suburbs, eventually breaking free near the Pointe du Roselier. From here, on a clear day, you have a good view across the Baie St-Brieuc to Cap Fréhel and beyond. It's a good point from which to see the tide race in, covering the shallow sands in a dramatically short time.

BEFORE YOU GO
Maps: IGN 1:100,000 Nos. 13, 14 and 16; IGN 1:25,000 Nos. 0415–16, 0515, 0615, 0714, 0814, 0915–16, 1015.

GETTING THERE
By sea: the most convenient ferry crossings are run by Brittany Ferries—from Portsmouth to St-Malo (at the eastern end) or from Plymouth to Roscoff (at the western end).
By car: D786 more or less follows Brittany's northern coastline, though a detour up D16 to Cap Fréhel is rewarding.
By rail: about 6 trains a day connect Paris (Gare Montparnasse) to Rennes, Lamballe, St-Brieuc, Guingamp and Plouret-Trégor. Connecting trains link Rennes with Dol and St-

Malo, while a local service runs from Dol to Dinan and Lamballe.
By bus: most places on the north coast can be reached by buses, which connect with trains at railway stations.

WHERE TO STAY
The main centres along this lengthy coastline are Dinard, St-Brieuc, Paimpol, Perros-Guirec and Lannion.
Outdoor living: the local tourist offices have lists of campsites.

ACTIVITIES
Walking: starting at Dinan, GR34 follows the entire length of the coastline, with a walk down the valley of the Rance to Dinard and continuing west as far as Toul-er-Hery, halfway between Lannion and Morlaix.

Cycling: you can rent bicycles at the railway stations of Dinard, Lamballe, Lannion, Morlaix, Roscoff, St-Brieuc and St-Malo.
Riding: information from Association des Cavaliers d'Extérieur des Côtes du Nord, St-Blaise, Plélo, Châtelaudren, T:86 74 21 86.

FURTHER INFORMATION
Tourist information:
Lamballe, pl Martray, T:96 31 05 38; Lannion, quai d'Aiguillon, T:96 37 07 35; Paimpol, pl de la République, T:96 20 83 16; Roscoff, rue Gambetta, T:98 69 70 70; St-Brieuc, 7 rue St-Guéno, T:96 33 32 50; St-Malo, esplanade St-Vincent, T:99 56 64 48.

The Baie du Mont St-Michel is noted for large flocks of lapwings and plovers.

Monts d'Arrée

Part of the Parc Régional d'Armorique

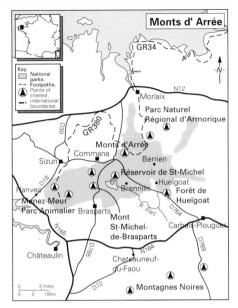

The morning frost still clung to the grass as I headed south out of Morlaix. The road climbs the valley towards the Monts d'Arrée, and as the sun melted the frost, clouds of mist hung in the combes and hollows. Locals say they are "going into the mountains" whenever they travel inland. With peaks around 300 metres (1,000 feet), none of these hills is high enough to warrant the claim, which has the ring of bar-room talk after several draughts of the local cider.

There are in fact two distinct ranges of hills. The Monts d'Arrée north of Carhaix-Plouguer are part of the Parc Régional d'Armorique. Further south, some 10 kilometres (six miles) beyond Carhaix (near Gourin), is a second range, the Montagnes Noires (Black Mountains). Mont St-Michel-des-Brasparts, in the Arrée range, is the highest peak at 391 metres (1,150 feet).

The hills are a mixture of farming, heathland and occasional woods with granite outcrops. These bare uplands have a forbidding feeling of doom; this is where the buzzards fly.

At the heart of these sombre hills lies the forest of Huelgoat. The word is said to be Breton for high forest; it is a relic of Argoat, the ancient forest that once covered the whole Brittany peninsula. Yew and larch mingle with oak, beech and silver birch, while ivy shrouds many of the trees. Despite the age of the forest, many of its trees are not well-founded; the soil is rocky, and there are plenty of trees with roots growing around rocks that protrude above the ground. The great storm that swept up the Channel in October 1987, devastating southern England, also tore across this exposed corner of Brittany. The gusting winds cut a swath through the forest, leaving thousands of uprooted trees in their wake. Slowly, foresters are removing the

fallen giants. Dead trees make a fertile breeding place for insects, and the lichens— of which there are a remarkable variety— care not whether a tree is dead or alive.

This ancient wood naturally has its legends. Dahud, the daughter of a 6th-century Breton king called Gradlon, was in the habit of throwing her lovers off a rock near Huelgoat. King Arthur is supposed to have slept in a forest cave. A hill-fort in the park has, inevitably, come to be called Le Camp d'Artus (Arthur's Camp).

The birdlife of both wood and hills is rich and varied. Buzzards, woodpeckers, jays and other common birds live in the forest. Salmon and otter revel in the clean waters of the rivers here. One of the country's most ambitious wildlife projects is the reintroduction of the European beaver to Brittany. Twenty years ago this animal had virtually disappeared from France, largely due to trapping. There were just a few colonies left in tributaries of the Rhône. But in the early 1970s, beavers were introduced just south of Huelgoat on the River Elez, and on the Roudouhir, near Hanvec. The colonies have spread naturally ever since. A beaver lodge is on public view at Brennilis, near the reservoir of St-Michel.

BEFORE YOU GO

Maps: IGN 1:100,000 Nos. 13–15; IGN 1:25,000 Nos. 0616–18 and 0717–18 (east and west).

GETTING THERE

By car: all roads, at least in Brittany, lead to Rennes. N12 follows the north coast around to Morlaix and Brest, while N24 joins the southern coast, heading west to Quimper. From Morlaix, D769 cuts through the forest of Huelgoat on its way to Carhaix, while D785 provides scenic mountain views before reaching Quimper. D764 links Carhaix with Huelgoat.
By rail: there are about 6 daily main-line trains from Paris (Gare Montparnasse) to Morlaix, Rosporden and Quimper. From Guingamp (the stop before Morlaix) a branch line runs to Carhaix.
By bus: SNCF runs 2 buses a day from Morlaix to Huelgoat and on to Carhaix-Plouguer. From Carhaix, daily buses also connect up with the railway stations of Rosporden, Loudéac and via Châteauneuf-du-Faou to Châteaulin.

WHERE TO STAY

Carhaix, Châteaulin and Morlaix are the nearest sizeable towns. In Huelgoat, the lakeside Hôtel du Lac (T:98 99 71 14) is a pleasant lunch stop out of season.
Outdoor living: the local tourist offices have lists of campsites.

ACTIVITIES

Walking: GR34 and GR380 cross the park; GR380 can be picked up at Morlaix or Sizun.
Cycling: bicycles are available at the railway stations of Châteaulin, Morlaix and Quimper.
Fishing: Châteauneuf-du-Faou, in the middle of the Black Mountains, is well known for its salmon fishing.
Riding: information from Centre Equestre des Monts d'Arrée, La Feuillée, Huelgoat, T:98 99 61 60; and Les Cavaliers de Kerjean St-Michel, Brasparts, T:98 81 40 08.
Museums: near the village of Commana, on D764, there is a museum of C17th life at the watermills of Kerouat. The 420-ha (1,000-acre) animal park at Ménez-Meur, Hanvec, has a herd of *aurochs* (a recreation of the region's ancient breed of domestic cattle), plus deer and wild boar. The fish museum (Maison de la Rivière, de l'Eau et de la Pêche) at the mills of Vergraon (near Sizun) features an experimental fish-farm for salmon and trout.

FURTHER INFORMATION

Tourist information: Brest, 1 pl de la Liberté, T:98 44 24 96; Châteaulin, quai Cosmao, T:98 86 02 11; Carhaix-Plouguer, rue Brizeux, T:98 93 04 42; Huelgoat, 14 pl Aristide-Briand, T:98 99 72 32; Morlaix, pl des Otages, T:98 62 14 94.
Park headquarters is at Ménez-Meur, Hanvec, Daoulas, T:98 21 90 69.

Iles d'Ouessant

Group of islands forming France's westernmost territory; part of Parc Naturel Régional d'Armorique

Finistère means the "end of the earth", though more prosaically it's the name given the westernmost region of mainland France. Just beyond the end of the earth lie the Iles d'Ouessant. They were first named the "western isles" around 330 BC by Pytheas, a Phoenician navigator sailing up the Atlantic coast in search of tin. The name has stuck. Nothing but sea, some 5,000 kilometres (3,000 miles) of it, lies between Ouessant and the Americas.

Two of the islands, Ouessant and Molène, have sizeable settlements. Many of the other islands in the group are now registered as a maritime reserve. Lacking any shelter from the prevailing westerlies, these islands get more than their fair share of bad weather, as the big Atlantic rollers create very rough and choppy seas. The islands sit on a shallow Continental shelf, so that even in fairly calm weather the sea can get up suddenly. Reefs abound in the shallows, sometimes erupting from the watery spray like giants' teeth. One of the better-selling lines in the tourist shops of Finistère is a poster map of the wrecks the sea has claimed.

The Iles d Ouessant, where Atlantic waters meet the Channel, are renowned for their gannets, razorbills and puffins.

There are compensations. The islands are, for the most part, blessedly deserted. The ferry is small, and can carry no more than two cars at a time. Given that the main road on Ouessant, the largest of the islands, is only about six kilometres (four miles) long, taking a car is pretty pointless. Even on fine summer days when the ferry is full the island is never unpleasantly overrun. There is a fair-sized settlement at Lampaul, the main town on Ouessant; in addition to the indigenous population, it has four hotels, though few visitors stray far from the main road. The only other inhabited island in the group, Molène, is much smaller, barely a mile in circumference. The other islands are mostly deserted.

Geologically the islands are similar to Finistère. They are crumbs broken off from the granite plateau of the mainland, which have somehow been left in mid-ocean. Cliffs tower dramatically on every side. The cliffs are a boon for connoisseurs of the sea: from a vantage point at the top you can study the ocean's moods, from its wilder rages to peaceful waves gently lapping the seaside rocks.

This is easy walking and cycling country; the bouncy turf is guaranteed to put a spring in your heels. There are few paths and fences, and you have to make your own way across the mat of heather and mossy turf.

The islands are a convenient stopping-off point for migratory birds, although nesting places are limited because of the buffeting sea. The ornithological centre has a list of 300 different species which have been spotted hereabouts. There are many rare birds on the list, including the yellow-browed warbler, squacco heron, the whiskered tern and the gyrfalcon. The puffin colony was almost wiped out by an oil slick in 1978, but the islands remain an important stop-over for migratory birds such as ring ouzel and wheatear.

The sea is the key to the islands' climate. They are warm in winter—February in Ouessant can be warmer than on the Riviera—and cool in summer because of the dominant westerlies. The few trees tend to nestle in hollows out of the wind, or hug the ground. The undergrowth shelters a large population of rabbits, and the islands provide grazing lands for a breed of dwarf sheep. In summer, the sun brings out lizards to laze on the dry stone walls that are the characteristic field division.

BEFORE YOU GO
Map: IGN 1:25,000 No. 0317 (west).

GETTING THERE
By air: there is a plane service to the main island of Ouessant in summer; contact Finist'air, T:98 84 64 87.
By sea: you can catch the daily ferry from either Brest or Le Conquet; from Brest the trip takes about 2hr. The car ferry (capacity 2 cars) takes twice as long; reservations are essential, T:98 80 24 68.

WHERE TO STAY
The 4 hotels in Lampaul, the main town on the island of Ouessant, are: Duchesse Ann (T:98 48 80 25), Le Fromveur (T:98 48 81 30), L'Océan (T:98 48 80 03) and Roc'h ar Mor (T:98 48 80 19). There are also rooms on the island of Molène. Reservations are a good idea if you plan to stay.
Outdoor living: there is a campsite on Ouessant.

ACTIVITIES
Walking: this is lovely walking country; there aren't any signposted paths, but none is needed.
Cycling: Ouessant's size, scarce traffic and flattish countryside make for ideal cycling. Bicycle stalls are situated near the quayside.
Birdwatching: Centre de Recherche Ornithologique (T:98 48 82 65) is open to the public.
Museum: the Ecomusée d'Ouessant, set in 2 restored houses, shows how the island's hardy inhabitants lived in the last century (closed Tues).

FURTHER INFORMATION
Tourist information: Lampaul (Ouessant), T:98 48 85 83.

The Presqu'île de Crozen features sheltered beaches backed by marram-covered dunes.

23

Presqu'île de Crozon

Includes part of the Parc Naturel Régional d'Armorique

The Presqu'île de Crozon, or Crozon Peninsula, is a long arm of land extending into the Atlantic between the Aulne estuary and the Bay of Douarnenez. At the landward end rises a range of hills, the highest of which, Ménez-Hom, rises to 330m (1,080ft), affording fine views of the peninsula. Along the southern coast, you can see the story of the earth's crust outlined in the tortured folds of the cliffs. At the seaward end, the peninsula splits into three long fingers: the Cap de la Chèvre pointing south, the Pointe de Penhir in the west, and the Pointe des Espagnols pointing north towards the harbour of Brest.

The peninsula is part of the Parc Naturel Régional d'Armorique, which extends to cover the Iles d'Ouessant. The coastline here boasts a remarkable dune system; in places, the Atlantic winds have swept the sand into dunes which rise up to 30m (100ft) over the underlying

The praying mantis is one of the curiosities of the rich insect fauna of the Forêt de Paimpont.

rocks. As the dunes are gradually colonized by marram grass and sea spurge, they are becoming more stable. But the very attractiveness of these beaches poses a threat to the delicate ecosystem as thousands of holidaymakers ignore the fences put up by the park authorities and trample the fragile grass cover.

The bulk of the tourists drive out of Camaret-sur-Mer to the point of Penhir. A far better alternative is to forsake the car and take the clifftop walk along the south of the peninsula, from Penhir to the main road near Kerloch. Although the path is well trodden, it also offers some spectacular vantage points over the Atlantic, away from the roar of the road and the smell of exhaust fumes.

Before you go *Maps:* IGN 1:100,000 No. 13; IGN 1:25,000 Nos. 0417–18 (east) and 0517 (west).

Getting there *By car:* N12 leads to Brest. From here take the N165 exit at Châteaulin and follow D787. From Quimper take N165 and D787.
By sea: ferries connect Brest with the port of Le Fret on the peninsula. A connecting bus runs to Crozon, Camaret-sur-Mer and Morgat. For further information, T:93 80 50 50.
By rail: Brest and Quimper are both on the main line from Paris. Local trains (about 6 daily) run between Brest and Quimper, stopping at Châteaulin, where you can rent bicycles.
By bus: during the week buses run from Quimper up the spine of the peninsula to Camaret-sur-Mer. There are

also buses from Brest to Camaret, but this is a long way around; the ferry is quicker.
Where to stay: the best bases are Quimper or Châteaulin, although Douarnenez and Locronan are more rural alternatives for those with cars. Brest is a soulless modern town, rebuilt after the war, with only its convenient location to recommend it.
Activities *Cycling:* bicycles are available from the railway stations at Brest, Châteaulin and Quimper.
Museum: the local geological museum, Maison des Minéraux, sells a geological map of the region, and is the starting point for guided tours. It's open in summer, and, by appointment only, in winter. Maison des Minéraux, rte du Cap de la Chèvre, St-Hernot, Crozon, T:98 27 19 73.
Further information *Tourist information:* Brest, 1 pl de la Liberté, T:98 44 24 96; Camaret-sur-Mer, quai Toudouze, T:98 27 93 60; Châteaulin, quai Cosmao, T:98 86 02 11; Crozon, pl Eglise, T:98 27 21 65; Douarnenez, 2 rue Docteur-Mével, T:98 92 13 35; Quimper, 3 rue du Roi-Gradlon, T:98 95 04 69.

Côte de Cornouaille and Côte Sauvage

Brittany's southern coastline

Past the Pointe du Raz, Brittany's equivalent of Land's End, the Breton coast becomes a south-facing one. The point itself is something of a tourist trap, although its spectacular chasms and sinkhole are worth seeing, as is the bleak and windswept Ile de Sein, 12km (8 miles) offshore. The main interest for naturalists, however, is the bird reserve at Cap Sizun, which shelters an impressive selection of seabirds, including razorbills, guillemots, shags, cormorants, shelduck, kittiwake, stormy petrel and chough.

From the Pointe du Raz, the coast curves steeply down to the Pointe de Penmarch. This is the old duchy of Cornouaille, where visitors are still likely to hear the ancient Breton language spoken. The coastline is one of wild and isolated cliffs, cut by deep inlets and still relatively uninhabited. On the estuary of the River Odet lies Quimper, the former capital of the duchy and still the area's major town. Although this coast is much favoured by yachtsmen, old fishing ports such as Concarneau still manage to retain a distinctly Breton maritime flavour. Several kilometres offshore lie the small, rocky Iles de Glénan; the largest, St-Nicolas, is a bird reserve.

Beyond Cornouaille, the Breton coast known as the Côte Sauvage stretches down to the Gulf of Morbihan, close to Vannes. There is no southern equivalent of the *grande randonnée* that runs along the northern coast, unfortunately. Indeed, the whole of the south coast seems to have been forgotten by the planners of long-distance footpaths, for there isn't one within striking distance of the sea.

There are also few coastal roads, as a series of deep inlets forced road builders to retreat inland. Between Gâvres and the peninsula of

Quiberon the coast is given over to a firing range. South of Port-Louis, the cliffs of the Ile de Groix rear out of the sea. A small fishing community coexists on the island with a bird reserve; the island's most dramatic sight is a chasm called the Trou de l'Enfer ("hole of Hell").

Farther south the coast becomes easier for travelling, and attracts more tourists. The Gulf of Morbihan's megaliths are famous, though Carnac is impossibly overrun with tourists. The tumulus (earth mound over an ancient grave) on the island of Gavrinis, however, makes an interesting visit, while south of the island stand some megaliths that are only revealed at low tide.

Belle Ile, flanked on its southern side by the Côte Sauvage, is also worth a visit, but not during the height of the tourist season in August. The island is only about 16km (10 miles) long and 8km (5 miles) wide, and has roughly 1,000 inhabitants.

Before you go *Maps:* IGN 1:100,000 Nos. 13 and 15; IGN 1:25,000 (east and west) 0419, 0519–20, 0620, 0720, 0821–22 and 0921.

Getting there *By sea:* frequent boats leave Lorient for the island of Groix; from Quiberon to Belle Isle; and from Audierne to the Ile de Sein. Boat trips around the Gulf of Morbihan originate in Vannes.
By car: D765/D784 stretches from Quimper to the Pointe du Raz; from here D2, D785, D44, D783 and D781 more or less skirt the coastline.
By rail: there are 6 trains a day from Paris to Quimper, stopping at Vannes, Auray, Quimperlé and Rosporden. In summer trains also run from Paris to Auray and Quiberon, the port for Belle Ile.

Ancient stone megaliths abound throughout the Gulf of Morbihan.

By bus: buses run from Quimper to Audierne, Pointe du Raz, St-Guénolé, Lesconil and Concarneau.
Where to stay: there are hundreds of hotels along the coast, though Auray and Vannes are good bases.
Activities *Walking:* in the absence of GRs, ask about walks at the tourist offices.
Cycling: bicycles are available from SNCF stations at Auray, Lorient, Quiberon, Quimper and Vannes.
Further information *Tourist information:* Audierne, pl Liberté, T:98 70 12 20; Concarneau, quai d'Aiguillon, T:98 56 97 09; Quimper, 3 rue du Roi-Gradlon, T:98 95 04 69; Rosporden, rue le Bas, T:98 59 27 26.

Forêt de Paimpont

8,000ha (20,000 acres) of ancient woodland near Rennes

Along with the forest of Huelgoat in the Monts d'Arrée, Paimpont is the only

25

surviving part of the ancient forest of Argoat, which once covered the inland areas of Brittany. In the Middle Ages the forest was known as Brocéliande, and provided the setting for Chrétien de Troyes's Arthurian stories, which English speakers are more likely to know in the form of Thomas Malory's *Morte d'Arthur*.

It is difficult to escape the legends. Joseph of Arimathea, one of Jesus Christ's disciples, came to Brittany with the Holy Grail and lived among the beeches and the oaks in days when the forest was really wild. Merlin the magician also supposedly lived here; the forest contains Merlin's Step, Merlin's Tomb and the Val sans Retour (Valley of No Return), where the witch Morgana (Morgan le Fay) trapped unwary youths at the Rocher des Faux Amants (Rock of the False Lovers).

Brush away the fables and the forest is much reduced in stature. Many trees were cut down to fulfil the demand for wood during World War I. This and the poor rocky soil have largely prevented the oak and beech wood from re-establishing itself, except in a few favourable locations. More recently, foresters have been planting scotch pines instead of the broadleaves. Fortunately, a few areas have remained relatively untouched, including the Val sans Retour.

The forest's flora is of great interest to botanists. Although the acidic soils can't support a great variety of species, the richness of this area is due to its range of micro-habitats—rocky outcrops, ravines, dry and wet areas—forming a fascinating mosaic. The fauna holds some surprises as well, with green woodpeckers, normally a forest bird, here at home alongside chats on the heathlands and reed and sedge warblers in the marshes. Insectlife includes two notable species, the praying mantis and the *Ephippigère*, a form of bush cricket more typical of southern climes.

Before you go *Maps:* IGN 1:100,000 No. 16; IGN 1:25,000 1018–19, (east) and 1119 (west).

Getting there *By car:* the forest lies north of N24, which runs from Rennes to Lorient. Turn right just after Plélan onto D38, which leads to the Abbaye de Paimpont. Then take D40, which wends into the forest; at the crossroads is the start of GR37.

By rail: there are 6 daily trains from Paris (Gare Montparnasse) to Rennes. The best option is to rent a bicycle from Rennes station, take it by train to Montfort-sur-Meu, and cycle to Paimpont from there.

By bus: the bus from Rennes to Ploërmel runs down N24. Ask to stop at Plélan, where you can pick up GR37 to the Val sans Retour.

Where to stay: Rennes, Montfort, Plélan and Paimpont all have hotels. *Outdoor living:* camping is allowed at Paimpont; or ask at tourist offices for a list of sites.

Activities *Walking:* GR37 runs from Montfort through the forest to Plélan, and back into the forest again, along the Val sans Retour.

Further information *Tourist information:* Rennes, Pont-de-Nemours, T:99 79 01 98.

La Brière, the second largest marshland in France after the Camargue, consists of an intricate network of reed-fringed channels, where eels are common.

Parc Naturel Régional de Brière

The European beaver, despite strict protection measures, remains a threatened species in France.

Regional park encompassing 400sq km (150sq miles) of almost impenetrable marshland; located 40km (25 miles) northwest of Nantes

Lodged between the mouth of the Loire and the base of the peninsula of Brittany is the Brière, one of the more interesting *parcs régionaux* in France simply because it is so hard to penetrate. Marshy meadows form a barrier between the southern edge of the park and the sprawling industrial town of St-Nazaire. The main roads circumnavigate the marsh, leaving the more enterprising explorer itching to get inside.

A few tracks cross the park. Most are unsuitable for motor vehicles; many are difficult for walkers. A firm path suddenly turns to marsh, and as you sink in up to your ankles frogs leap effortlessly out of your way. Don't expect to hike vast distances. In racing jargon the going is slow, to the point

of bringing everything on two feet to a halt. Sometimes a reed swamp of phragmites will force you to retrace your steps and try another entry, but more often it will be one of the many waterways, mostly drainage ditches or canals, barring the way. The waterways are themselves probably the best way to get about the Brière, if you can persuade a kindly local to rent out one of the flat-bottom punts.

There's a reward for all this difficulty in movement. For the real enjoyment of the marsh is in just sitting and waiting for the wildlife to recover from the disturbance of your arrival and to resume their daily lives.

For the avid birdwatcher, few places can match the Brière, although in the vastness of the marsh you can feel overwhelmed. On the southwestern corner of the park a good place to visit is the Marais de Guérande and Traict du Croisic. Throughout this complex of salines and marshes you'll see plenty of bluethroats, for here they reach a very high density, as well as reed buntings and stonechats. The tracks which cut into the marshes are excellent vantage points for observing

28

the huge variety of waders and wildfowl, while in late summer and autumn a visit to the coast, at the Pointe du Croisic, offers excellent seabird watching. You can count on good numbers of those marvellous flying gannets, so sturdy yet very agile and elegant on the wing. Numerous skuas and shearwaters also pass through.

BEFORE YOU GO
Maps: IGN 1:100,000 No. 24; IGN 1:25,000 Nos. 1022–23 (east) and 1122 (west).
Guidebooks: the park publishes an ornithological map and booklets on the flora and fauna of the Brière.

GETTING THERE
By air: Nantes is the nearest airport.
By car: main roads enclose the regional park. N165 from Nantes to Vannes is the border on the northeast side while D773 and D774 circle the park to the south and west.
By rail: St-Nazaire has about 5 trains a day from Paris's Gare Montparnasse. There are also local trains to Pontchâteau from Nantes.

WHERE TO STAY
St-Nazaire is not an attractive place to stay, as the old town was destroyed in 1943. Other large towns with a wide range of hotels are La Baule, Nantes and Redon.

2 *auberge rurales* accommodate visitors to the park: Auberge de Kerhinet, St-Lyphard, Herbignac, T:40 24 86 46, and Auberge du Haut-Marland, St-André-des-Eaux, St-Nazaire, T:40 01 24 63.
Outdoor living: the tourist offices listed below have lists of campsites in the area.

ACTIVITIES
Walking: the park offices have details of recommended walks. Guided walks are organized in July and August by the Syndicat d'Initiative Briéron (address below).
Cycling: the quiet roads that cross the marsh are ideal for cycling. You can rent bicycles at the station in St-Nazaire.
Fishing: permits from the Commission Syndicale de Grande Brière Mottière, Mairie de Donges, T:40 88 65 47.
Riding: information from L'Association Régionale de Tourisme Equestre, 5 rue de Santeuil, Nantes,

T:40 73 57 19. Riding tours available from Le Centre du Sabot d'Or, Les Carroix de Cuneix, St-Nazaire, T:40 66 08 00.
Boats: tours are organized by boatyards in Chaussée-Neuve, Rosé, Fossés-Blancs, Bréca and Clos d'Orange.
Museums: there are a number of exhibitions around the park, including an ecomuseum at Kerhinet, near Saint-Lyphard, featuring a restored *briéron* village, as well as an animal park, Parc Animalier de Rozé, at St-Malo-de-Guersac.

FURTHER INFORMATION
Tourist information: La Baule, 8 pl de la Victoire, T:40 24 34 44; St-Nazaire, pl de l'Hôtel de Ville, T:40 22 40 65.
  Park headquarters is at 180 île de Fédrun, St-Joachim, T:40 88 42 72. Another useful information source is the Syndicat d'Initiative Briéron, Maison du Sabotier, 2 rue des Ecluses, La Chapelle-des-Marais, T:40 66 85 01.

THE BEAVER

The European beaver came close to extinction earlier this century. Although its only natural enemies are dogs and foxes, its fur is prized; hunting nearly provided the beaver's death warrant. It was one of the first animals in France to be protected, in 1905.

  Despite its considerable size, up to 80cm (2½ feet) long and 30kg (66lb) in weight, this rodent is not easy to see. It is discreet, wary of humans and almost exclusively nocturnal. It spends the day in its bank-side lodge. The European beaver's dams are a relatively modest construction, unlike the vast construction works of its North American cousins. The beaver is vegetarian, eating leaves and aquatic plants.

  There are now between 1,000 and 5,000 beavers left in France, mainly in the Parc Régional d'Armorique and in the Cévennes.

CHAPTER 2

The Northeast

When asked to explore the wild places of Northeast France I had doubts about just how much the area had to offer. Like most people, I associated the area first and foremost with Paris, apart from the coast whose ports are always busy with cross-Channel travellers. But I needn't have worried; my search was rewarded by a surprisingly wide variety of landscapes. I drove from seaside to mountains along straight roads lined with tall poplars and plane trees, crossing wide rolling plains and wooded ridges. Vast areas are forested; while a quarter of France is covered with trees, the proportion in Alsace and the Meuse (western Lorraine) rises to over a third.

The flora and fauna are correspondingly diverse. In Picardy, the northernmost tip of France, the flowers and grasses of the fragile dunes provide a fascinating contrast to the brilliant alpine plants of the *chaumes*, the high pastures in the Vosges mountains. In addition, there are curiosities such as the gnarled old beeches in the forests of the Montagne de Reims, or the pink seaweed that grows, amazingly, 400 kilometres (240 miles) from the sea on the salty marshes of Lorraine. Amid the vast expanses of farmland, milky white cows stand knee-deep in meadows of wildflowers. Beside the roads, too, wide verges are left uncut, often speckled with brilliant poppies.

The coastal bays, like the inland lakes and *étangs* (shallow lakes), attract many bird species as they migrate across Europe. In the Ardennes, on the Belgian border, birds of prey

The sun rises over the Vosges mountains, a haven for some of France's rarest and most secretive wildlife, including red and roe deer, and both pine and beech martens.

The delicate yellow flowers of the cowslip are a welcome springtime sight in wild pastures.

such as hawks, red kites and buzzards circle the forests, swooping for food along the meandering valleys of the Meuse and Semoy. Boars, wildcats and martens still inhabit the forests of the Vosges.

Admittedly, the Northeast is only unspoiled in patches, as it also encompasses the great conurbation of Paris, the flat industrial northern plain, and the broad sunny hillsides whose chalky soil has been covered since the 12th century in one of France's best-known and most valuable crops—the vines of Champagne. To the south of the wine-growing region is the "wet" part of Champagne, so called because of its many lakes and rivers. This is where you can really feel out in the country—en province—as you absorb the atmosphere of rural France.

The Vosges mountains in Alsace, on France's eastern border with Germany, were the largest stretch of wildness I discovered in the Northeast. While less extensive and lower than the Alps and less remote than the Pyrenees, they are nonetheless one of France's most beautiful mountainous areas, offering dense forests and secluded lakes, pretty walking trails and traditional villages.

With its curious German-sounding place names and red-roofed villages, Alsace seems removed from the rest of France. Annexed to the German empire in 1870, it only became French again after World War I.

In fact the whole of the Northeast echoes with memories of war. Over the centuries, the armies of Caesar, Charlemagne, Napoleon and Hitler have all marched across the wide plains and ridges of Champagne, Lorraine and Picardy, where the open countryside provides ideal battle-grounds. Who hasn't heard of the battles of Verdun and the Marne?

Though the scars of battle have now healed, the countryside and its wildlife were changed in the process. Woods were felled for the war effort, and the fragile dunes along the coast were trampled by the Allied armies arriving from Britain. Now farmers have become the main threat to the environment. So much marshland has been drained to make way for crops that special areas such as the canals and marshes of the Ried, the old flood plain of the Rhine at the foot of the Vosges, have all but disappeared. So, too, have the storks that once nested in the roof-tops there. Traditionally, their arrival in March was a sign of good luck, but their numbers have steadily dwindled during the last 25 years.

Tourism, too, is taking its toll, particularly in the Vosges, where ski resorts are being developed. Around Paris, there are of course similar pressures on land for visitor attractions as well as housing and industry. Sadly, cavalier attitudes towards building restrictions are doing nothing to enhance the environment, particularly in areas such as the superb natural forests north of the capital.

GETTING THERE

By air: the main airports are Paris-Charles de Gaulle and Paris-Orly. Strasbourg also has some international flights while Lille is on the internal network.

By sea: there are cross-Channel ferries from Dover and Folkestone to Boulogne and Calais.

By car: from Paris, A1 runs north through Lille, with A26 branching off near Arras for Calais and A25 at Lille for Dunkerque. Another is planned through Amiens and Boulogne to link up with the Channel Tunnel at Calais. East from Paris, A4 cuts through Reims and Metz to Strasbourg.

By rail: SNCF (French Railways) operates frequent services between the Gare du Nord in Paris and the Channel ports. The main routes east from Gare de l'Est (Paris) are through Châlons-sur-Marne and Nancy to Strasbourg, and through Troyes and Chaumont to Belfort and Mulhouse.

By bus: most towns have local services but country areas are often served only once a day, and not at all on Sun.

WHEN TO GO

Spring and autumn are peak periods for birdwatchers, as migratory birds stop over in large numbers along the coast or on the inland reservoirs and lakes. Wildflowers are in bloom Mar–Nov, but are most abundant in spring. The region never has extremes of weather, although some mountain roads are impassable when there is heavy snow in the Vosges.

WHERE TO STAY

There is no shortage of hotels, inns, hostels and *chambres d'hôtes* (bed and breakfast at farms and private houses). Lists are available at tourist offices. For a small fee you can book accommodation at Accueil de France tourist offices in Calais, Lille, Metz, Nancy, Reims and Strasbourg.

Many towns have a municipal campsite. Camping is permitted at some farms.

ACTIVITIES

Walking: several *grande randonnée* footpaths cross the Northeast, or you can walk along the coast south from the Belgian border to Etaples. There are 6 *parcs naturels régionaux* in the area—the Ballon des Vosges, Forêt de l'Orient, Lorraine, Montagne de Reims, Nord-Pas-de-Calais and Vosges du Nord—all with marked nature trails and footpaths.

Cycling: bicycles are available at railway stations, campsites and cycle shops.

Riding: stables offer short as well as longer treks.

Watersports: sailing and windsurfing are available on the Forêt de l'Orient and Der-Chantecoq lakes and on the Madine *étang* in Lorraine; also on the sea at the Somme bay and the beaches around Le Touquet. There is canoeing on the rivers in the Ardennes.

Fishing: permits can be bought locally for rivers and lakes. Enquire at tourist offices or town halls.

Skiing: cross-country pistes are marked out when the snow is adequate in the Ardennes and Vosges, where there are also some downhill runs.

FURTHER INFORMATION

Information is available from the head office of the French Government Tourist Office, 127 av des Champs Elysées, Paris, T:47 23 61 72.

Côte d'Opale and Baie de la Somme

Varied habitat for migrating birds in surprisingly secluded coastline by France's busy cross-Channel ferry ports

The easily accessible coastline around the Channel ports of Calais and Boulogne, known as the Côte d'Opale or Opal Coast, is as busy a spot for migratory birds as for people and boats. The grass-topped cliffs, sandy beaches and wide estuaries are among France's richest areas for ornithologists. As cross-Channel tourists rush to and from their ferries, few are aware of the natural delights just beyond the docks.

Nature lovers and birdwatchers may find it all too tempting to speed off down the *autoroute* in search of more exotic locations. But if you have time to spare, do not write off this bit of coastline. Even before you set foot in France there is plenty to see by scanning the swirling flocks of gulls as your ferry slips in to Boulogne harbour. This is degree-level birdwatching to be sure, but for those eager for a challenge, there is always the chance of spotting something unusual, such as a glaucous gull in winter, or little gull in late summer.

Once on land, it's a difficult choice of either turning left for the impressive white cliffs of Cap Gris-Nez and Cap Blanc-Nez and some of the best migrant birdwatching along the Channel coast, or right for the salt marshes and estuarine wildlife of the Canche and the Somme. Dunkerque may seem less enticing for the wildlife enthusiast, but again you would be wrong. Even the stark, forbidding east jetty on the new port provides one of the best vantage points for watching migrant sea birds—divers, grebes, skuas and ducks—while the Braek dyke is noted for its wintering flocks of snow bunting, and all sorts of rarities which turn up in the adjacent lagoon. The paradox of so many exciting wild birds seeking out such desolate industrial landscapes imparts a curious sense of wilderness difficult to find in many more picturesque locations.

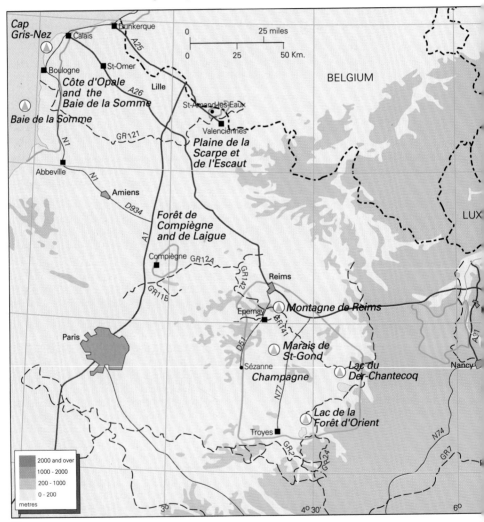

Just along the coast, east of Dunkerque, is a small nature reserve at La Dune Marchand. This covers 120 hectares (296 acres) of sand dune and maritime scrub with scattered damp hollows (dune slacks), presenting a welcome break along the heavily industrialized coast. The site offers a classic example of natural dune formation, ranging from the wind-buffeted seaward frontal dunes of golden sand, to the so-called grey dunes, with their luxuriant carpet of lichens and mosses. Here you'll find such relics of glacial times as sand pansy and early forget-me-not dotted among the open areas, which nestle between the dense thickets of sea buckthorn, creeping willow and wild privet. But the most exciting features of this little reserve are another group of glacial relict flowers growing in the damp dune slacks, and even in old bomb craters; these include three species of rare orchid—fen orchid, musk orchid and marsh helleborine—as well as the delicate mauve flowers of autumn gentian and the inaptly named grass of Parnassus, which, with its five-petalled white flowers, bears more similarity to saxifrage than grass.

Between the little resorts of Wimereux and Ambleteuse, a sandy footpath leads over the dunes of the nature reserve around the Slack estuary. Small, explanatory signs mark the spiky reeds and grasses, fleshy green plants, and delicate flowers that naturally colonize dunes as long as they're not too heavily trampled.

One of the most striking features of this coastline is the band of dunes that stretches for two kilometres (over a mile) inland in places. Having survived the ravages of two World Wars and haphazard building development, their fragile vegetation is now protected as they are part of the Parc Naturel Régional Nord-Pas-de-Calais, which covers the coast south from Calais to Le Touquet. The park also encompasses the canals and marshes around St-Omer, and these have their own distinct wildlife.

The coastal path that runs all along the clifftops and dunes from the Belgian border in the north to the Baie d'Authie (south of Le Touquet) is regarded by many as the most beautiful in France, offering glorious Channel views and wide inland vistas of rolling farmland. At several points you can scramble down the rocky path to the sea itself. Though spring and autumn are the most spectacular periods for passage birds, there is plenty to observe here throughout the year.

The shallow bays between Calais and the Somme are home for a rich variety of sea birds and vegetation all year long. So, too, are the cliffs, dunes and marshes of Gris-Nez, Blanc-Nez and Platier d'Oye. An expedition to Cap Gris-Nez, halfway

Northeast France

Key
— Exploration zones.
▨ National parks.
— Roads.
- - Footpaths.
Ⓐ Points of interest.
—•— International boundaries.

GERMANY

Parc Naturel Régional des Vosges du Nord

Bitche

GR53

49⁰

Strasbourg

N420

Dié

Vosges

Colmar

48⁰

Mulhouse 7⁰ 30'

-N-between Calais and Boulogne, may not sound all that adventurous, but the area ranks as one of the most ecologically interesting sites in northern France, with an abundance of shrews, voles, field mice, harvest mice and even the rare dormouse. Look out for newts and the rare natterjack toad where the cliffs have crumbled. The area is also a must for anyone interested in tiger beetles, fast-running insects with huge eyes and jaws. Also, if you get bitten, take comfort in that you may have nourished a very rare native especies of horsefly.

Most nature enthusiasts visiting the towering cliffs of Cap Gris-Nez and Cap Blanc-Nez are birdwatchers. There are few spectacles more impressive than wave after wave of migrant birds looming out of an October morning mist, and from such a vantage point you can almost feel part of this great avian transit.

The Baie de la Somme, located south of the Côte d'Opale, is another remarkable spot, particularly when the tide recedes, leaving small rivulets and miles of sand. From the steep pebbly beach at Le Hourdel, at the southern end of the bay, you can watch as the on-rushing tide quickly transforms the sandbanks to a vast expanse of water.

The Somme bay is a vast place, with expanses of mud flats and salines stretching away for miles. There may be plenty of activity—flotillas of northern ducks out on the river or in some of the lagoons, and innumerable small brown waders resting on some slightly elevated mud bank—but identifying these birds is another matter. It's best to savour the peculiar ambience of the estuary, a natural larder for millions of migratory wildfowl and waders.

There is some visual relief on the north side of the bay, which forms part of the large and privately owned bird reserve, the Parc du Marquenterre. Nature trails guide visitors around to some excellent vantage points for observing a selection of the hundreds of species of birds which occur here each year, and also wind their way into the impressive towering sand dunes, which extend a considerable distance up the coast to the north.

BEFORE YOU GO

Maps: IGN 1:100,000 No. 1; IGN 1:25,000 Nos. 2202–6; Michelin 1:200,000 Nos. 51 and 52.

Guidebooks: there is a *Topo-Guide Provisoire* on the Littoral Pas-de-Calais with maps and notes on the coastal path. *La Nature en Baie de Somme* is one of the Ouest France series of natural history booklets. The *parc naturel* has leaflets on the wildlife of the dunes and cliffs; its *Promenade dans le Marais Audomarois* describes the marshes near St-Omer and their history.

GETTING THERE

By sea: cross-Channel car ferries run throughout the day from Dover and Folkestone to Boulogne and Calais (Sealink and P&O); also Ramsgate to Dunkerque

(Sally). There is a Hoverspeed hovercraft service, taking 40mins from Dover to Boulogne or Calais.

By car: the N1 coast road runs from the Belgian border through to Abbeville at the head of the Somme canal. A new *autoroute*, A16, is being built from Calais to Paris to link up with the Channel Tunnel.

By rail: main-line services link Paris to Calais (via St-Omer), Boulogne and Dunkerque. Other trains run along the coast from Abbeville.

By bus: there are regular services in and between the main resorts on the coast and inland to St-Omer, Montreuil and Abbeville.

WHERE TO STAY

The area has a good range of places to stay from well-appointed hotels such as the 4-star Westminster in Le Touquet (T:21 05 48 48) to *chambres d'hôtes* (bed and breakfast), hostels and farms. In the 2-star category well placed for seeing the coast or exploring inland is the Hostellerie du Château des Tourelles in the village of Le Wast, T:21 33 34 78. Boulogne Youth Hostel, T:21 31 48 22.

Outdoor living: campsite La Bien-Assise (T:21 35 20 77) is in an attractive château setting at Guines and also has pine chalets.

ACTIVITIES

Walking: you can join the 148-km (90-mile) coast path anywhere from the Belgian border to Conchil-le-Temple. Several other long-distance paths (GR120, 121, 123, 124, 127 and 128) run inland. The Parc du Marquenterre has

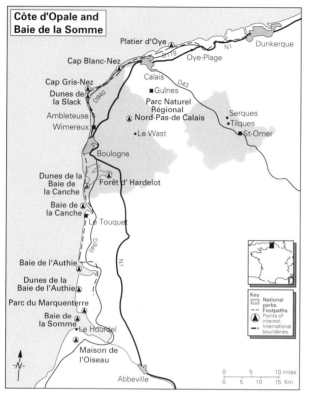

Côte d'Opale and Baie de la Somme

Plaine de la Scarpe et de l'Escaut

Nature is reclaiming this former coal-mining area on the Belgian border, 45km (27 miles) southeast of Lille

One of the least likely places I expected to find nature in the wild was France's industrial northeast along the border with Belgium. Yet the plain of the canalized rivers Scarpe and Escaut has woods, marshes, ponds and streams, where visitors can feel buried in the depths of the countryside.

The Plaine de la Scarpe et de l'Escaut is the largest part of the three areas which together form the Parc Naturel Régional Nord-Pas-de-Calais. Once a coal-mining area stretching for 40km (25 miles) east to west, and 15km (10 miles) north to south, it comprises three main areas: woodland (mostly oaks, pines and beeches), farmland and marshy ponds. At the centre is the old spa town of St-Amand-les-Eaux. The wide variations in both the acidity of the soil and the humidity have encouraged an enormous diversity of wildlife, particularly birds, insects and plants, now that the mines have closed and nature has been able to take over again.

Having crunched my way up a black gritty path on a disused coal heap beside the Mare à Goriaux, I surveyed a scene as wild as any in France: a lake, which has grown, thanks to mining subsidence, from three marshy ponds, bordered by alder and willow. Its banks

several short circular trails.
Fishing: all along the coast, people fish in the sea with lines, particularly at the bays of the Somme and Canche. Deep-sea fishing is possible from Boulogne.
Watersports: the sandy beaches, particularly between Le Touquet and the Somme, are ideal for windsurfing and sailing. Canoeing is available on the Canche estuary at Etaples. There are barge cruises on the Audomarois canals around St-Omer.
Ornithology: tableaux of birds set against seascape backgrounds are displayed at the Maison de l'Oiseau at the Carrefour du Hourdel on D204 near St-Valéry (T:22 26 93 93); open daily Mar–mid-Nov. The Parc Ornithologique du

Marquenterre has 2 ornithological trails in an extensive wooded park; open daily end-May–mid-Nov with guides at each of the hides during July and Aug. During the shooting season the park is closed, though permits are sold for its reserve on the Somme bay.

FURTHER INFORMATION
Tourist information:
Abbeville, pl Libération, T:22 24 27 92; Boulogne, pont Marguet, T:23 31 68 38; Calais, 12 blvd Clemenceau, T:21 96 62 40; St-Omer, blvd Pierre-Guillain, T:21 98 40 88.

Pas-de-Calais Tourisme, 44 Grande-Rue, Boulogne, T:21 31 98 58. Parc Naturel Régional Pas-de-Calais, Station Marine, 28 av Foch, Wimereux, T:21 32 13 74.

are thickly lined with reeds, bulrushes and waterlilies, providing a haven for waterfowl and insects, while the shallow waters conceal carp, bream and perch. On the flat-topped slag heap itself, young birches flourish and in spring the woods are carpeted with anemones, as well as bluebells and blueberries. Sweet-smelling lily of the valley appear by May.

Over 200 species of bird have been observed here since the park was created. Wild duck, grebe and heron thrive on the shallow warm water, while all around you see and hear finches, larks and nightingales.

In the autumn and spring, the lake and woods become a dormitory for large numbers of migratory bird. If you're really lucky, in spring you

The tidal estuary of the Somme is a vast desolate landscape but also home to countless thousands of wetland birds.

might see an osprey swooping on to the water, although its stay in the area is always brief. Every October, wild duck reappear, in some years as many as 2,000.

At the centre of the park, the Forêt de Raismes-St-Amand-Wallers, the largest area of woodland, was largely replanted with firs after substantial felling during World War I. However, an avenue of 180-year-old beeches remains, regally lining one of the roads through the forest. Acacias were also planted to improve the soil, which now supports oak, hornbeam and hawthorn. In five special botanic reserve areas, there are the diminutive carnivorous sundew, broom and mosses.

Access to the special nature reserves is restricted for the general public as there are no roads or footpaths, but you can drive for miles along the narrow lanes which criss-cross the park, and there are marked walking trails.

Early morning frost sparkles in the winter landscape on the margins of the Forêt de Compiègne.

Between the Amaury lake and the River Escaut, near the village of Hergnies, a centre for watersports, walks and educational visits has been set up.
Before you go *Maps:* IGN 1:100,000 No. 2; IGN 1:50,000 Nos. 2605, 2606, 2506 and 2505; Michelin 1:200,000 No. 51.
Guidebooks: Espace Naturel Régional publishes various leaflets entitled *La Vie en Vert*; these deal with the wildlife and geology as well as walking trails.
Getting there *By car:* the nearest town is Valenciennes, 5km (3 miles) south of the park boundary. A23 (Valenciennes–Lille) passes near the Mare à Goriaux, while D169 (Valenciennes–Tournai) and D935 also cross it.
By rail: the nearest station is Valenciennes.

By bus: a half-hourly service, Ligne 4H, runs from the station to the edge of the Forêt de Raismes and near the Centre d'Amaury, Hergnies.
Where to stay: there are several hotels in St-Amand-les-Eaux, including the 2-star Grand Hôtel de Paris (T:27 48 21 00) or, near the Forêt de Raismes, the Hôtel Thermale (T:27 48 50 37), a grand spa establishment with a pool and casino.

Hostel accommodation is available at the Maison du Parc Le Luron, once a hunting lodge (T:27 27 88 27) and at the Centre d'Amaury (T:27 25 28 85).
Outdoor living: try Camping Mont des Bruyères (T:48 96 09 36).
Activities: the Centre d'Amaury is the main centre for organized activities. Sailing boats, windsurfers, canoes and bicycles are available, and you can fish in the lake.
Walking: trails wind through the Forêt de Raismes, around the Mare à Goriaux, and beside the lake and canals at the Amaury centre. The GR121 long-distance footpath crosses the park.
Cycling: bicycles are available at St-Amand-les-Eaux, Maulde and the Centre d'Amaury, Hergnies. Several forest lanes closed to vehicles are open to cyclists.
Further information *Tourist information:* St-Amand-les-Eaux, Tour Abbatiale, T:27 27 85 00.

Parc Naturel Régional Nord-Pas-de-Calais, Plaine de la Scarpe et de l'Escaut, Maison du Parc Le Luron, 357 rue Notre-Dame-d'Amour, St-Amand-les-Eaux, T:27 27 88 27. Centre d'Amaury, Hergnies, T:27 25 28 85.

40

BEECH FORESTS OF NORTHERN FRANCE

The imposing beech is most at home in central Europe, but in northern France through to Belgium it forms the major component of many of the great forests. Typically the trees have been subject to selective felling, leaving great stands of towering, even-aged trees. They occur mostly on shallow, porous soil, which, combined with the very low light penetration to the ground in high summer, makes for a very open, if rather dark, interior. The straight, grey trunks stretching up to the high canopy impart a mysterious air, like being in some natural cathedral. Birdlife is hard to track down, being mostly hidden in the upper canopy, but where there are mixed stands with hornbeam and oak and great rides cut through the forest, you may catch a glimpse of some of the raptors, such as goshawk, sparrowhawk or honey buzzard.

Forêt de Compiègne and Forêt de Laigue

Former royal hunting grounds, now preserving their rich wildlife; dense forests located 80km (50 miles) north of Paris

The ancient forests that surround Paris number among the country's most attractive. Despite the millions who live in the area and seek recreation outdoors, these forests are often remarkably wild, with footpaths that lead into thick woods where silence is only disturbed by the rustling of the wind. Among them, the beech and oak Forêt de Compiègne is one of the largest in the country, covering 14,458ha (35,700 acres). It is less frequented than those nearer the capital, though criss-crossed by a well-marked network of footpaths, bridleways and cycle-tracks, as well as paved roads. Adjoining it across the River

Aisne is the Forêt de Laigue, which covers another 3,827ha (9,450 acres).

Sturdy wooden signposts, painted white with small pointers, caught my eye as I drove into the forest area along the avenue des Beaux-Monts, which leads straight from Compiègne's impressive National Palace. The *poteaux* (posts) stand reassuringly at every crossing of the many straight sandy tracks leading through the forest. The tourist office's explanation for the posts dates from the middle of the 19th century. Out on a hunting expedition, the Empress Eugénie, wife of Napoléon III, got hopelessly lost, not surprising as the leafy alleyways all look remarkably similar. To prevent a repetition, the emperor immediately ordered the posts to be erected. Though some are by now dilapidated, if you look closely you can see that each bears a red spot. Stand with your back to it and the way ahead always leads back to Compiègne.

Both forests were at the heart of the vast Sylvancestes woods that covered the entire area in Roman times; due to their proximity to the capital, successive French kings jealously preserved them for hunting. The oldest oak woods in the Beaux-Monts area, on the northern side of the forest, were planted by François I during the 16th century. During the 18th and 19th centuries, 3,000 more hectares (7,400 acres) of oaks were planted, together with pines in places where the soil is poorer. Beeches predominate in the hillier parts, where the forest trails are particularly pleasant for walking; sunlight streams through the branches, making the undergrowth a vibrant jumble of wildflowers.

The highest points, from which there are remarkably lovely views, are inappropriately called *monts* (mountains), yet rise to no more than 120m (400ft)! At the lowest levels are small tranquil lakes where fishing is allowed. Their reedy banks provide a haven for large numbers of wild ducks, herons and a regular passage of migrant waterfowl. The trees are also home for a wide range of forest birds, but when walking through the imposing columns of the high beech forest you are more likely to experience a blanketing silence; the occasional robin or chaffinch may call, but the only movement is a faint rustle of leaves in the wind. The specialities—the woodpeckers, owls and raptors—stay hidden. Wild boar and roe and red deer are common in the remoter parts of the forests, particularly on the Mont des Singes in Laigue.

In springtime the ground is carpeted with wild anemones and bluebells, while the Laigue's southeast-facing slopes are covered in sweet-smelling lily of the valley. In autumn, the forests turn a stunning amber, thanks to the beeches.

Before you go *Maps:* IGN 1:25,000 No. 403; Michelin 1:200,000 No. 56.

Getting there *By car:* 80km (50 miles) north of Paris, N31 leads from the A1 into Compiègne. The D932, D973, D332 and N31 lead into the Forêt de Compiègne, while the D85 and the D130 cross it. D130 also crosses the Forêt de Laigue.

By rail: there are regular services to Compiègne from Paris.

By bus: regular bus services operate throughout the area from Compiègne.

Where to stay: Compiègne has a good selection of hotels at various prices. The 2-star Hôtel de Flandre (T:44 83 24 40) is near the station and overlooks the River Aisne. More central is the 2-star Hôtel de France in rue Eugène-Floquet, T:44 40 02 74. There are also rural Gîtes d'Etape in the area, included on walking and cycling routes.

Outdoor living: camping is permitted in designated areas within the forests.

Activities *Walking:* the 2 forests are criss-crossed by marked trails, including GR124-A from Paris to Belgium. There is a 10-km (6-mile) ecological circuit around the Mont St-Pierre.

Cycling: marked tracks run through the forests. A popular excursion is to Pierrefonds, about 25km (15 miles) round trip. Bicycles are available at the railway station.

Riding: there are bridlepaths in the forests; riders are not allowed on footpaths. Information on treks from the tourist office in Compiègne (address below).

Fishing: permits for the Aisne

The fragrant lily of the valley is one of the characteristic spring flowers of natural beech woodland.

and Oise rivers and forest ponds from the Fédération Départementale des Associations de Pêche et de Pisciculture de l'Oise, 10 rue Pasteur, Compiègne, T:44 40 46 41.

Exhibition: there is a small information centre with displays on wildlife and trees in the Maison Forestière des Etangs St-Pierre, open Mon–Sat.

Sightseeing: the most famous part of Compiègne forest is Clairière de l'Armistice, Armistice Clearing, where Marshal Foch, Commander-in-Chief of the Allied Forces, headed the delegation that on 11 November 1918 signed the Armistice ending World War I. The ceremony took place in a railway carriage, a reconstruction of which stands here as a small museum.

Further information *Tourist information:* Compiègne, pl de l'Hôtel de Ville, T:44 40 01 00; Pierrefonds, pl de l'Hôtel de Ville, T:44 42 80 38.

Champagne

The lakes and forests of "wet"
Champagne contrast with the familiar
image of intensive viticulture in the "dry"
part

The sturdy green vines that have made Champagne famous stretch in ruler-straight lines over hillside after hillside in the "dry" northern part of the region. As I was soon to discover, "wet" Champagne to the south presents a very different land-scape: a land of forests and vast lakes, pastures and crops, with half-timbered vil-lages throughout.

"Dry" Champagne refers to the chalk areas. Formerly a desolate wasteland, these are now widely cultivated and only the inac-cessible military lands lend any clue to the old natural landscape. However, over the large expanse of open, cultivated dry land conditions are still favourable for two of Europe's most exciting "steppe" birds—the stone curlew and little bustard. Despite their size, they are almost impossible to pick out, being perfectly camouflaged against the grey and brown stony ground. Much commoner are grey partridge and quail, to be heard but rarely seen. You will also see crested larks and corn buntings, typical of arable France.

Reference literature proclaims that over 24,000 hectares (59,300 acres) of vineyards on Champagne's chalky ridges are dedi-cated to producing 200 million bottles of France's most sought-after wine each year. So it doesn't seem likely that the area might allow itself the luxury of leaving any corner of the precious soil uncultivated, let alone wild. Yet between the towns of Epernay and Reims, the hilly forests of the Mon-tagne de Reims provide a sharp contrast to the vineyards. The area is not so much a

Poppies grow wild in the Champagne region in
defiance of farmers' cultivation.

mountain as a plateau, the highest point being 228 metres (750 feet) at Mount Sinai, which affords a spectacular view over the Champagne plain.

The ancient beech woods at Verzy, on the northeastern side of the Montagne de Reims, are a particular curiosity as they are known to have existed since the 6th century. The oldest trees, mutations of the common beech, are probably more than 500 years old. With the passage of time their branches have become so intertwined they form a domed ceiling, while the thick gnarled trunks, with their grotesque bumps and twists, are like something out of a Disney cartoon. Footpaths lead into the woods from special parking areas, but, dispelling any air of fantasy, the trees are now protected by fences.

Bilberries carpet the undergrowth, while in the marshy areas sundew thrives with its curious round carnivorous leaves. Roe and red deer populate the woods but the arrival of nearby *autoroutes* has severely limited the number of wild boar that once settled here from forests farther north.

As you approach the wet region to the south of the vineyards, the soil turns to clay. This leads to a much greener lusher vegeta-

The chanterelle (*Cantharellus cibarius*) is a highly-prized and tasty mushroom. Its vivid orange trumpets are abundant in broad-leaved deciduous forests.

tion, also largely agricultural, but punctuated with oak woods, lakes and marshes. Only a small patch of the St-Gond marshes, which once covered the plain to the south of Epernay, survive. Laced with rivulets and canals, the boggy land has been greatly exploited for peat. However, the marshes that have survived beside the road from Bannes to Joches are rich in wildlife, particularly birds: little owls, nightjars, great grey shrikes and several species of woodpecker, including wryneck. The tall plantations of poplars are the place to stop and look for golden orioles—or rather, listen, for despite their gaudy plumage they usually remain well concealed. In the few marshy fragments left the elegant hen harrier and Montagu's harrier still cling on, but only just.

With the creation of two large reservoirs, the Lac de l'Orient and the Lac du Der-Chantecoq (and a third, the Aube, nearing completion), the countryside of this "wet" Champagne area has seen considerable changes since the 1960s. Forests, farmland and villages have disappeared underwater, which is now popular with many local people for watersports. At the same time, parts of both lakes have areas protected as ornithological reserves (though in summer the birds are disturbed by all the leisure activities and the lower water levels). Red kites nest in the ash woods around the lakes. Other common nesters here include the great crested grebe and, to a lesser extent, shoveller ducks, pochards and teal. In the dense mixed woodland of the Forêt d'Orient are up to 350 different types of mushroom.

In the last decade, the Lac du Der-Chantecoq—the country's largest stretch of water, with a perimeter of 77 kilometres (46 miles)—has become one of the country's major sites for migrating cranes. In autumn and spring, around 50,000 cross France on a 200-kilometre (125-mile) front on the migrating route between Sweden and Spain. Champagne has always figured on the route, but since the lake, which is near St-Dizier, was created in 1974, increasingly large numbers have been stopping there, estimated as up to 70 per cent in some years.

BEFORE YOU GO

Maps: IGN 1:100,000 No. 22; Michelin 1:200,000 No. 61.
Guidebooks: booklets on the two natural regional parks are on sale at park information centres and local bookshops. They include walking and cycling trails in the Montagne de Reims, a scientific report on the Forêt de l'Orient and *La Grue Cendrée* (the crane) *dans les Grands Lacs de Champagne.*

The Golden oriole is hard to spot high up in the dense woodland canopy, despite the bright plumage of the males.

GETTING THERE

By car: the east–west Autoroute de l'Est (A4) from Paris crosses the Montagne de Reims near Reims, as do N4 and D51. Various scenic circular routes are signposted. The Orient lake and forest border N19 between Troyes and Bar-le-Duc; there is also a scenic route around the lake. The Der-Chantecoq lake lies due west of D384, 18km (10 miles) south of St-Dizier.
By rail: there are direct services from Paris-Est to Epernay, with connections to Reims and St-Dizier.
By bus: for the Forêt d'Orient, a service links Troyes and Vendeuvre; for Der-Chantecoq there are buses from St-Dizier to Eclaron and Braucourt.

WHERE TO STAY

There is a choice of hotels in Troyes, Reims, St-Dizier and Epernay, as well as country inns throughout the area. The auberge Cheval Blanc du Lac (T:26 72 62 65) is near the dam Der-Chantecoq in the half-timbered village of Giffaumont-Champaubert.

There are youth hostels in St-Dizier, St-Julien-les-Villas and Vendeuvre-sur-Barse.
Outdoor living: Camping de la Presqu'île de Champaubert (T:25 04 13 20) is beside the Der-Chantecoq lake. Near Reims on the rte de Châlons-sur-Marne is the Champagne campsite (T: 26 85 41 22).

ACTIVITIES

Walking: marked trails traverse the Forêt d'Orient, including one around the spot where the Order of Templars settled in the C13th, giving the forest its name. The GR24 long-distance footpath crosses the Orient forest and the GR 14, 141 and 142 cross the Montagne de Reims, where there are also 8 marked routes, from 2–20km (1–12 miles), encompassing the villages, views, wildlife and architecture. There are also 12 short walks in the Verzy and Hautvillers woods.
Cycling: information on recommended rides from the Maison du Parc at Piney or, with bike hire as well, from the Maison du Parc, Pourcy.
Watersports: several clubs are based on the lakes, offering sailing, waterskiing, windsurfing and scuba diving. Fishing is allowed on both lakes. There are sandy beaches at Geraudot and Mesnil-Saint-Père.
Reserves/museums: in the Forêt d'Orient, an animal reserve has red and roe deer and wild boar; also bird sanctuaries with observation points beside each lake. The open-air Museum Village of Ste-Marie-du-Lac features half-timbered buildings typical of the Champagne countryside. There is also an exhibition on the natural history of the Montagne de Reims at the Maison du Parc in Pourcy, and a museum devoted to forestry, La Maison du Bûcheron, in the village of Germaine.

FURTHER INFORMATION

Tourist information: Troyes, 16 blvd Carnot, T:25 73 00 36; St-Rémy-en-Bouzemont, Lac du Der-Chantecoq, Maison du Lac, Port-de-Giffaumont, T:26 72 62 80.
Regional tourist office for Champagne-Ardennes, 5 rue de Jéricho, Châlons-sur-Marne, T:26 64 35 92.
Regional Nature Parks: Montagne de Reims, Maison du Parc, Pourcy, T:26 59 44 44; Forêt d'Orient, Maison du Parc, Piney, T:25 41 35 57.

Parc Naturel Régional de Lorraine

Forests, salt ponds and grassy hillside oases give this park, located near Strasbourg, a singular identity

There I was, 400km (250 miles) from the sea in the heart of Lorraine, yet a small patch of saltwort was growing beside other marine plants in a sandy beach-like dell. Its tiny distinctive leaves, spiky and a delicate pink colour, looked decidedly out of place so far from the coast.

This is just one of the remarkable quirks of nature found in the extensive Parc Naturel Régional de Lorraine, which lies on either side of the River Moselle. The salt beneath the soil, on the vast plain between the Moselle to the west and the Vosges in the east, rises to the surface in several places at shallow *mares salées* (salt ponds), which evaporate in summer. Most plants cannot tolerate the salinity, so only those that thrive by the sea grow here. On the edge of the village of Marsal, a short trail enables visitors to observe these fragile plants in a small botanic reserve. They need protection not only from people, but also the hardier reeds and grasses that would otherwise overwhelm them.

Lorraine is also notable for its *pelouses calcaires*. These are patches of grass on sheltered hillsides where the limestone is topped by a thin layer of comparatively poor sandy soil, which supports an exceptional variety of exotic

and rare wildflowers. A typical example lies near the village of Génicourt-sur-Meuse, where you can follow a marked trail at the foot of a disused quarry below the hillside. Twenty different varieties of wild orchid bloom here between May and September, when their delicate and exquisitely marked petals mingle with over 30 other varieties of flower. Around them are broom, hawthorn and hazel, as well as saplings of oak and birch.

Another characteristic of Lorraine, particularly on the eastern side, is its large shallow *étangs* (lakes). Though too big to be called ponds, they are never more than waist-deep, so the water warms through to the bottom in summer. Some *étangs* are used extensively for watersports, but others are kept strictly for the birds and fish. The still waters of the innumerable lagoons and their reed fringes offer an attractive stopping point to all kinds of birds of passage: black storks, black-winged stilts and, in winter, the very rare white-tailed eagle are among the specialities.

Of the 500 species of birds seen in France, around 320 have been sighted at the large Etang de Lindre; 120 actually nest here, including the elusive and now rare bittern. Otters occur here, too, but count yourself lucky if you see one. Surrounded by woods and fields, the habitat is varied and wonderfully undisturbed as public access is severely restricted; most of it is surrounded by privately owned farmland with no roads across. A good spot from which to observe is the old dam in the village of Lindre-Basse at the western end, where you can walk for

a short distance beside the water. You can also try the other end, at Guermange, where there is a hide.

Another must is the Etang de Gondrexange. Like many others in the region, it is noted as a place for migrant birds, but for many people the most magical time is spring, when the dawn chorus is in full flood, pouring across the still waters from the dense forests and reed beds. You can simply admire the rich symphony of bird calls, dominated by two virtuosi— the nightingale and the golden

oriole—but if you pay closer attention you may be rewarded with the short and simple song of the collared flycatcher, in one of its very few localities in France.

Before you go *Maps:* IGN 1:100,000 Nos. 11 and 12; Michelin 1:200,000 Nos. 57 and 62.

Guidebooks: Guide du Parc Naturel Régional de Lorraine (Créer).

Getting there *By car:* the east–west A4 and north–south A31 cross Lorraine at Metz. *By rail:* main stations are Metz, Nancy and Sarrebourg.

By bus: there is a network of local services radiating from Metz and Nancy, but you cannot rely on being able to get one to every small village; many services stop on Sun.

Where to stay: accommodation of all standards is available in Nancy or Metz, and there are many smaller towns and villages with 1- and 2-star hotels. Pont-à-Mousson on the Moselle lies between the 2 parts of the regional park. Sarrebourg and Sarre-Union are convenient for the east side, St-Mihiel for the west.

Open water, marshland and forest support abundant and varied wildlife in the Etang de Gondrexange.

Outdoor living: campsites include Camping de la Base de Plein Air de St-Mihiel (T:29 89 03 59) and the Municipal de Brabois at Villers-lès-Nancy (T:83 27 18 28).

Activities *Walking:* the regional park organizes nature walks throughout the summer, with themes including birdwatching, the *mares salées* and *pelouses* *calcaires*. GR5 crosses the east part of the regional park. There is a trail to the *mare salée* at Marsal, a marked woodland walk at Mulcey, and a nature trail beside the *pelouse calcaire* at Génicourt-sur-Meuse.

Fishing: carp, pike and eel are plentiful in the *étangs*; details of fishing permits from local tourist offices.

Courses: the St-Mihiel activity centre (T:29 89 03 59) runs courses in canoeing, caving and archery; it also organizes walking and biking excursions.

Further information *Tourist information:* Pont-à-Mousson, pl Duroc, T:83 81 06 90; Metz, 1 pl St-Clément, T:87 33 60 00.

   Parc Naturel Régional de Lorraine, Domaine de Charmilly, chemin des Clôs, Pont-à-Mousson, T:83 81 11 91.

Vosges

Wild high point—literally—of the Northeast, with wooded mountains rising 1,400m (4,600ft) above the Rhine valley south of Strasbourg

Why do the beeches grow on the upper slopes of the Vosges above the fir trees? It's a phenomenon that has puzzled many visitors to this mountainous area to the west of the wide flat valley of the Rhine on France's eastern border. The explanation seems to be that the firs cannot tolerate the combination of humidity and low winter temperatures in the Vosges. The Alps, for example, are much drier.

   The Vosges stretch for about 100 kilometres (60 miles) from north to south and 50 kilometres (30 miles) across. Rising to 1,424 metres (4,700 feet) at Le Grand Ballon and dotted with small glacial lakes and bogs, they are the most extensive area of wildness in Northeast France. However, they are attracting more and more tourists, particularly in winter for skiing.

   It takes skill and patience to spot any wildlife in the Vosges, as the slopes are so thickly wooded, mostly right up to their softly rounded tops. Six species of tits nest in these high forests, as well as Europe's two smallest songbirds, the gold- and firecrests. Honey buzzards arrive in the high forests in June, and there are sparrowhawks and goshawks, as well as speckled Tengmalm's owls. Hazelhens thrive in areas of young conifers, burrowing in to the winter

snow. Red and roe deer are increasing in number, and there are good populations of pine and beech martens. Mountain goats have been reintroduced here.

   As three-quarters of the Vosges are forested, wide views are hard to come by, though you get glimpses down over pristine valleys and lakes as you twist around hair-

Tengmalm's owl has recently spread from upland forest to beech woodland.

pin bends over mountain passes such as the Col de la Schlucht. Most spectacular of all is the Route des Crêtes, which follows the ridges along the north–south backbone. The views are particularly dramatic at the south end of the route, where the road is highest: on a clear day you can see right across the Rhine plain to the Black Forest in Germany. Halfway along the road, at Hohneck, 1,362 metres (4,100 feet) high, a small botanical garden of alpine plants has been laid out.

Flowers thrive on the sunny mountain-tops where trees have been felled to create grassy summit pastures, or *chaumes*, another feature of the Vosges. These clear-ings, warmed by the dry wind known as the *foehn*, are reputed to date back to the 7th century, when Irish monks settled in Mun-ster and wanted grass for their cattle in summer. Farmers have done the same ever since, though the custom is now becoming less popular because it is uneconomic com-pared with modern farming methods. As a result the *chaumes* are under threat from the encroaching trees. The Gazon du Faing *chaume* near Le Valtin is among several areas that have recently been designated as nature reserves by the newly created Parc Naturel Régional des Ballons des Vosges.

The Vosges locals are also proud of their bogs, even though these are small com-pared with those, say, in Scotland. But what they lack in size, they make up in numbers on both hilltops and slopes. Andromeda, a protected species from the heather family, thrives in these marshy wet areas, as do all the four vacciniums (wild bilberry, blue-berry, cowberry and cranberry) and also

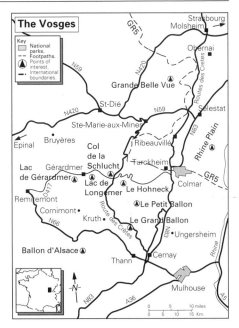

A RETURN TO THE PAST

Symbolizing the area's traditions, storks are being reintroduced at the open-air Ecomusée at Ungersheim. Numbers have dwindled in recent years, largely because it has become a sport to shoot them during their winter migration in North Africa. Young birds are kept in an enclosure at the Ecomusée for their first three years to curb their migratory instinct; after, they are content to winter in the area. It's good to see them nesting in the chimney pots again.

sundew, one of the carnivorous *Drosera* species.

The east-facing slopes of the Vosges have for centuries been anything but wild. Here the vineyards that produce Alsace's famous wines stretch for miles.

While the stork is the emblem of Alsace (see box), the present-day nature enthusiast would be better advised to concentrate on the wildlife along the Rhine valley. Despite its notorious industrial image, the Rhine retains many areas of ecological interest. Most notable is the Ried, an area of rich damp meadows on alluvial deposits along the valley floor, which are flooded in spring and autumn. Botanically these water meadows are a source of great interest, with even minor variations in elevation sufficient to reveal distinct differences in the flora. In fact the Ried has a number of botanical points in common with Siberia, but the most characteristic species are the low, delicate spikes of green-winged orchids and the Chiltern gentian.

(*Overleaf*) A typical winter landscape at Lac du Forlet in the Vosges mountains.

49

CHAPTER 2: THE NORTHEAST

BEFORE YOU GO
Maps: IGN 1:100,000 No. 31; various IGN 1:25,000 and 1:50,000, edited by the Club Vosgien; Michelin 1:200,000 Nos. 62 and 87.
Guidebooks: *Bonjour les Vosges* (Comité Départemental du Tourisme); Norbert Lefranc, *Les Oiseaux des Vosges* (Kruch).

GETTING THERE
By car: several main east–west roads cross the Vosges, but these are steep and twisting in mountainous stretches. The north–south routes are much slower but extremely scenic; these include the Route du Vin, through the vineyards and picturesque wine-making villages, and the Route des Crêtes between Ste-Marie-aux-Mines and Cernay.

The capercaillie, a retiring and secretive bird of the forested uplands, nevertheless exhibits a spectacular mating display.

Drivers can rely on even the narrowest, remotest mountain roads being in good condition.
By rail: there are main-line services to Strasbourg, Colmar, Mulhouse, Belfort and Epinal, with connections into the Vosges as far as Metzeral, Kruth, Cornimont and Bruyères. Services between Lunéville and Sélestat cross the Vosges via St-Dié.
By bus: towns and villages along the main valleys are served by buses at least once a day.

WHERE TO STAY
The area has a good selection of hotels and inns, particularly in the main tourist resorts of Gérardmer, Ribeauvillé and Turckheim. Farmhouses along the valleys also offer accommodation, often a centuries-old tradition, and there are *gîtes* for self-catering.
Outdoor living: many villages have a municipal campsite; these include Munster (T:89 77 31 08), Turckheim (T:89 27 02 00) and Obernai (T:88 95 38 48). Tourist offices have a full list.

ACTIVITIES
Walking: there are marked trails in the forests and across the open pastures. The Club Vosgien organizes walking tours and also sells marked-up IGN maps. GR5 follows the north–south ridges, passing Hohneck and the alpine botanical garden.
Fishing: permits are available for lakes and rivers; details from the local town halls.
Cycling: ordinary and mountain bikes are available in various centres; there are guided tours.
Riding: centres in Gérardmer, St-Dié, Munster, Turckheim and Markstein.
Watersports: the lakes at Gérardmer and Xonrupt-Longemer have sailing boats.
Skiing: the Vosges are best suited to cross-country, but there are several downhill centres, including La Bresse, Gérardmer and Le Ballon d'Alsace.
Exhibitions: in the open-air Ecomusée, 42 furnished old buildings from Alsace are on display and there are regular demonstrations of local crafts; it is at Ungersheim near Ensisheim on the Rhine plain, T:89 48 23 44.

FURTHER INFORMATION
Tourist information: Colmar, Hôtel du Département, T:89 22 68 00; Gérardmer, pl des Déportés, T:29 63 08 74; Strasbourg (main regional office), 9 rue du Dôme, T:88 22 01 02.
Parc Naturel Régional des Ballons des Vosges, 1 rue de l'Eglise, Munster, T:89 77 29 04.

Parc Naturel Régional des Vosges du Nord

Site of the ill-fated Maginot Line; now a secluded backwater with varied flora and fauna

Driving through the pretty northern Vosges region of Alsace, I wondered how it had managed to escape an invasion by tourists. Perhaps the answer is that it is relatively tucked away, though by no means cut off, in France's northeast corner.

Its soft misty horizons of wooded hillsides dotted with curiously shaped sandstone rocks and ruined medieval castles are not really spectacular, but they have a certain charm and beauty. With ubiquitous huge piles of logs for winter fires and meadows of wildflowers, the Vosges du Nord bears a distinctly alpine feel, yet the cliffs and soil are red, more reminiscent of the Mediterranean. Nor does the area feel particularly French; place names are Germanic, reflecting that the whole of Alsace was once under German jurisdiction. The ugly concrete fortifications near the border are part of the ill-fated Maginot Line, built between the two World Wars.

The fact that the regional nature park in the northern Vosges has recently become one of UNESCO's 276 international biosphere reserves reflects not only the wealth of its flora and fauna, but also the conservation and environmental programmes ٠ being undertaken here.

Beech, Scotch pine and oak predominate in the 72,000ha (177,900 acres) of woodland. Twice as I drove along, a deer hurried across the road just in front of me. Wild boar are also common, but sightings of wildcats and martens are rare. In fact, the wealth of game animals reflects the stricter hunting controls, a relic of former German influences on Alsace. In holes on the sandstone cliffs, four pairs of peregrine falcons are nesting; one of the places where they can be seen is the rocky crags of Erbsenfelsen.

With moors, peatbogs, marshes and sandy grasslands, the plants that thrive are extremely varied, ranging from delicate pink alpine laurels to the curious round-leaf sundew. The rare lily-like water arum and wood's grape-fern are found, too.

In the well-placed hide in the bushes and reeds around the pretty lake at Baerenthal, there is an identification chart showing 27 species of bird and the best spots to look out for them. It includes those that nest here, such as kingfishers, great crested grebe and coots; those that winter here, such as teal and tufted duck; or migrants, such as grey herons and occasionally ospreys. The observation book in which visitors can record what they saw is fascinating reading.

Before you go *Maps:* IGN 1:100,000 No. 12; Michelin 1:200,000 No. 87.
Guidebooks: park headquarters has guides to the deer, birds and castles; it also has leaflets on the wildlife and walking trails.
Getting there *By car:* the A4 *autoroute* runs along the south of the area between Metz and Strasbourg; N62 crosses it from Haguenau to Bitche.
By rail: Saverne is on the

main Paris–Strasbourg line or there are services from Strasbourg to Sarreguemines with connections to Bitche, Niederbronn and Haguenau.
By bus: hourly services operate between some villages, including Ingwiller and La Petite-Pierre.
Where to stay: the main tourist centres are Bitche and Niederbronn-les-Bains, where the 2-star Muller, 16 av de la Libération, T:88 09 70 00, is renowned for its cuisine.
Outdoor living: there is a site in Baerenthal (T:87 06 50 73/ 26) and others in Bitche, Saverne, Oberbronn and the Etang de Hanau.
Activities: the regional park has a programme of excursions with themes such as natural history, archaeology and history.
Walking: there are marked trails in the forests and across the open pastures. Club Vosgien organizes walking tours and also sells marked-up IGN maps. GR53 crosses the Vosges du Nord via La Petite-Pierre and Oberbronn. There are marked nature trails at Geyerstein near La Petite-Pierre and around the lake at Hanau. Bird hide at the Etang de Baerenthal (collect the key from the town hall, between 8–12 and 2–6).
Cycling: bicycles can be rented in various centres, and mountain bikes are available at Wingen-sur-Moder.
Exhibitions: there are displays on water, sandstone and forest in the castle at La Petite-Pierre and on the flora and fauna at the Maison de la Forêt at Hanau lake.
Further information *Tourist information:* Bitche, T:87 96 00 13; Niederbronn-les-Bains, 2 pl de l'Hôtel-de-Ville, T:88 09 17 00.
Parc Naturel Régional des Vosges du Nord, La Petite-Pierre, T:88 70 46 55.

The Alps

Over 200 million years ago dinosaurs lived out their last days in a temperate region by the edge of an ocean known as Tethys, which covered the area where the Alps now stand. The movement of giant continental plates on the surface of the earth spelt the end for this ancient sun trap, and the dinosaurs. The land mass south of Tethys pushed north, causing the sea to dry up as it went. Where continental plates clashed, the Alps heaved high into the air.

Evidence that these mountains were once sea bed shows itself even to the casual hiker in these parts. Walking in the Ecrins National Park, I turned over some limestone at the side of the path. There on the other side of the stone was a fossil ammonite, an extinct marine creature related to the modern nautilus and squid. When this creature died the area was sea, yet the hardened rock that retained its outline was now nearly a kilometre above sea level.

The Alps are spectacular. The mountains tower dramatically above the valleys below, dwarfing people, fields and entire towns by their sheer scale. A patchwork of meadows and woods covers the lower slopes, but your eyes naturally turn upwards to some distant summit high above the treeline where the rocks stand raw and naked.

The Alps are shaped like a crescent moon around the north of Italy, and form the natural boundary between Italy and neighbouring France, Switzerland, Austria and Yugoslavia. France holds the highest peak in the range, Mont Blanc, which at 4,807

The Massif de Chartreuse, whose impressive limestone cliffs dominate the dense mixed forest lying below, is home to many rare species such as the wild cat, eagle owl and raven.

CHAPTER 3: THE ALPS

metres (15,760 feet) is Europe's highest mountain. Most of the other well-known peaks, such as the Matterhorn, stand farther east beyond France's borders.

The French Alpine region divides fairly naturally into five parts. The Alpes Maritimes (Maritime Alps) lie at the southernmost end of the range, closest to the sea, and fall within the Parc National du Mercantour. These mountains are more Mediterranean than Alpine in their climate and vegetation; lower, warmer and drier than those in the heart of the range. To the north, in the Ecrins and Queyras, you come into the high mountain scenery of the western Alps proper. Beyond this region lies Savoie, with the remote and spectacular peaks of the Vanoise, and the Mont Blanc massif.

The French Alps are fringed to the west by a chain of foothills, or Préalpes: the foothills of Haute-Provence in the south, the rugged plateau of the Vercors, and the Massif de Chartreuse. On the other side of Lake Geneva and the Rhône valley is the Jura.

The higher you ascend these mountains the colder it gets. At altitudes above 3,100 metres (10,000 feet) there is likely to be permanent snow, although the precise snowline will depend on local geographical features.

In the highest parts glaciers can still be found. Glaciation has been a major influence on the mountain landscape. In the Ice Ages the glaciers swept down from the mountains, hollowing out deep valleys.

The sheer height of the Alps has kept them remote and helped to preserve their wildlife, though hunting has always been a major threat. Modern naturalists' concern has focused on the Alpine ibex — a goat-like creature that is one of Europe's rarest animals — and the more common chamois (a type of antelope). This concern led to the establishment of France's first national park, the Vanoise, in 1963. The number of ibex has increased considerably since.

One of the most characteristic Alpine creatures is the marmot, a ground-based relative of the squirrel that is similar to the American groundhog. When the winter freeze sets in this rodent hibernates in a complex underground burrow, during which time its heartrate slows dramatically. When alarmed, marmots emit a shrill whistle, warning friends and family of impending danger. The golden eagle would certainly make a marmot whistle. This majestic bird (the French call it the *aigle royale*) still nests in the more remote parts of the Alps; marmots are part of its staple diet.

The nimble ibex, the chamois and the marmot are all Alpine fauna found above the treeline, about 2,100 metres (7,000 feet). At this height the growing season is short, usually only a few months. Beneath 2,100 metres, in woods of pine and larch, the flora and fauna are sub-Alpine. Beech woods proliferate still farther down the mountain, beneath 1,600 metres (5,000 feet).

The climate of the Alps is typical of mountainous terrain. The Jura has more rain and snow (over 150 centimetres/58 inches annually) than any other part of France. On the other hand, the Mercantour national park is one of the country's sunniest areas.

The Alpine habitat is vulnerable, and the last 20 years has seen a new threat to the wilderness in the growth of downhill skiing. New ski lifts and access roads open regularly, taking more and more people into previously wild areas. The massif of Mont Blanc, for example, is surrounded by ski lifts, which have now reduced Europe's mightiest peak to a park playground.

GETTING THERE

By air: the main airports are all some way from the mountains, at Mulhouse (the closest airport for the Jura), Lyon and Nice.

By car: the Autoroute du Soleil (A6) is as much for skiers as for sun worshippers; exit on to A36, near Beaune, for Besançon and the Jura, or A40 for the Haute Savoie. Farther south, A43 at Lyon leads to Grenoble. N85 heads north out of Nice through the Alpine foothills to Gap and Grenoble.

By rail: the quickest way south is via the TGV (*train à grande vitesse*) from Paris's Gare de Lyon. Once in Lyon, change onto the network that services the mountains. There are direct trains from Paris to Chambéry, Modane, Bourg-St-Maurice, Annecy and St-Gervais (for Mont Blanc); they also run to Grenoble, a convenient centre for exploring the Alps.

By bus: for schedules, contact the bus station at Chambéry, 9 pl de la Gare, T:79 75 43 99.

WHEN TO GO

The Alps make a spectacular destination whatever the time of year, whether for summer hill-walking, or winter skiing.

WHERE TO STAY

Both road and rail networks tend to follow the valleys, where most of the towns are sited. See individual exploring sections for details of the best places to set up base. The tourist offices at Besançon, Digne, Grenoble and Lyon will book rooms for you.

ACTIVITIES

Walking: you must expect some stiff climbs in the Alps, though no special equipment is needed to walk on a *grande randonnée* (GR).

Climbing: the Club Alpin Français is the best source of information. Contact them at 9 rue La Boétie, Paris, T:47 42 38 46. Some local addresses for the club are given under the heading "refuges".

Adventure holidays: the UCPA (l'Union Nationale des Centres Sportifs de Plein Air) offers walking, skiing, canoeing and climbing holidays at more than a dozen centres in the Alps and Jura. Further information from the UCPA, 62 rue de la Glacière, Paris, T:43 36 05 20.

Caving: the massifs of Chartreuse and Vercors are classic sites for cavers. See details in individual sections.

Fishing: information on restrictions and licences from Le Conseil Supérieur de la Pêche, 135 av Malakoff, Paris, T:45 01 20 20.

Skiing: information on cross-country skiing from Centre Information Montagne et Sentiers, 7 rue Voltaire, Grenoble, T:76 51 76 00.

FURTHER INFORMATION

Tourist information:
Besançon, 2 pl 1ère-Armée-Française, T:81 80 92 55; Bourg-en-Bresse, 6 av Alsace-Lorraine, T:74 22 49 40; Briançon, Porte Pignerol, T:92 21 08 50; Chambéry, 24 blvd de la Colonne, T:79 33 42 47; Digne, le Rond-Point, T:92 31 42 73; Gap, 5 rue Carnot, T:92 51 57 03; Grenoble, 14 rue République, T:76 54 34 36; Lyon, pl Bellecour, T:78 42 25 75.

FURTHER READING

La Faune des Alpes, published by the Vanoise National Park; Jean-François Dejonghe, *Les Oiseaux de Montagne* (La Société Nationale de Protection de la Nature).

The agile and alert marmot is an inhabitant of Alpine pastures.

Alpes de Provence

Barren hills and plateaus with heavily wooded valleys in the foothills of the Alps

My introduction to the Alpine foothills was unforgettable. For a youth from the south of England, the scenery was remarkable: Telegraph Hill and Windmill Hill were but molehills compared to these 5,000-foot monsters. And these weren't even the Alps proper.

I hitched a lift just east of Avignon. This was before the Autoroute du Soleil had reached the south coast; my driver chose the cross-country route through the Alpes de Provence simply because, at the time, it was the shortest route. The switchback bends, as the road climbed and wound its way through the foothills, dictated a relatively slow speed. My driver, however, was intent on averaging 60 miles an hour. He took each bend as though he were driving in the 24-hour marathon at Le Mans: on the inside, regardless of whether that meant driving on the right or the left of the road.

The drive took my mind off the scenery. *Autostop* (hitching), I concluded, was not the best way to see France. I swore the next time I would make the journey more sedately.

It took me 20 years to return to the Alps. The train from Nice to Digne, known locally as *le train des pignes*, and run by a private railway company, has many qualities. Speed is not one of them. But there is plenty of time to examine the *pignes* (pine cones) and the scenery during the three-hour twenty-minute journey. For the first two hours out of Digne, the ride is one of the most spectacular in Europe, passing bluffs, canyons and ravines, and layers of rocks thrown up at crazy angles. But the perspective from the train, as it winds through the densely wooded valleys, is misleading. Up on the hills the land is arid and there are few trees. This is one of the most deserted parts of the Alpine foothills.

The Alpes de Provence lie some 80 kilometres (50 miles) east of Avignon, and are roughly centred around the town of Digne, west of the great national parks of Mercantour and Ecrins. They are not as high or celebrated as the peaks in the national parks, but they are every bit as wild.

The limestone around Digne is particularly rich in fossils. The area was made a geological reserve in 1979 to protect the rocks from fossil hunters. There is also a palaeontological laboratory at Digne. Close by is a remarkable collection of giant ammonites, about 600 embedded in the rock.

BEFORE YOU GO
Maps: IGN 1:100,000 Nos. 60–61; IGN 1:25,000 (east and west) Nos. 3340–41, 3440–41 and 3541–42.

GETTING THERE
By car: N85 runs from Grenoble to Gap and Digne. From Paris, take A10, and turn off on to A43 for Grenoble.
By rail: SNCF trains link Digne with Grenoble. The Chemins de Fer de la Provence run trains to Digne from Nice (station is 10mins from SNCF in Nice).

WHERE TO STAY
Digne is the most central base, though Sisteron and Seyne lie on the GR running through the area. Château-Arnoux is another possibility.
Outdoor living: local tourist offices have lists of campsites.

ACTIVITIES
Walking: GR6 runs from Sisteron to Seyne, north of Digne. There are a number of other paths leading into the hills from stations on the Nice–Digne railway.
Cycling: rent bicycles at the railway station at Digne.

Riding: horse-back tours and rides at Ferme Equestre La Fénière, Quartier Champarlaud, Peipin, T:96 64 37 96. Further information from Association Départementale de Tourisme Equestre, 4 rue des Charrois, Digne, T:92 31 18 83.

FURTHER INFORMATION
Tourist information: Digne, pl du Tampinet, T:92 31 42 73; Sisteron, Hôtel de Ville, T:92 61 12 03.

For taped weather forecasts telephone Nice, T:93 83 91 11.

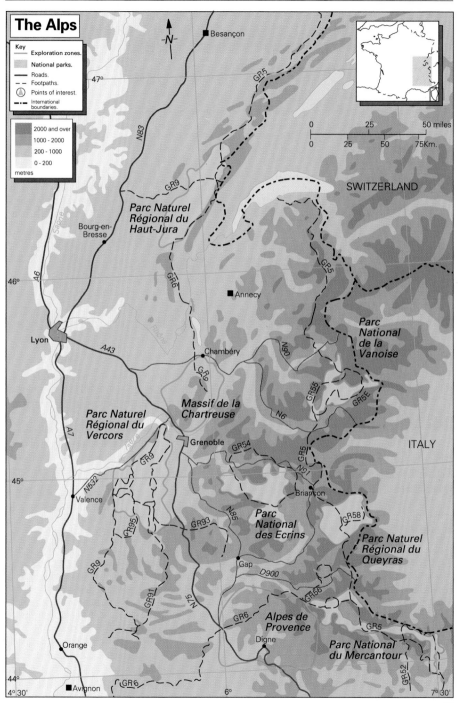

The Alps

Key
- Exploration zones.
- National parks.
- Roads.
- Footpaths.
- Points of interest.
- International boundaries.

2000 and over
1000 - 2000
200 - 1000
0 - 200
metres

0   25   50 miles
0   25   50   75Km.

-N-

Besançon

47°

SWITZERLAND

GR5

GR9

N83

Parc Naturel Régional du Haut-Jura

46°

Bourg-en-Bresse

Annecy

GR6

GR5

Parc National de la Vanoise

Lyon

A43

A6

Saône

Rhône

Chambéry

GR9

N90

GR55

GR5E

ITALY

Parc Naturel Régional du Vercors

Massif de la Chartreuse

N6

N91

45°

A7

Isère

GR9

Grenoble

GR54

GR5

Valence

N532

N85

Briançon

Parc National des Ecrins

GR58

GR95

GR93

Parc Naturel Régional du Queyras

GR9

GR91

N75

Gap

D900

GR56

Alpes de Provence

GR5

Orange

GR6

Digne

Parc National du Mercantour

GR52

44°

4° 30'

Avignon

GR6

6°

7° 30'

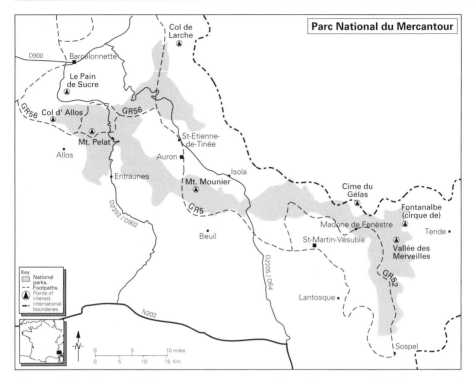

Parc National du Mercantour

Key
- National parks.
- Footpaths.
- Points of interest.
- International boundaries.

0   5   10 miles
0   5   10   15 Km.

Parc National du Mercantour

Sunny, arid parc national *stretching from the high Alps to the Mediterranean foothills; central zone covers 68,500ha (169,265 acres)*

It was the way you could almost smell the heat that brought the memories back. My companion and I were sitting down for a picnic, near the southern end of the Parc National du Mercantour. This is where the park takes on a Mediterranean feel: the soil is dry, and everywhere the vegetation shows signs of the heat. Grass is coarse and sparse, and interspersed with succulents, plants that speak eloquently of the need to hang on to water. Pine trees grow where they can,
60

severally and in copses. Only the crowns of snow on distant peaks served to remind us that this was the Alps.

We sheltered under some conifers to keep cool, and I unpacked my lunch: half a baguette, a lump of cheese and a tomato. Twenty years ago, on my first trip through the Alps, I had enjoyed the same lunch on an Alpine hillside just a few miles away. Then, the ingredients for my sandwich had cost one franc; now they cost ten. There is inflation for you. The other difference was that 20 years ago it was enough food for the day. Now I saw it as a stop-gap, and still looked forward to a large evening meal. That is middle age for you.

The smell that brought back these memories is hard to define. Every little breeze smells new and different as the tang of the pines and cypresses mixes with the scent of the occasional herb. Nearby, too, was Grasse, centre of the French perfume industry. I can't help thinking that some scent may have floated up from the perfumeries and, much diffused, added to the heady mixture I inhaled.

The Parc National du Mercantour is a long thin slice of the Alpes Maritimes (Maritime Alps) that stretches for 80 kilometres (50 miles) along the Italian border. The French government designated the area a national park in 1979, then only the sixth area to achieve that status. Across the Italian border is the nature reserve of Argentera, but from a geographical or ecological point of view these parks are really one. Mercantour also straddles the borders of two French *départements*: the Alpes Maritimes in the south and the Alpes-de-Haute-Provence in the north.

At its southern end the park is barely 16 kilometres (10 miles) from the Mediterranean. Holm oaks can be found under about 700 metres (2,300 feet), while olive trees are grown on terraces lower down the slopes. At its northern end the park is less than 24 kilometres (15 miles) from the mountains of Queyras. Above the pine treeline, around 2,500 metres (8,000 feet), there is rhododendron heathland.

Fire is one of the biggest threats to a hot dry park such as Mercantour. The southern borders suffered from fire a few years back, but are now making a reasonable recovery; however it takes about 30 years for this type of forest to regenerate itself.

The highest mountain in the park is Gélas, which at 3,134 metres (10,300 feet) is a moderate Alpine peak. The park's GR takes you past Gélas. Around this point, the route picks up an old salt transport road, connecting Piedmont in the Italian Alps with the Mediterranean. Despite being so close to the tourist traps of the Riviera, the central area of the park has no permanent inhabitants.

The lack of human habitation makes the park a refuge for wildlife. In summer about 100 ibex cross from Italy into the park to join the indigenous marmots and mountain hares. About a third of the golden eagles in France nest in this park, and chamois are found in the most remote corners. The richness of the park's animal life is equalled by its flora; about 40 species of plant found in the park are specific to this Alpine zone.

The park also has two sites of considerable archaeological interest. In the Vallée des Merveilles (Valley of Marvels) and the Cirque de Fontanalbe, both near Tende, are a collection of more than 100,000 open-air rock engravings in grey-green schists, dating from the early Bronze Age (about 1800 to 1500 BC). Archaeologists are still puzzling over why these prehistoric people retreated to such an out-of-the-way place, 1,850 metres (6,000 feet) above the sea, which today is uninhabited.

BEFORE YOU GO
Maps: IGN 1:100,000 No. 61; IGN 1:25,000 (east and west) Nos. 3640, 3741–42 and 3841.

GETTING THERE
By air: Nice is the nearest airport.
By car: from Gap D900 runs up the valley to Barcelonnette at the park's northern end; D2204 from Nice leads to Sospel at the southern end. Several scenic roads cross the park: D2205 runs from N202 to Isola and on to St-Etienne-de-Tinée (it meets D64, which passes through the park a second time before joining D900); while D2202 climbs to 2,300m (7,400ft) before hugging the northern edge of the park and dropping down to Barcelonnette.
By rail: the nearest station is Sospel, only 33km (20 miles) from Nice, but an hour by train. From the station it's a 5-km (3-mile) walk up D2568 or GR52 to the park's southern tip.
By bus: there are buses from both Gap and Digne to Barcelonnette, as well as a service from Digne to Allos.

WHERE TO STAY
Barcelonnette is the nearest town of any size, though Sospel is a much prettier base. Closer to the park proper are St-Etienne-de-Tinée, Auron, Entraunes, Isola, Beuil, St-Martin-Vésubie and Lantosque.
Outdoor living: camping is only allowed in the park's buffer zone.
Refuges: the park information office has a list of refuges; or contact the Club Alpin Français at 14 av Mirabeau, Nice, T:93 62 59 99.

ACTIVITIES
Walking: GR52 runs up the southern spine of the park from Sospel to St-Martin-Vésubie. GR5 crosses the park from St-Sauveur-sur-Tinée to join up with GR56, which loops through the northern sector of the park

from the Col d'Allos to Col de Larche. In addition there are more than 600km (360 miles) of local footpaths.

Climbing: the best book for serious climbs is Robin Collomb's *Mercantour Park—Maritime Alps* (West Col).

Canoeing: the Roya is navigable Mar–Oct; information from tourist office at Tende.

Cycling: rent bikes in Sospel.

Skiing: the massif of Sanguinière is excellent for cross-country skiing.

Nature walks: during summer park officials organize walks to study Mercantour's natural history.

FURTHER INFORMATION

Tourist information:
Barcelonnette, pl 7 Portes, T:92 81 04 71; Sospel, Vieux Pont, T:93 04 00 19; Tende, T:93 04 73 71.

The park's headquarters is in Nice, 23 rue d'Italie, T:93 87 86 10. Local offices are at Barcelonnette, T:92 81 21 31; St-Etienne-de-Tinée, T:93 02 42 27; and Péone-Valberg, T:93 02 58 23.

For taped weather forecasts telephone Nice, T:93 83 91 11.

Parc Naturel Régional du Queyras

A 60,000-ha (148,000-acre) regional nature park above the Durance valley

Most Alpine valleys are today covered in development of one form or another; quarries

Snow lingers late in the year on the peaks of the Parc Naturel Régional du Queyras.

and industry vie with tourist chalets for each square foot of valley soil. Climbing into the mountains is the only way to escape this development and get to the wilder parts. As I made my way up from the Durance valley on an ill-frequented forest path, I heard a sudden movement and spotted the tail of a marmot disappearing into the undergrowth. In more touristy areas of the Alps, the marmots will eat cake out of your hands, like squirrels in a suburban park. My marmot clearly had not seen many tourists.

The light in these mountains is remarkable, especially when the sun shines hot and bright. When climbing in summer, nothing can be more welcome than the occasional breezes that ripple the leaves of the trees, giving them a fleeting iridescence. Away from industrial pollution, the Alpine air is so clear that distant snowy peaks seem to be situated in the next valley.

The park of Queyras is roughly rectangular: its eastern edge is defined by the Italian border, the western by the valley of the Durance, which separates Queyras from the Ecrins National Park.

The hills of the Queyras have always been a natural fortress. They spelled safety for marauders, and provided a base from which to prey on travellers on the trade route along the Durance valley. The fort at Château-Queyras was for a while the centre of Europe's first republic—or *escarton*—in the 14th century. The price of independence was not cheap; the *escartons* had to pay an annual rent of 4,000 golden ducats to the dauphin of France.

During the industrial revolution Queyras became

64

COUNTRYSIDE CARE

To protect this fragile environment the park rules forbid camping (other than overnight stops for hikers); making fires; picking or digging up plants; and motor vehicles (other than on public roads). Cigarettes must be extinguished carefully.

depopulated. By the 1960s the population of the 650sq km (250sq miles) that now constitute the regional park had dropped to fewer than 2,000, a quarter of the number that lived here a century ago. With so little human interference, the mountains became a stronghold for wildlife. There are said to be some half a dozen nesting pairs of golden eagles, who prey on the marmots. Of the larger mammals, the only rarity is the chamois. But a wide variety of game birds can be found here, including the ptarmigan which, like the mountain hare, changes colour in winter. The Spanish moon moth can be found in the Scotch pine woods; this large exotic creature, closely related to tropical silk moths, being found in only one locality in France.

Running along part of the southern border of the park is the nature reserve of the Val d'Escreins. The reserve has an exceptionally rich collection of flora, and is only open to the public in summer. Even in June, there will still be snow on the hills, as spring comes very late to the Queyras.

Before you go *Maps:* IGN 1:100,000 No. 54; IGN 1:25,000 Nos. 245–46, 3537–38 (east) and 3637 (west).

Getting there *By car:* D902

runs south from Briançon through the park and out its western boundary; D2051 cuts through to the Italian border; D947 leads to the castle of Queyras and Abriès and affords some good views. Note that many park roads swiftly turn into unpaved tracks.

By rail: the nearest railway station with a regular service is Mont-Dauphin, on the line from Gap to Briançon; the park boundary is 2km (4 miles) away. Alternatively, a footpath passes by the closed station of St-Crépin, which is served by 2 daily buses from Gap and Mont-Dauphin.

By bus: regular buses connect with trains at Mont-Dauphin station, running to Guillestre, Château-Queyras, Ceillac, Abriès, Arvieux and Vars-les-Claux.

Where to stay: you have a choice of hotels in Briançon, Mont-Dauphin, Guillestre and Les Claux. Inside the park try Ceillac, Château-Queyras, Molines-en-Queyras, St-Véran, Abriès, Aiguilles or Arvieux.

Outdoor living: the park office at Guillestre has a list of campsites.

Refuges: the park office has a list.

Activities *Walking:* GR5 from Briançon crosses the park from north to south; GR58 makes a tour of the park. Local tourist offices have details of less energetic hikes. In summer there are guided walks.

Climbing: Ceillac lies at the foot of La Font Sancte (3,387m/11,000ft), a noteworthy challenge.

Canoeing: in summer you can canoe down the Guil and Durance. Contact Fédération de Canoë-Kayak, Embrun, T:92 48 08 68.

Cycling: the high point of the Tour de France is the Col

d'Izoard on the park's northern boundary. Less ambitious souls can hire mountain bikes in Ceillac.

Further information *Tourist information:* Briançon, Porte Pignerol, T:92 21 08 50; Ceillac, Mairie, T:92 45 05 74; Guillestre, pl Salva, T:92 45 04 37; Molines-en-Queyras, T:92 45 83 22; St-Véran, pl du Tour, T:92 45 82 21.

You can listen to taped weather forecasts on T:92 20 10 00. For mountain guides, call the Bureau des Guides, Molines, T:92 45 71 09; in Ceillac, T:92 45 05 74.

Park headquarters are at av de la Gare, Guillestre, T:92 45 06 23.

Parc National des Ecrins

A 93,000-ha (230,000-acre) national park of majestic mountains, in the high Alps some 50km (30 miles) southeast of Grenoble

The first person I saw the day I climbed the hills of the Ecrins was a lean, grey-haired man in his fifties. Nothing unusual in this. But his outfit was odd: swimming trunks topped by a short-sleeved pullover. From the amiable look on his face, I predicted he would want to stop and chat.

This man was no casual rambler, though; he lived here. His cabin was farther down the valley, in a remote spot 8km (5 miles) from the nearest village. At this altitude (1,600m/5,000ft), in

winter the snow would lie waist-high at his cabin door, so he retreated to another cabin lower down. Neither summer nor winter cabin had electricity or a telephone, and gas lamps and wood fire were his sources of light and heat. I couldn't help feeling I'd run into the modern French equivalent of Henry David Thoreau, who, despairing of progress, retreated into the woods to find fresh inspiration for his writing.

The mountains of the Ecrins were designated a national park in 1973. Proud peaks dominate the skyline, and are snowcapped throughout the year. Even in summer, snow lies thick in the more sheltered gullies that crease the range. In common with the country's other natural parks, the Ecrins is divided in two: the central zone is the park proper, which has strict rules designed to protect wildlife and habitat; a buffer zone runs the periphery of the park. Three river valleys mark the park boundary—the Romanche to the north, the Drac to the west and the Durance from Briançon to the south.

The highest peaks stand in the granite Massif de Pelvoux, which comprises the northern half of the park proper. The Barre des Ecrins, roughly due west of Briançon, is the highest point of the park at 4,102m (13,460ft). The sedimentary rocks of the Massif du Champsaur form the park's southeastern sector. This massif is lower than its northen counterpart; the summit of Rougnoux, its highest point, reaches 3,179m (10,430ft).

For the most part, the park's central zone has few trees. Glaciers radiate out from the highest peaks; ice

The Spanish moon moth is also known as the *papillon d'Isabelle.*

covers about a tenth of the inner core. Nevertheless, something like half of the plant species of France can be found in this one park. Differences in the distribution of plants and trees reflect the climatic variations within the region. The park's colder northern edges are covered with spruces, while the wetter west is thick with beeches. Larches favour the drier eastern slopes and lavender the more Mediterranean conditions that prevail in the valley of the Durance.

Before you go *Maps:* IGN 1:100,000 No. 54; IGN 1:25,000 Nos. 241–43.
Guidebook: Robin Collomb, *Dauphiné Alps* (West Col Productions).

Getting there *By car:* N85 from Grenoble runs along the edge of the park's buffer zone to Gap; from here N94 circles the park on the southern side around to Briançon. Alternatively, N91 forks off N85 at Vizille, south of Grenoble, and runs around the north of the park. A number of secondary roads lead into the buffer zone, but almost all stop at the boundary of the park proper. *By rail:* there is a regular train service to Gap and Briançon from Grenoble, Marseille and Valence.

Argentière, Mont-Dauphin and Briançon are the best disembarkation points.
By bus: SNCF runs 2 daily buses from Gap to Embrun, Mont-Dauphin and St-Crépin; the last is useful to hikers as GR54 passes by the station.
Where to stay Gap, Briançon, Mont-Dauphin and Embrun are the main towns, and offer a range of accommodation. Good bases in the buffer zone include St-Maurice-en-

The "Demoiselle Coiffée" is a remarkable geological feature of this limestone area.

Valgaudemar, Freissinières, Puy-St-Vincent, Pelvoux and St-Antoine.
Refuges: the park office has a list, or contact the Club Alpin Français at 6 av René-Froger, Briançon, T:92 20 16 52.
Activities *Walking:* GR54 passes through the park; pick up the path at Mont-Dauphin or St-Crépin. GR5 skirts the park buffer zone, north of Briançon.
Viewpoints: the Glacier Blanc (White Glacier) and popular Serre Chevalier can be reached by cable car from Chantemerle, on N91.

Goats roam freely among scattered rocks and scrub vegetation.

Further information *Tourist information:* Briançon, Porte Pignerol, T:92 21 08 50; Embrun, Général-Dosse, T:92 43 01 80; Gap, 5 rue Carnot, T:92 51 57 03; Grenoble, 14 rue République, T:76 54 34 36; Guillestre, pl Salva, T:92 45 04 37.
Taped weather forecasts, T:92 20 10 00.
Park headquarters: 7 rue Colonel-Roux, Gap, T:92 51 40 71.

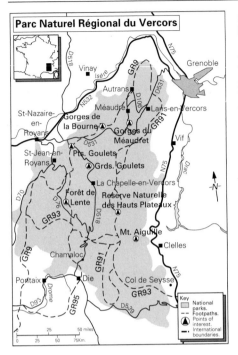

Parc Naturel Régional du Vercors

Parc Naturel Régional du Vercors

Mountainous plateau on the western edge of the Alps; a regional nature park of 135,000ha (333,000 acres)

The day had started the same as many others on the trip. My companion and I had been dogged by poor weather, and now the weather forecasters were on strike. "It won't make the weather any different," said the hotelkeeper.

Clouds hung low over the hills as we walked up the valley. Only rarely did the clouds thin out enough to yield a glimpse of our target, the Col de Seysse. Patches of blue sky appeared then vanished in swirls of cloud. It was easy walking terrain on grassy moorland, but fearing a total loss of visibility later on we located a water course

to follow back down if we became engulfed in cloud.

Fifty metres (150 feet) below the *col*, visibility was just as poor as it had been below; but as we reached the Col de Seysse, it was as though a curtain had been raised. Where we'd come from, the hills were wreathed in low cloud and it looked like rain. But to the other side, above the hills and ridges of the Vercors, the sky was cloudless. The valleys beneath were bathed in brilliant summer sunshine, and we could see for miles. The view was spectacular. Straight ahead there unfolded a series of peaks, touched by the odd circle of cloud or cap of snow; to the right was the rugged high plateau of the Vercors.

The Parc Naturel Régional du Vercors, created in 1970, lies to the south and west of Grenoble. The valleys of the Drac, Drôme and the Isère are the natural boundaries of this roughly triangular tract of mountains. The centrepiece of the park is the 17,000 hectares (42,000 acres) of the high plateau of Vercors, the largest nature reserve in France. The edge of the plateau is a spectacle in itself. Where it is cleanly cleft, the cliffs resemble a medieval fortress. Yet erosion has many quirks. One such is Mont Aiguille, the "needle mountain", which protrudes from the plateau like a peninsula over the sea of sylvan hills below.

The plateau itself is of limestone that has become so eroded that it looks like coarse foam rubber. Rain rapidly drains away through fissures in the rocks, so that the plateau holds little water near its surface. Instead, it acts as a huge reservoir, supplying water for the valleys below. Some 20,000 sheep come to the plateau to graze during the summer months.

The internal erosion of the plateau has created a vast network of explorable caves. These labyrinthine tunnels helped to shelter resistance fighters during the last war, making the plateau one of their greatest strongholds.

The Vercors also used to be a stronghold of bears, lynx and wolves, but sadly all are now extinct in the park. The last bear in these hills was killed in 1921; its skull is now in Grenoble's natural history museum.

Nevertheless, the mountain hare can still be found here, as can the marmot. The park authorities have recently introduced more marmots from the mountains of the Vanoise and Ecrins, to strengthen their numbers. The most ambitious attempt to re- introduce a species into the park began in 1989, when a small number of ibex, taken from the Vanoise National Park, were released. Since 1983 the park authorities have also been studying the prospects of reintroducing bears, but at the time of writing this study had yet to be completed.

BEFORE YOU GO
Maps: IGN 1:100,000 No. 52; IGN 1:25,000 Nos. 226–229.

GETTING THERE
By car: the eastern edge of the park is only 5km (3 miles) from Grenoble, on the A48 *autoroute*. South of Grenoble, N75 follows the park boundary. The southern edge of the park is more or less described by D539 and D93.

One of the more spectacular drives through the park runs from D531 turn-off on N532, near St-Nazaire-en-Royans. The road skirts the Gorges de la Bourne before turning off on to D106 for a tour of the Gorges du Méaudret; it rejoins D531 for the descent into Grenoble.

By rail: there are no stations in the park, but plenty within easy walking distance, notably Grenoble. Local trains on the Grenoble–Valence line stop at Vinay and St-Hilaire-St-Nazaire, both just a few kilometres from the park. On the eastern flank trains stop at half a dozen stations between Vif and Lus-la-Croix-Haute; Clelles is close to Mont Aiguille.

By bus: there are regular buses from Grenoble to villages in the park—Autrans, Lans-en-Vercors and Villard-de-Lans are all points to pick up GR9.

WHERE TO STAY
The Bon Accueil at St-Maurice-en-Trièves (T:76 34 72 28) is cheap, comfortable and convenient.

Grenoble and Valence are the area's largest towns, Romans-sur-Isère the next down the scale.

Outdoor living: tourist offices have lists of campsites.
Refuges: contact Club Alpin Français at 32 av Félix-Viallet, Grenoble, T:76 87 03 73.

ACTIVITIES
Walking: GR9, GR91 and GR93 run through the park. Pick up GR9 and 91 off D106, just over the river from Grenoble; join GR95 at Die, where it runs north to link with GR93.
Caving: the high plateau of the Vercors is a centre for caving. Details from Maison de la Spéléologie, La-Chapelle-en-Vercors, T:75 48 22 38.
Riding: La Renardière, at Villard-de-Lans (T:76 95 13 10) offers everything from children's lessons to organized tours, in summer; in winter they operate out of Sassenage, nearer Grenoble (T:76 26 47 26).
Viewpoint: the Col de Seysse, on GR93, offers a spectacular view over the southern end of the Vercors plateau.
Scenic tour: a tourist train runs (summer only) from the SNCF station at St-Georges-de-Commiers. Small train, large spectacle, says the advertising.

FURTHER INFORMATION
Tourist information: Autrans, rte de Méaudre, T:76 95 30 70; La Chapelle-en-Vercors, Mairie, T:75 48 22 54; Die, pl St-Pierre, T:75 22 03 03; Grenoble, 14 rue République, T:76 54 34 36; Lans-en-Vercors, pl Eglise, T:76 95 42 62; Valence, pl du Général-Leclerc, T:75 43 04 88.

Park information: Chemin des Fusillés, Lans-en-Vercors, T:76 95 40 33. For guides contact the local office in Méaudre town hall, T:76 95 20 16. Weather reports on T:76 51 11 11 (Grenoble).

Massif de Chartreuse

A well-wooded limestone plateau alongside the River Isère

In a word association game it would be hard to avoid linking Chartreuse with the alcoholic drink of the same name. The monks of Grande Chartreuse created this sweet green liqueur in 1605. The monastery was the first of the Carthusian order when it was founded by Saint Bruno in about 1084. It is in the abundantly wooded, lozenge-shaped Massif de Chartreuse that any search would begin for the 130 aromatic and medicinal plants required by the original recipe.

The eastern boundary of the plateau is the River Isère.

There are two main routes from Chambéry to Grenoble: the eastern route follows the river; the western route, nowadays N6 and A48, defines the western boundary of the massif.

Chartreuse is what the French term the *Préalpes*—the foothills to the Alps. The limestone plateau has been moulded over time by glaciers and water. Unfortunately it has also taken a battering from the development of skiing. Ski lifts and paved roads have made the region more accessible, and correspondingly less wild. Despite this, and the proximity of Chambéry and Grenoble, Chartreuse has some lovely scenery, a mixture of wooded escarpments interspersed with valleys and waterfalls. Once away from the roads, the footpaths lead you into some still-tranquil walking country.

The highest peak on the massif, Chamechaude, at 2,082m (6,830ft), is relatively low by Alpine standards. There is a good view of Chamechaude and most of the other summits of both the Chartreuse and Vercors massifs, from the top of Charmant Som, which can be reached by D57-d. Like Vercors, the pitted limestone plateau of Chartreuse has many grottoes and underground passages that attract cavers.

Before you go *Maps:* IGN 1:100,000 No. 53; IGN 1:25,000 Nos. 3233–34 and 3333 (east and west).

Getting there *By car:* 3 roads enclose the massif—A41, N6 and A48.

By rail: 2 railways take the same route as the main roads around the park. Take a local train from Grenoble to either Chambéry or Moirans, get off at an intermediate station,

and hike from there.

By cable car: the quickest way out of the valleys is via the cable car (*la téléphérique*) from the riverside up to the forest overlooking Grenoble.

By bus: buses run from Grenoble to St-Laurent-du-Pont, Les Echelles and St-Pierre-de-Chartreuse.

Where to stay: despite its size Grenoble is a pleasant base; Hôtel Royal is comfortable and quiet (T:76 46 18 92). Towns on the massif itself include Les Echelles, St-Laurent-du-Pont, Le Sappey-en-Chartreuse, St-Pierre-de-Chartreuse and St-Pierre-d'Entremont.

Mist-shrouded peaks tower above glaciers in the Ecrins.

Outdoor living: lists of campsites available from local tourist offices.
Activities *Walking:* GR9 runs up the spine of the massif.
Caving: information from Centre National de Spéléologie, St-Martin-en-Vercors, T:75 45 50 05.
Skiing: main centres are Le Sappey, La Ruchère, Les Entremonts and St-Pierre-de-Chartreuse.
Further information *Tourist information:* Chambéry, 24 blvd de la Colonne, T:79 33 42 47; Challes-les-Eaux, av Chambéry, T:79 72 86 19; Les Echelles, Mairie, T:79 36 60 49; Grenoble, 14 rue République, T:76 54 34 36;.St-Pierre-de-Chartreuse, T:76 88 62 08; Le Sappey-en-Chartreuse, T:76 88 82 73.
   Weather forecasts (Grenoble) T:76 51 11 11.

71

Parc National de la Vanoise

A remote mountainous area running along the north of the Arc valley to the Italian border; the national park's central area covers 53,000ha (130,000 acres)

We had 2,500 feet to climb to get beyond the treeline. It had been an unusually warm June across Europe—the English newspapers were already bringing out their "Phew!" headlines—and here in the Alps that constituted a very sweaty climb. Our reward was the view, once we were well clear of the trees. The green grassy valley floor was surrounded by sheer mountains and scree. On one side plunged a deep ravine, which you heard before you saw because of the gurgling waters. The mountains on the far side of this divide had snow at the same level as we were. I had to pinch myself. This was summer; the sun was burning hot; that was snow.

Chamois (top) and Alpine ibex (below) inhabit the high rocky slopes of the Alps. The rarer ibex numbers less than 1,000 in the whole of France.

The surrounding peaks were among the biggest in the French Alps, sharp points that prodded the sky. White clouds hung over some of the highest ones, making it hard to discern where the cloud ended and the snow began. Looking back down into the valley on our way up was something of a culture shock. This was where we had come from, but it was hard to identify with that low landscape, so small and insignificant, with its tapestry of pastures.

The Parc National de la Vanoise was the first of the French national parks. The idea for its establishment dated from the 1930s, when naturalists wanted to create a reserve to help protect the Alpine ibex. Italy had already created a national park (the Gran Paradiso) on its side of the border, but the ibex had no protection from the hunters' bullets once they crossed the geopolitical divide into France.

Arguments between naturalists, who wanted a large park, and locals, who wanted a small park which did not unduly restrict their activities, were not resolved until the 1960s. The compromise between these two positions set a pattern for subsequent parks. When the Vanoise was created in 1963, it had a central zone where there were strict regulations to minimize human disturbance of the environment, and a less stringently protected buffer zone encircling it.

Today there is no permanent human habitation in the central zone, which covers almost 53,000 hectares (130,000 acres). The peripheral zone, nearly three times as large, has fewer than 30,000 human inhabitants. Together with the Italian Parco Nazionale del Gran Paradiso, it is part of the largest environmentally protected area in Western Europe.

The Alpine ibex still survives in the park, and in 1989 some 15 animals were transferred to the Ecrins and Vercors parks in the hope of re-introducing the animal there. When the national park was first set up there were only about 40 ibex. The park now has the largest colony—some 700 strong—of these animals in France. There are also about 5,000 chamois living here in 1963 there were only 400 of them.

In contrast to the flora, which is at its most luxuriant at the Alpine pasture level, the birdlife becomes more spectacular as you climb to the higher zones. The upper forests are chiefly home to vast numbers of chaffinches and dunnocks, while at the sub-Alpine level the main species to look for are ring ousel, nutcracker, redpoll and black grouse. Farther up among the grasslands are water pipits, rock thrushes and wheatears. The ptarmigan, alpine accentor and snow finch are the only winged inhabitants above the snowline.

In summer the Vanoise is a popular walking centre, and the paths are well trodden, especially those within easy reach of a road. The more distant parts of the park are still quite wild, although they grow less so with the development of each new ski resort.

The blue eryngo, or queen of the Alps, is one of the many delights of the abundant and varied natural flora to be found higher in the Alpine meadows.

BEFORE YOU GO
Maps: IGN 1:100,000 No. 53; IGN 1:25,000 (east and west) Nos. 3532–34 and 3632–33.
Guidebooks: the park office publishes several local guides.

GETTING THERE
By car: from Chambéry or Grenoble take the N6 turn-off from the A41 *autoroute*. The route splits close to St-Pierre-d'Albigny; N90 follows the valley of the River Isère to Bourg-St-Maurice, on the northern edge; N6 dives down to Modane, in the south.
By rail: there are regular services from Paris and Chambéry to Bourg-St-Maurice and Modane.
By bus: there are buses from Modane to Bonneval-sur-Arc.

In high summer there are also buses from Bourg-St-Maurice to Val d'Isère and Les Arcs; from the SNCF station at Moutiers to Pralognan and to Val-Thorens.

WHERE TO STAY
Bourg-St-Maurice is on the expensive side; Modane is scruffier and cheaper. Bonneville-sur-Arc, Bessans, Pralognan-la-Vanoise and Val d'Isère also have a choice of hotels.
Outdoor living: camping allowed in the peripheral zone.
Refuges: there are 42 refuges in the park; reserve in advance, T:79 33 05 52.

ACTIVITIES
Walking: GR55 runs from Val d'Isère up some stiff inclines to Pralognan-la-Vanoise, and joins GR58 near Modane. GR5 and 5E run from Val d'Isère to Modane in a less strenuous route.
Climbing: the guide to climbs in the park (as well as walking) is *Vanoise Park* by Robin Collomb (West Col).

FURTHER INFORMATION
Tourist information: Bonneval-sur-Arc, T:79 05 95 95; Bourg-St-Maurice, pl Gare, T:79 07 04 92; Modane, pl Replaton, T:79 05 22 35; Pralognan-la-Vanoise, T:79 08 71 68; Val d'Isère, T:79 06 10 83.

The park office is at 135 rue du Dr-Julian, Chambéry, T:79 62 30 54.

ALPINE FLOWERS

The wildflowers of the Alpine meadows and pastures are delightful. Exotic species such as the lady's slipper orchid thrive alongside the saxifrage as well as the more common buttercups and dandelions. These meadows have not seen intensive farming in modern times. The result is a staggering profusion of flowers; green meadows blaze with the violet, trumpet-shaped gentian, yellow anemone and blue thistle. This last is known as *la reine des Alpes*—the queen of the Alps.

National parks such as the Vanoise, Mercantour and Ecrins contain nearly half of all the plant species found in France, and French law, by forbidding their digging or uprooting, seeks to protect them within their natural habitat.

Parc Naturel Régional du Haut-Jura

A range of lush wooded mountains 50km (30 miles) northwest of Geneva; the regional nature park covers 62,000ha (153,000 acres)

The hills of the Jura are composed of sedimentary rock, mostly limestone or chalk. Originally, there was a plain here, but during the formation of the Alps, it was squashed between an irresistible force and an immovable object—the mountains to the south and the solid Massif Central to the west. The result was that the rocks of the Jura were folded into hills that resemble a ruffled rug on a floor.

The Jura limestone is pierced by underground caverns, and their chambers have been found to have a curious effect on the mountains' watercourses. The true source of the River Loue, for example, was only discovered in 1901 when a young Frenchman caught a whiff of anise on the air; the river reeked of Pernod. The Pernod distillery, on the upper reaches of another river, the Doubs, had had a large spillage several days earlier. When the Loue became Pernod-infused, too, it was the first anyone knew of an underground connection between the two rivers.

The Jura mountains are heavily forested. The name Jura means forest, and comes from an extinct Gaulish language 2,000 years old, yet the description still fits. The Jura mountains, although only half the height of the Alps, remain covered with a lush forest that thrives on the area's heavy rainfall, and in winter, snowfall. (It is France's wettest region, but does have a dry spell in high summer.) The densely wooded gorges that line the Jura make for spectacular scenic drives and train journeys.

The gently rolling lower slopes of the Parc Naturel Régional du Haut-Jura provide excellent walking country.

The Jura range in fact gave its name to an epoch. The Jurassic period of the earth's history—the central period of the Mesozoic era—took place about 200 million years ago. This was the age of the dinosaurs; the mountains here were formed while they still roamed the earth. The distinctive line of fossils in the Jura chalk was first recognized in the earlier half of the 19th century, and hence the Jurassic period was named after these mountains. Some of the richest deposits are in the hills of Le Bugey, to the south of the park near the village of Marchamp. The rocks here, discovered in 1830, produce a fantastic yield of fish and dinosaur remains.

Until recently the Jura was quite wild. However, since World War II a number of new roads have been built, and there are no longer inaccessible areas. Even the remotest parts are quite an easy walk from the nearest paved road.

Nevertheless, this is one area of France where the lynx can still be seen. This cat was extinct in the Alps at the end of the last century, and it only just clings on in the French Pyrenees. However, since they have been re-introduced in Switzerland, lynx do sometimes cross the border into France.

The high rainfall and glaciation history account for one of the curiosities of the Jura, in that being limestone mountains, they surprisingly contain a large number of bogs. The peat bogs are typically dominated by sphagnum mosses and among these grow a number of carnivorous plants. Most familiar is the sundew, but equally common is the blue-flowered butterwort. Other wet habitats on the Jura plateau are dominated by sedges, home to tree pipits, whinchats and snipe, as well as the Apollo butterfly.

In contrast to the rather Nordic atmosphere of the plateau, at the western border of the massif is the famous geological site of Cirque de Baume-les-Messieurs. Under the towering limestone cliffs grows a forest of white oak and box, imparting a Mediterranean feeling to the scenery. The forest supports a typically sub-Mediterranean bird fauna, including the short-toed eagle, Alpine swift, crag martin, rock bunting, ortolan and Bonelli's warbler.

In France the mountain hare is confined to the Alps, where, in winter, its coat turns almost totally white, with the exception of the ears which remain black.

The Apollo butterfly, a rare inhabitant of the Massif Central and the Alps, is prized for its dramatic beauty.

BEFORE YOU GO
Maps: IGN 1:100,000 Nos. 37, 38 and 44; IGN 1:25,000 (east and west) Nos. 3327–28.

GETTING THERE
By car: N83 from Bourg-en-Bresse to Lons-le-Saunier and Besançon runs roughly parallel to the Jura mountains. At right angles to this run the roads that cross the mountain range into Switzerland: D72, N5, N78 and A40. It is the turnings off these roads that take you into the heart of the hills. D437 north of St-Claude and D984 from Bellegarde to St-Laurent along the Swiss border are notably scenic.
By rail: there are regular train services between Bourg-en-Bresse, Lons-le Saunier and Besançon. Pontarlier has direct trains from Paris. About 4 trains a day run from Bourg-en-Bresse up to St-Claude; the ride is slow and spectacular. Equally slow are the trains north from St-Claude to Morez and Andelot.
By bus: regular buses run from Morez to La Cure, on the Swiss border; from St-Claude to La Cure and from Morez to Bois d'Amont. Buses from St-Claude also run to Clairvaux.

WHERE TO STAY
St-Claude is relatively central; most of the better hotels lie on the outskirts. Champagnole, Lons-le-Saunier, Pontarlier and Poligny are other convenient bases.

ACTIVITIES
Walking: GR9 follows the eastern boundary of the park until it meets GR5. At this junction GR5 takes up the northerly line heading towards Annecy, while GR9 turns west to cross the park. There are also local paths; one is centred on St-Claude.
Cycling: the railway stations at Bourg-en-Bresse, Besançon, Pontarlier and St-Claude rent out bicycles.
Fishing: the streams here offer some of the best trout fishing in France. The lakes have tench, bream and carp.
Riding: the Ranch des Balmettes, Ambérieu-en-Bugey (T:74 38 14 67) has organized tours in the Bugey hills. There is also a 700-km (420-mile) figure-eight ride, set up with the assistance of the Comité Départemental du Tourisme; information on "Le Grand Huit" from Jura du Grand Huit, Lavigny, Voiteur, T:84 25 31 89.
Fossils: Near Marchamp (on D87) is one of the richest fossil deposits (both fish and dinosaurs) in France.

FURTHER INFORMATION
Tourist information: Bourg-en-Bresse, 6 av Alsace-Lorraine, T:74 22 49 40; Champagnole, Hôtel de Ville, T:84 52 43 67; Lons-le-Saunier, 1 rue Pasteur, T:84 24 65 01; Poligny, 85 Grande-Rue, T:84 37 24 21 (summer only); Pontarlier, 56 rue République, T:81 46 48 33; St-Claude, 1 av Belfort, T:84 45 34 24.
    Weather forecasts (Besançon) T:81 88 44 44.

CHAPTER 4

Central France

"**O**n the opposite bank of the Allier the land kept mounting for miles to the horizon; a tanned and fallow autumn landscape with black blots of fir-wood and white roads wandering through the hills. Over all this the clouds shed a uniform and purplish shadow, sad, somewhat menacing, exaggerating height and distance and throwing into still higher relief the twisted ribbon of the highways. It was a cheerless prospect but one that is stimulating to the traveller."

This description of the Cévennes was written more than a hundred years ago by Robert Louis Stevenson, in *Travels with a Donkey*. Stevenson's account of his wanderings within central France could almost have been written yesterday, however. This vast area still attracts ramblers seeking stark scenery, rare wildlife or just solitude.

The Massif Central is the heart of France as the source of the country's major river arteries. Ancient granite and crystalline rocks are the main ingredients of this huge plateau. Although dwarfed by the Alps, the region is still mountainous and enjoys a montane climate, with skiing in winter and sudden cloudbursts in summer.

From a landscape point of view, the chief characteristics of the Massif are its plateaus and gorges. The two aspects could scarcely be more dissimilar. The plateau is almost a temperate desert: often waterless, normally arid, with few trees and frequent fierce winds. Villages are few, and houses often turn out to be deserted. Trees line the gorges, on the other hand, on all but

The Jonte gorges, Causse Noir, forms part of a series of limestone plateaux, 200 million years old. As the Ice Age receded, rivers, like the Jonte, cut deep gorges through the landscape.

the steepest precipices; while water runs headlong downhill, pausing only for the occasional hydroelectric dam. Many of the region's towns are found in the gorges, where for centuries people farmed terraces cut into the hillsides.

Our chapter title, Central France, is a broad definition for in addition to the wilds of the Massif Central this chapter also ranges west into quieter rural areas — the Dordogne and the Armagnac region of Gascony. These regions capture the popular conception of how pastoral countryside ought to look — green forests and meadows.

The Massif Central is a mix of granite and limestone. The granite centre is immensely old. No fossils lie hidden in these rocks, formed before identifiable life existed on earth. The limestone plateaus, known as *causses*, lie in two distinct patches south and west of the granite Massif. Those in the southern part of the Cévennes, such as Méjean or Larzac, are known as the Grands Causses and are higher and larger than the *causses* of Quercy and Périgord farther west. In geological terms these are recent rocks, about 200 million years old. The *causses* were once the sea bed, until the formation of the eastern-lying Alps thrust them 300 metres (1,000 feet) or more into the air.

During the Ice Ages, glaciers covered the Massif, rounding its hills and smoothing the rocks. When the glaciers retreated and vanished, streams and rivers took their place, cutting deep into the landscape. West-flowing rivers, such as the Dordogne and the Tarn, came up against the *causses*, eroding the limestone to create gorges with very steep sides.

Springs characterize the Massif Central and are the source of many of France's rivers. To the west the Massif feeds the Dordogne and the Tarn; to the north the Loire and its tributaries. The eastward-flowing streams, such as the Ardèche, lead to the Rhône; while to the south the Hérault and the Orb funnel down to the Mediterranean.

The limestone *causses* are some of the most desolate and deserted wildernesses in France. These are the French equivalent of the Russian steppes, wild and rugged landscapes of rock and coarse grass, which soon yellows in summer due to the dearth of water. In winter the *causses* are cold and inhospitable. Because they are so devoid of cover, these uplands are not always good for birdwatching; the narrow valleys provide better opportunities. The rare bearded vulture, for example, inhabits the gorges of the Tarn and Jonte. Some of the richest birdwatching I have experienced was not in the remotest areas but in the relatively well-populated valley of the River Allier, between the regional parks of the Volcans d'Auvergne and Livradois-Forez. Birds of prey that live in the region include Montagu's harrier and peregrine. As for mammals, the mountains provide sanctuary for both boar and wildcats, though both are largely nocturnal and you will need good fortune and persistence to glimpse either. One of the delights of the Massif Central is its wide variety of wildflowers. At Le Bouchet-St-Nicolas I was staggered by a profusion of cowslips, meadow sweet and blue campion. Higher up in the mountains the flora becomes sub-Alpine.

Travelling in the Massif Central these days is more comfortable than it was for Stevenson and his donkey. Many roads and some railways run along the thickly wooded gorges. It's worth seeking out minor roads, rather than *autoroutes*, and choosing slow local trains in preference to expresses if you want to relish the scenery. When Stevenson walked through the Massif he began at Le Monastier, south of Le Puy and what is now the regional nature park of Livradois-Forez. He then continued roughly southeast to Langogne, over the granite massif of Mont Lozère and on to Florac and the walk's end at St-Jean-du-Gard. From here he took a carriage to the railway town of Alès.

This is only the merest sketch of his journey. But it is easy enough to retrace Stevenson's steps, as his path is marked on the Institut Géographique National (IGN) maps. Authenticity may be a mite more difficult to achieve, however. These days there aren't many donkeys for sale hereabouts, and renting a carriage for the final leg may prove a problem. The good news is that there is a bus from St-Jean to Alès.

GETTING THERE
By air: the region's main airports are at Clermont-Ferrand, Lyon and Toulouse.
By car: the Autoroute du Soleil (A6) is the main route from Paris south to Lyon. The more direct (and less crowded) route for Clermont-Ferrand is to take N7 out of Paris and switch to N9 at Moulins. For the west of central France follow A71 south of Orléans, then N20 down to Limoges, Cahors and Toulouse.
By rail: speeding from Paris to Lyon in just 2hr, the TGV (*train à grande vitesse*) is the easiest way to travel south. Lyon has frequent connections to St-Etienne and other towns in the east of the Massif. There are 6 daily main-line trains from Paris's Gare de Lyon to Clermont-Ferrand, with connections for Nîmes, Béziers, Aurillac and Brive. Trains for Limoges, Cahors and Toulouse start from Gare d'Austerlitz.

For train information in English call Paris, T:45 82 08 41.
By bus: local services are sparse. For schedule information, contact the bus stations at Clermont-Ferrand (T:73 91 42 68); Limoges, (T:55 77 57 65); Toulouse (T:61 62 56 11); or Montpellier (T:67 34 23 02).

WHEN TO GO
Summers tend to be stultifyingly hot; winters freezing cold. Spring and autumn make better times for visiting.

WHERE TO STAY
Most travellers will approach the region through Clermont-Ferrand in the centre, Limoges in the west or the Rhône Valley in the east. Local tourist offices have details of hotels.

ACTIVITIES
Walking: there are some stiffish climbs in the Massif, from valley bottom to plateau table, but for the most part the walking is easy. The long-distance footpaths *grande randonnée* (GR) footpaths are a trusty guide to the best scenery.
Climbing: The Club Alpin Français maintains some refuges in the region. Their headquarters is at 9 rue La Boétie, Paris, T:47 42 38 46.

The rare nocturnal heron inhabits riverbanks and lake margins.

Caving: the underground rivers and tunnels of the *causses* are classic sites for caving. Get in touch with the Fédération Française de Spéléologie, 130 rue St-Maur, Paris, T:43 57 56 54.
Riding: there are plenty of opportunities for riding, and it's also possible to rent a *calèche*, a horse-drawn wagon. Contact the Fédération Française d'Equitation, 15 rue de Bruxelles, Paris, T:42 81 42 82.
Adventure holidays: the Union Nationale des Centres Sportifs de Plein Air offers hill-walking, hang-gliding and cycling holidays at half a dozen centres in the Massif. Contact them at 62 rue de la Glacière, Paris, T:43 36 05 20.
Fishing: salmon can be fished in the Allier and Garonne

SAFETY
The weather can change alarmingly fast in the mountains of the Massif, even in summer. A waterproof, warm clothing and sturdy footwear are essential.

during spring, and most rivers have trout. Information on restrictions and licences from Le Conseil Supérieur de la Pêche, 135 av Malakoff, Paris, T:45 01 20 20. **Skiing:** the mountains of the Auvergne and the Cévennes have cross-country skiing trails, notably around Mont-

Dore, the Cantal and the Massif Lozère.

FURTHER INFORMATION

Tourist information: for general information, contact the regional tourist offices— Auvergne, 45 av Julien, Clermont-Ferrand, T:73 93 04 03; Limousin, 8

cours Bugeaud, Limoges, T:55 79 57 12; Rhône-Loire, 5 pl de Baleine, Lyon, T:78 42 50 04.

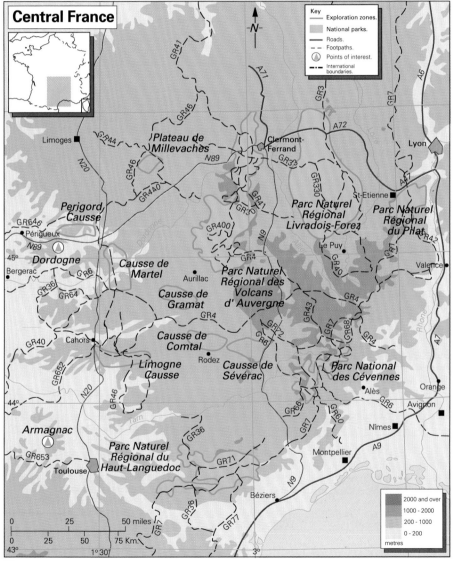

Central France

Key
— Exploration zones.
National parks.
— Roads.
--- Footpaths.
Ⓘ Points of interest.
-··- International boundaries.

-N-

GR41
A71
A6
GR3
GR7
GR46
A72
Limoges
GR44
Plateau de Millevaches
Clermont-Ferrand
N89
Lyon
N20
GR46
GR33
GR330
St-Etienne
A47
GR440
GR41
GR30
Parc Naturel Régional Livradois-Forez
Parc Naturel Régional du Pilat
GR42
Perigord Causse
GR646
GR400
N9
Le Puy
Périgueux
N89
45°
Dordogne
GR4
Valence
Bergerac
GR6
Causse de Martel
Aurillac
Parc Naturel Régional des Volcans d'Auvergne
GR40
GR36
GR64
Causse de Gramat
GR4
GR43
GR4
GR7
GR68
GR4
Rhône
A7
GR40
Cahors
Causse de Comtal
Rodez
GR2
GR6
Parc National des Cévennes
GR652
Limogne Causse
Causse de Sévérac
Orange
Alès
N20
44°
GR46
Tarn
GR6
GR7
GR60
Avignon
Nîmes
Armagnac
GR36
A9
GR653
Parc Naturel Régional du Haut-Languedoc
GR71
Montpellier
Toulouse
GR36
N9
Béziers
GR7
GR77

0	25	50 miles
0	25	50	75 Km.

43°
1°30'
3°

2000 and over
1000 - 2000
200 - 1000
0 - 200
metres

Parc Naturel Régional des Volcans d'Auvergne

Plateau of volcanic rock and dramatic peaks covering 3,500sq km (1,350sq miles)

While the volcanic peaks of the Auvergne no longer rain down lava, brooding thunder clouds can build up suddenly over this dramatic landscape and then open up with Wagnerian force. I learned this to my cost once when I ignored a hotel barometer I assumed was stuck on "variable" and set off for a long walk on the plateau. After an hour the heavens opened. Drenched and chastened, I made my way back, only to find the hot sun re-emerging just as I had the hotel within sight.

This is a cautionary tale, the weather can change very quickly in the mountains, and a forecast that talks of occasional thunder storms should be heeded. Even if there is

only one in the whole of the Massif Central, you could easily wind up in the middle of it.

The Auvergne is a wide-ranging region lying south of Clermont-Ferrand. The regional national park, containing the volcanoes, is shaped like a diamond, stretching north from Aurillac for 120 kilometres (75 miles) to Clermont-Ferrand. Extinct volcanoes dominate the park; the Puy-de-Sancy, at 1,886 metres (6,190 feet), is the highest of these ancient volcanoes, and the source of the River Dordogne. Three million years ago these volcanoes erupted regularly, throwing out streams of molten lava. The cooling lava and dead volcanoes together have moulded the landscape of Auvergne today.

The Volcans d'Auvergne could be part of a lunar landscape. The countryside is desolate and seemingly interminable, a forlorn relic of another world. The main volcanic *puys* (French for "peaks") lie to the north of the park, from Volvic down to Mont-Dore. Puy-de-Dôme, 12 kilometres (seven miles) west of Clermont-Ferrand, is the most celebrated: the climb to its summit is one of

The typical lunar landscape of the Auvergne was moulded by the lava of, now, extinct volcanoes.

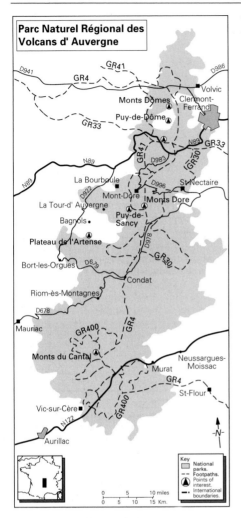

Parc Naturel Régional des Volcans d' Auvergne

Key
National parks.
Footpaths.
Points of interest.
International boundaries.

0   5   10 miles
0   5   10   15 Km.

water. The Cézallier plateau is also volcanic, linking the Cantal with the northern *puys*. Its chief town, Bort-les-Orgues, is so named because the cooled lava solidified into a ridge of basalt resembling organ pipes. The only part of the regional park not of volcanic origin is the granite plateau of Artense, in the northwest of the park.

To sit in the middle of Clermont-Ferrand, surrounded by these mountains, is like being on a stage. The scenery is awe-inspiring , a perfect setting for a rather ordinary town. In *Fat Man on a Bicycle*, author Tom Vernon describes it vividly: "... and suddenly there before me were the real mountains, the volcanoes of the Auvergne mist shrouded in the distance even in the sun, layer upon layer of blue shapes stretching back like stage mountains, cut-outs behind successive layers of gorse".

Stockraising is an important way of life in the Volcans d'Auvergne, and much of the ground is given over to pasture. Fences are few, however, so one of the characteristic sounds is the clanking of brass cowbells. Ramblers will also come across a large number of lizards, which lie on stone to soak up the sun, and scramble away when humans pass. The short-toed eagle, whose staple diet is small reptiles, also lives here.

The edge of the park produced some of the best birdwatching when I last visited. I saw a huge variety of birds in one short afternoon walk. A Montagu's harrier flew past, larks rose from fields, and in a thicket a great tit called persistently. The reason soon became clear: a red-backed shrike. Sitting on a dead branch in a thorn thicket, the bird surveyed its prospects and swooped on some unfortunate before taking it off to its larder. The shrike is known as the "butcher bird" because it stores its food. In the past it impaled its prey on thorns and came back later for its meal, though nowadays the store is as likely to be a barbed-wire fence. Later on that day a golden oriole flew past. Despite their striking yellow colour, these birds are rarely seen because they blend in surprisingly well with sunlight and leaves. To cap the afternoon's entertainment I caught sight of a couple of kestrels and a red kite.

the most gruelling in the Tour de France.

The *puys* have a characteristic shape, rising cone-like from the landscape. But the summit is often missing, blown off by some ancient eruption. The resultant craters have filled with water, creating calm lakes where lava once spurted. Unfortunately, few of these lakes are wild, having been taken over by pedal-boats or anglers.

In the southern end of the park lie the Monts du Cantal, formed by the cooling lava from just one volcano. The landscape here has since been reworked extensively by large-scale erosion, both by glaciers and

BEFORE YOU GO
Maps: IGN 1:100,000 No. 49;
IGN 1:25,000 Nos. 2432–36
and 2531–35.
Guidebook: *Walks in the Auvergne*, an English-language guide to the *grande randonnée* footpaths (Robertson McCarta).

GETTING THERE
By car: from Clermont-Ferrand D983 heads to Mont-Dore by way of Randanne (site of park headquarters). Farther south, D996 cuts across the park. Turning left onto D978 takes you over the top of the hills to Condat; D679 continues to Bort-les-Orgues, D678 to Mauriac.

At the park's southern boundary, N122 from Aurillac to Murat takes a scenic route up the valley that divides the Cantal massif.
By rail: 2 main lines cross the park. The journey from Aurillac to Neussargues-

GORGES OF THE MASSIF CENTRAL

One of the natural glories of France must be its gorges. The Gorges du Tarn, in particular, number among the country's best-known tourist sights, a Gallic version of the Grand Canyon. The scenery is staggering: the colour of the cliffs changes shades with the light and according to the minerals in the limestone sides.

It's possible to travel up most of the gorges by car, and some have quiet roads well suited for cycling. Surprisingly few are scaled by long-distance footpaths, although there is a scenic path that runs along the Gorges du Chavanon. The best view of the Gorges du Allier is via the railway.

But the best place to feel the full majesty of the gorges is from the water; consider renting a canoe. Some stretches of rapids are strictly for experienced canoeists, however.

Moissac is one of the most spectacular in Europe. The line from Neussargues to Bort-les-Orgues winds straight through the heart of the park, via Riom-ès-Montagnes, leaving plenty of time ($1\frac{1}{2}$hr) to take in the scenery.
By bus: regular buses connect with trains at Ussel and run to Bort-les-Orgues. There is

also a service (not Sun) from Clermont-Ferrand to La Tour d'Auvergne and Bagnols.

WHERE TO STAY
Clermont-Ferrand is central, but not particularly attractive. The main alternatives are scattered around the park periphery: touristy Aurillac, Mauriac, La Bourboule, Murat and St-Flour. Mont-Dore, Neussargues, Riom-ès-Montagnes, St-Nectaire and Vic-sur-Cère are the best options inside the park.
Outdoor living: there is no restriction on camping in the park.

ACTIVITIES
Walking: 5 of France's long-distance footpaths cross the park—GR4, GR30, GR33, GR400 and GR41.
Cycling: information from La Ligue d'Auvergne de la FFCT, 27 rue des Chandiots, Clermont-Ferrand. You can rent bicycles at the railway stations of Aurillac, La Bourboule, Mont-Dore and St-Flour.
Riding: information from Association Départementale de Tourisme Equestre, 12 av Edouard-Michelin, Clermont-Ferrand, T:73 90 08 10.
Skiing: the park is ideal for both cross-country and

CAUSSES OF THE MASSIF CENTRAL

The vast upland limestone plateaus of the Massif Central form one of the most striking landscapes in France. Likewise they hold a very special nature conservation value, being host to a diverse yet specialized flora and fauna. The *causses* are the domain of scrub and scattered small trees: white oaks and Scotch pines intermingle with junipers, box, hazel and brambles, while more open still are vast areas of heath with low spiny shrubs and an open ground flora of herbs and grassy tussocks.

Over this seemingly barren landscape fly reasonable numbers of Montagu's harriers, and this is the stronghold of the chough. Across the open herbaceous plateaus are little bustards and vast numbers of larks, but this hot, dry area is particularly favoured by reptiles: the impressive ocellated lizard is very much at home among these stony and thorny scrub habitats, while the smaller, brown Iberian wall lizard has recently been found on the eastern side of the *causses*. Insects, too, are of special interest, especially grasshoppers and crickets, several species of which occur here in complete isolation from their main range.

In addition to the Grands Causses of the Cévennes, there are smaller *causses* lying northwest: the Causse de Sévérac and the Causse du Comtal (known as the Petits Causses), and the Causses de Quercy.

downhill skiing. Information from Comité Régional de la Fédération Française de Ski, pl des Bughes, Clermont-Ferrand, T:73 92 17 05.
Viewpoint: Puy-de-Dôme offers a superb panorama over the volcanoes; you can see about 70 peaks in all. The *puy* also has Roman ruins.

FURTHER INFORMATION
Tourist information: Aurillac, pl Square, T:71 48 46 58; Bort-les-Orgues, pl Marmontel, T:55 96 02 49; La Bourboule, pl Hôtel de Ville, T:73 81 07 99; Clermont-Ferrand, 69 blvd Gergovia, T:73 93 30 20; Mauriac, pl Georges-Pompidou, T:71 67 30 26; Mont-Dore, av Libération, T:73 65 20 21; Murat, av Dr-Mallet, T:71 20 03 80; St-Flour, 2 pl Armes, T:71 60 22 50; Vic-sur-Cère, av Mercier, T:71 47 50 68.

Park offices are at: Montlosier près Randanne, Rochefort Montagne, T:73 21 27 19; 10 rue du Président-Delzons, Aurillac, T:71 48 68 60; and 28 rue St-Esprit, Clermont-Ferrand, T:73 92 42 42.

86

Parc Naturel Régional Livradois-Forez

Forested 300,000-ha (740,000-acre) park linking 2 ranges of hills; located between Clermont-Ferrand and St-Etienne

The Parc Naturel Régional Livradois-Forez is, if not the wildest part of France, certainly among the more rural. The park is a pleasing mix of fields and hills, of agriculture and woodland. This is not an isolated wilderness, where walkers can hike for miles without seeing any sign of life. Instead it is quietly pastoral: isolated farmsteads, surrounded by a patchwork of fields and meadows, lie in the valleys, while a mixed woodland of oaks and pines covers the hills. Two ranges of hills make up the park. The

The Massif de Sancy lies among ancient volcanic mountains, well known for their spring waters.

wooded Monts du Livradois and their southern continuation, the Monts du Velay, lie between the valleys of the River Allier and the River Dore. To the east of the wide valley of the River Dore are the granite Monts du Forez. Two *grande randonnée* footpaths meander through the park: GR330 tours Livradois-Forez, while GR60 gives good views of the Velay.

Livradois-Forez numbers among the country's latest generation of regional nature parks, being set up in 1983 to capitalize on its rural assets and to attract tourism. It is the second of these parks in the Auvergne; the other is the Volcans d'Auvergne, whose distant purple peaks line the horizon like a row of giant's fangs. The park lies to the east of Clermont-Ferrand and the valley of the Allier, which separates Livradois-Forez from the Volcans d'Auvergne regional park. The eastern boundary is followed by N89 and the railway from Thiers to St-Etienne; both routes afford good views. The Ardèche valley marks the park's southern end.

Before you go *Maps:* IGN 1:100,000 Nos. 49 and 50; IGN 1:25,000 Nos. 2630–34, 2730–34 and 2830–34 (east and west).

Getting there *By car:* D906 runs north–south through the park. Several roads cross east–west, including D996 and D558.

By rail: SNCF runs 4 daily trains from Clermont-Ferrand to Thiers or Pont-de-Dore in the northern end of the park. The line from Clermont-Ferrand to Le Puy skirts the park's southwestern edge.

By bus: buses connect with trains at Thiers, running south through the park to Ambert and Arlanc. Another continues south to La Chaise-Dieu, meeting the railway at Darsac.

Where to stay: Hôtel Robert at Vollore-Ville (T:73 53 71 27) is welcoming and right in the middle of the park. Other convenient centres are La Chaise-Dieu, Ambert, Thiers, Le Puy and Brioude.

Outdoor living: lists from local tourist offices.

Activities: an organization known as "Chamina" will provide information on cycle paths and riding and ski trails. Contact them at 5 rue Pierre-le-Vénérable, Clermont-Ferrand, T:73 92 82 60.

Museum: Ambert has a museum of old agricultural machinery appropriately sited in rue de l'Industrie (T:73 82 43 88). The museum also organizes summer train tours over the Auvergne and Cévennes; pick up the train at Ambert or Clermont-Ferrand.

Further information *Tourist information:* Ambert, 4 pl

Hôtel-de-Ville, T:73 82 01 55; Brioude, blvd Champanne, T:71 50 05 35; La Chaise-Dieu, pl Mairie, T:71 00 01 16; Montbrison, cloître des Cordeliers, T:77 96 08 69; Le Puy, pl du Breuil, T:71 09 38 41; Thiers, pl du Pirou, T:73 80 10 74.

Park headquarters is at St-Gervais-sous-Meymont, Olliergues, T:73 95 54 31.

Parc Naturel Régional du Pilat

65,000ha (160,000 acres) of rounded hills between Lyon and St-Etienne; eastern outpost of the Massif Central

The Parc Naturel Régional du Pilat was set up in 1974, and is a curious and welcome survival in an area once poised to be a victim of urban sprawl. An eastern outpost of the Massif Central, it is separated from the main massif but shares its geological features. The high point of the park is the peak of Perdrix, at 1,434m (4,700ft). This is a rounded ancient landscape, which has been slowly shaped by weather and time, wearing away the sharp edges and smoothing off the corners. Mixed forests of conifers and deciduous trees cover many of the higher hills, intermixed with pasture and arable farming on the lower slopes.

As the Montagu's harrier flies, the distance from Lyon to St-Etienne is only about 60km (35 miles). At first glance it seems scarcely credible that the outward spread of two such large

Spectacular rock formations characterize the impressive granite plateaux of the Monts du Forez.

towns could have left anything remotely resembling wilderness. Yet during an entire day in these hills I saw no more than three people.

The clue to this relative isolation is, of course, the height. Development has largely been contained along the valley of the River Gier, which forms the northwest boundary of this crudely triangular park. Its varied climate, ranging from Mediterranean to sub-Alpine, stems from a mixture of uplands and south-facing valleys.

This wild part of France is holding its own. Deer had vanished from the park; they have now returned. Wild boar, too, can be glimpsed here, and I saw several formidable dragonflies.

Before you go *Maps:* IGN 1:100,000 Nos. 50 and 51; IGN 1:25,000 Nos. 2933–34 and 3032–34. The park office sells a map of the park at 1:50,000 scale. *Guidebooks:* the park office has guides to the flora and birdlife of Pilat. **Getting there** *By air:* Lyon receives international and domestic flights. *By car:* the wildest part of the park lies in a triangle bounded on 2 sides by *autoroutes* — A7 and A47. The third side is hemmed by N82 from St-Etienne to Annonay, which cuts through the park. *By rail:* the best approach is the line from Lyon to St-Etienne, which tracks the border of the park. **Where to stay:** the 1-star Lion d'Or is an old coaching inn in

St-Chamond, with a *fin-de-siècle* atmosphere (T:77 22 01 38). Lyon, St-Etienne and Vienne are the largest towns surrounding the park; Annonay, Givors and Roussillon are smaller possibilities. Bourg-Argental is the best bet inside the park. *Outdoor living:* The tourist offices have lists of campsites. **Activity** *Walking:* the park office has details of a number of walks, including an 18-km (11-mile) botanical tour. 2 long-distance footpaths, GR7 and G42, cross the park. **Further information** *Tourist information:* Annonay, pl des Cordeliers, T:75 33 24 51; Bourg-Argental, pl Liberté, T:77 39 63 49 (summer only); Lyon, pl Bellecour, T:78 42 25 75; St-Etienne, 12 rue Gérentet, T:77 25 12 14.

Parc National des Cévennes

Sparsely populated national park covering 1,000 sq km (390 sq miles) of arid plateaus and moors in the southeast of the Massif Central

🦅🦅🦅

One good rule of thumb for discovering France's wild places is to make for the high ground, preferably somewhere at the end of a stiff climb along a few miles of footpath. I can scarcely claim the Cévennes as a discovery. It is, after all, a *parc national*. And long before I was born, Robert Louis Stevenson took his donkey, Modestine, through these hills.

Fortunately, not much has changed since Stevenson's time; most traces of habitation, from towns to paved roads, are confined to the valleys. Villefort, in the valley of the Allier, is one such example. The town is

THE LAMMERGEIER

The bearded vulture, also known as the lammergeier, is an immense bird. Even with a wingspan of up to 2.8m (9ft) it still welcomes the updraught of a thermal to help it fly. Consequently, vultures tend to favour warm cliffs and sunny gorges, where the sun warming up the valley bottom creates an updraught as the hot air rises.

There were bearded vultures in the Gorges du Tarn and de la Jonte until 1940. Hunters were partly responsible for their subsequent demise, but as important was the local farmers' new-found respect for hygiene, which meant they disposed of dead cattle, leaving no carrion to be picked clean.

The bearded vulture was once common in mountainous areas through southern and central Europe. But by the late 1960s the population was down to a few pairs, scattered across the Mediterranean countries and into North Africa. Their reintroduction to these gorges has been a slow one, but by 1985 there were more than 50 of these great birds patrolling the heights.

hemmed in by hills, so the way out of it along the *grande randonnée* is mercifully brief. The path rises steeply: a 225-metre (750-foot) climb in less than three kilometres (two miles). The vegetation changes as you climb. At first the woodland is mostly deciduous. Farther up it becomes mixed, as conifers take over. The woods gradually become almost entirely pines, interspersed with some small birch trees. Finally you emerge above the treeline onto a moor.

It is only when you have cleared the treeline that you first have a view. Before that you are climbing blind, with only glimpses through the upper branches to a distant hill on the other side of the valley. The view at the top, though, repays all your patience and exertion. Snow still covers the distant peaks at the end of May. All around, as far as the eye can see, the plateau stretches into the distance, changing hues from green and brown to a grey and purple on the horizon: a wasteland virtually devoid of any sign of human presence.

Parts of these hills are truly wild. The Parc National des Cévennes was created in 1970, the fourth of the six that have been set up so far. The central zone is the high ground that runs more or less south–south-west in a straight line between Mende and Villefort, roughly as far as Le Vigan, covering an area of 900 square kilometres (350 square miles). The borders of the buffer zone form a crude pentagon, from Mende to Les Vans, to Alès, Alzon and La Malène.

The park's central zone falls fairly naturally into three parts. The rounded old granite of Mont Lozère, in the north of the park, close to the town of Villefort, is the high point of the park, with a height of 1,699 metres (5,570 feet). It is high enough to be covered with snow for more than a quarter of the year. The massif of Mont Aigoual, south of Mont Lozère, is a mixture of granite and schist. Here the climate and plant life is almost Mediterranean; with long dry summers the sweet chestnut trees prosper. The areas of older rocks are shaped like an hourglass on the maps, with a slender neck at Barre-des-Cévennes linking the massifs of Lozère with Aigoual.

The lammergeier, or bearded vulture, is one of France's rarest raptors and has been the focus of intense conservation activity in recent years.

To the south and west of the granite are a series of deeply dissected limestone plateaus. These are the *causses* of Sauveterre, Méjean, Noir and Larzac—collectively known as the Grands Causses ("large plateaus"). These grassy expanses, green in spring and turning brown by late summer, stretch far into the distance, broken only by an occasional stone wall or building and rocky quarters, where there is not even enough soil to support a blade of grass. The *causses* are defined by the gorges that form their natural boundaries.

Despite the high rainfall on the *causses* there is little groundwater, save the odd dew pond. Any rain immediately seeps into the rock underground, carving vast sculptured caverns filled with stalagmites and stalactites. Sometimes the roof of one of these caverns caves in, and the result is a sinkhole—a sudden deep drop from the plateau into the underworld.

The climate of the *causses* is one of extremes. The eastern portion of the Causse Méjean is more than 1,000 metres (3,300 feet) high; in winter it's freezing cold, in summer baking hot. Local farmers use the *causses* for summertime pasture.

With their networks of natural tunnels and channels, the *causses* are frequently likened to Swiss cheese. In fact they are instrumental in the production of another type of cheese—Roquefort—made from the milk of ewes that graze on the high plateau. The cheese is stored in the caves above the village of Roquefort, close to the Causse du Larzac.

The caves at Aven Armand, on the Causse Méjean, are among the most celebrated in France. Most of the caves hereabout are strictly for experienced cavers, and require specialized equipment, but those at Aven Armand are open to the public. They make fascinating viewing: the more than 400 stalagmites, often attaining heights in excess of 20 metres (66 feet), glimmer with remarkably delicate shadings.

The mixing of Mediterranean, mountain and continental climates in the Cévennes gives rise to a wide range of habitats that in turn support an impressive fauna. Bird-watchers can hope to see the black wood-pecker and the short-toed eagle, which both nest in the park. The short-toed eagle feeds on reptiles, for which the Cévennes is particularly noteworthy. The warmer southern slopes represent the northernmost range of the typically Mediterranean Montpellier snake, while altitude separates out the two vipers: the commoner asp frequents forest-edge habitats up to about 1,000 metres (3,300 feet) altitude, the rarer adder taking over from about 900 metres (3,000 feet) to the upper treeline. The Cévennes is also one of the few noted areas where both species of smooth snake occur together.

The holes and small caves on the limestone *causses* are convenient dwellings for a host of mammals: rabbits, foxes and mice. The park has pursued an active programme of reintroducing species that used to live in the Cévennes. It has successfully reintroduced European beavers into the rivers of the Tarn and the Tarnon, and bearded vultures in the Gorges de la Jonte and Gorges du Tarn. Several threatened birds of prey, including the golden eagle, also nest in the Gorges du Tarn.

Parc National des Cévennes

GR4
GR7
GR65
GR43
La Bastide-Puylaurent
Marvejols
GR7
GR72
Le Monastier-Pin-Moriès
Mende
GR68
GR6
GR60
N106
GR4
Les Vans
Mont Lozère
Villefort
Causse de Sauveterre
GR72
Gorges du Tarn
Florac
Génolhac
La Malène
St-Laurent-de-Trèves
GR7
Bessèges
Causse Méjean
Aven Armand
GR60
Col des Faysses
Barre-des-Cévennes
N106
Gorges de la Jonte
Meyrueis
D9
St-Roman-de-Tousque
Causse Noir
Mont Aigoual
D907/D983
St-Jean-du-Gard
Millau
Alès
GR66
GR6
La Cavalerie
Le Vigan
Alzon
Causse du Larzac

Key
National parks.
Footpaths.
Points of interest.
International boundaries.

0   5   10 miles
0   5   10   15 Km.
-N-

BEFORE YOU GO
Maps: IGN 1:100,000 Nos. 58, 59 and 65, also the 1:100,000 map of the Cévennes; IGN 1:25,000 Nos. 2738–40 (east) and 2638–40 (west).

GETTING THERE
By car: N9 runs south from Clermont-Ferrand, picking up N106 to Mende, then wends through the Cévennes to Florac and Alès. For a more scenic route, turn off N106 onto D907/D983 about 5km (3 miles) south of Florac. At St-Laurent-de-Trèves, D9 cuts through the pass of Faisses and continues to the village of St-Roman-de-Tousque; it rejoins N106 south of Alès.
By rail: the railway from Clermont-Ferrand to Alès takes a more northerly route

In the Cévennes mountains, deciduous trees blend with evergreen pines.

Plateau de Millevaches

A remote granite plateau on the northwest edge of the Massif Central; its springs are the source of several rivers

The Tour d'Eygurande is one of France's long-distance footpaths. About an hour's walk out of Merlines the footpath picks up the route of a disused railway, following the woody gorges of the River Chavanon. Beneath the path vigorous waters gush over the rocky river bed, while shafts of sunlight glint on the water.

For most of its route the path is on the plateau of Millevaches ("a thousand cows"). At first sight the name is an absurdity. This is an infertile and remote upland, far from the gadding waters of the river valleys: the wilderness seems to lack the wherewithal to support one cow, let alone a thousand. But the name, has nothing to do with cattle, but is a corruption of a Celtic word for spring (*batz*). This immediately makes sense, for the plateau is the source of several important rivers, including the Vienne and the Creuse, as well as a couple of tributaries of the Dordogne.

The source of the Vienne is about a 30min walk north of the village of Millevaches, the settlement which gave its name to the plateau. The plateau is not officially protected (it lies outside the boundary of the regional nature park of the Volcans d'Auvergne), but the peat bog of Longéroux, near the town of Meymac, is a nature

than the 2 roads running the length of the park. Trains also run up into the hills from Alès to Bessèges.
By bus: there is a regular service from Alès to Florac and St-Jean-du-Gard; Le Puy to Langogne and Mende; Florac to Mende, Millau and Génolhac; and Nîmes to Le Vigan. 4 buses a day run from Sévérac to Rodez, and on to Millau, Cahors and Espalion.

WHERE TO STAY
Villefort is a good base for exploring the Cévennes; the 2-star Hôtel Balme (pl du Portalet, T:66 46 80 14) has an excellent restaurant. Alès is another convenient base. More central possibilities include La Bastide-Puylaurent, Florac, Génolhac, Meyrueis and Les Vans.
Outdoor living: camping is forbidden in the park centre; there are plenty of campsites on the periphery.
Refuges: the park office has a list of stops on GRs through the park.

ACTIVITIES
Walking: a series of GR long-distance footpaths criss-cross the park (see map). There is also a footpath that follows Stevenson's walk.

The Corsican mouflon now inhabits upland areas of mainland France.

Cycling: bicycles are available at the railway stations of Alès, La Bastide-Puylaurent, Langogne, Marvejols, Mende and Villefort.
Canoeing: many of the park's rivers are good for canoeing; the park office has a leaflet detailing possibilities.
Riding: the park features over 500km (300 miles) of bridle paths; contact the Association Lozérienne de Tourisme Equestre, Ste-Enimie, T:66 48 53 71.
Viewpoints: a 38-km (23-mile) tour of the ridges (D998) from Génolhac to Les Bastides, returning on D35 and D906) takes in splendid views. The whole of the park can be seen from the Can de L'Hospitalet, south of St-Laurent-de-Trèves.

FURTHER INFORMATION
Tourist information: Alès, 2 rue Michelet, T:66 78 49 10; Florac, av J-Monastier, T:66 45 01 14; Mende, 16 blvd Soubeyran, T:66 65 02 69; Villefort, rue Eglise, T:66 46 87 30 (summer only).
Park headquarters at Florac, T:66 45 01 75.

The lesser-spotted woodpecker is an elusive but widespread species in broad-leaved forests.

reserve. Conifers mix with oaks in the woods near Meymac, providing an excellent habitat for blueberries (*myrtilles*), the local "cash crop".

The berries also are a food source for birds; re-emerging from cover after a rain shower during my walk along the Tour d'Eygurande, I noticed the increased birdsong. As I made tracks for lunch a lesser spotted woodpecker and a kestrel flew past in the space of a few minutes.

Before you go *Maps:* IGN 1:100,000 No. 41; IGN 1:25,000 Nos. 2232 and 2331–32.

Getting there *By car:* N89 from Clermont-Ferrand to Tulle is the plateau's southern boundary.
By rail: the railway line from Clermont-Ferrand to Brive passes through Ussel and Tulle. The line from Ussel to Bugeat, Eymoutiers and Limoges crosses the plateau.
By bus: SNCF runs a bus service from Ussel north to Felletin.

Where to stay: Ussel is the hub of both road and rail services in the area. La Courtine, Egletons, Felletin, Merlines, Meymac, Tarnac and Treignac are other options.

Activities *Walking:* GR44 and GR440 cross the plateau ending up at Limoges. The Tour d'Eygurande is the eastern side of the plateau; pick up the tour at Merlines or Ussel.
Cycling: bicycles are available at Meymac station.

Further information *Tourist information:* Ussel, pl Voltaire, T:55 72 11 50.

Dordogne

Restful, gentle region of lush river valleys, located between Limoges and Bordeaux

The Dordogne may not be the wildest part of France, but it is exceptionally rural, a tranquil blend of woodland and agriculture. It is a gentle yet rich landscape of small hills where herds of deer peer warily at passing strangers from the safety of the woodland edge.

The River Dordogne lies at the centre of the region, flowing from the granite of the Auvergne before meandering west to the Atlantic. "Just to glimpse", as Henry Miller observed, "the black, mysterious river at Domme from the beautiful bluff at the edge of the town is something to be grateful for all one's life." Thousands of visitors annually share Miller's view, and at times it is hard to hear a word of French spoken; the pastoral view, however, remains unchanged.

One of the Dordogne's most striking man-made contributions are the prehistoric cave paintings at Les Eyzies. The best of these paintings, at Lascaux a few kilometres up the road, were discovered by accident in 1940 by four boys searching for a lost dog. The paintings are remarkable not only for their vivid portrayal of Stone Age animals but also for their uncanny state of preservation.

People lived in these caves in the middle of the last Ice Age, and the pictures depict the wildlife of the times: bison, reindeer and mammoths. These paintings survived in their pristine state

TRUFFLES AND MUSHROOMS

The regions of Limousin and Périgord are noted for their immense variety of wild fungi. Most distinguished is the truffle, of which a dozen or so species occur in Périgord. Most widespread is the truffle *Tuber melanosporum*. It generally occurs around field edges where the ploughed and hard soils meet. But being mostly underground it is not particularly easy to locate. Look for circular patches in which the soil is bare and as though freshly dug, with stones paler than elsewhere. But in the end, it's far easier to train an animal to sniff them out for you.

for about 20,000 years thanks to the evaporation of water, which covered the walls with a kind of lacqueur.

On its way west from its source high in the Massif Central, the River Dordogne passes through Périgord Noir, its name a slight exaggeration of the dark oak woods there. Neighbouring Périgord Blanc, north of the River Isle, takes its name—with a bit more accuracy—from the whiteness of the limestone.

The Dordogne is a highly agricultural region, with its most prized produce gathered in winter, when pigs and specially trained dogs root out truffles. There are about 30 varieties of truffle, and those of Périgord are especially valued.

Two areas of the Dordogne are noted for their vineyards: the red wines of Bergerac come from the lower reaches of the Dordogne, while farther southeast are the wines of Cahors, a town on the River Lot.

Before you go *Maps:* IGN 1:100,000 No. 48; IGN 1:25,000 Nos. 1834–37, 1934–38, 2034–39 and 2134–39.

Getting there *By car:* roads radiate out from Sarlat—D47 leads to Périgueux, while D703 heads west to Bergerac, east to Souillac.
By rail: 3 trains a day run south from Périgueux to Les Eyzies and Le Buisson. The line east from Bergerac follows the River Dordogne to Le Buisson and Sarlat. Main-line trains from Paris run through Brive to Souillac and Cahors.
By bus: 3 daily buses link Souillac to Sarlat.
Where to stay: L'Auberge sans Frontière at Dégagnac (T:65 41 52 88) is a splendid village hotel, and a good base for tours in the region. The main towns are Périgueux,
94

Brive-la-Gaillarde, Bergerac and Sarlat; other possibilities include Les Eyzies, Montignac, Domme and St-Cyprien.
Outdoor living: practically every town has a municipal campsite.
Activities *Walking:* several *grande randonnée* paths cross this lovely walking country— GR6, GR46, GR36, GR64 and GR652.
Cycling: railway stations at Bergerac, Cahors, Les Eyzies, Périgueux, Sarlat and Souillac rent out bicycles.
Riding: information from Association Départementale de Tourisme Equestre de Dordogne, 4–6 pl Francheville, Périgueux, T:53 09 26 26.
Sightseeing: the hilltop village of St-Cirq-Lapopie is one of the best preserved in France.
Further information *Tourist information:* Bergerac, 97 rue Neuve-d'Argenson, T:53 57 03 11; Les Eyzies-de-Tayac, pl Mairie, T:53 06 97 05 (summer only); Périgueux, 1 av Aquitaine, T:53 53 10 63; Sarlat, pl Liberté, T:53 59 27 67; Souillac, blvd Malvy, T:65 37 81 56.

Armagnac

Rural gem in southwest France; frequently overlooked by travellers speeding to the Pyrenees

The western outpost of Gascony is Les Landes, that vast forest on the Atlantic

Poplar trees grow along the bank of the Dordogne near Beynac.

coast. Armagnac is the area east of Les Landes, sandwiched between the River Garonne to the north and the Pyrenees to the south, an extended version of the modern *département* of Gers. This is where Armagnac, the southern rival of Cognac, is distilled.

A series of rivers stretch out like fingers to cross Gascony, rising in the mountains of the Pyrenees and heading for the valley of the Garonne, which is also the route of the Canal du Midi. The Garonne is clean enough to have salmon. Armagnac is far from being the wildest part of France. It is, nevertheless, off the beaten track; the countryside is rustic, quiet and relatively free of tourists—certainly by comparison with the Dordogne to the north.

The region holds a number of forests, including the 2,000-ha (5,000-acre) Forêt de Bouconne west of Toulouse, while in the *département* of Gers lies the Forêt de Berdoues, south of Mirande. The nature reserve of Puntous is close by.

Before you go *Maps:* IGN 1:100,000 No. 63; IGN 1:25,000 Nos. 1542–45, 1642–45, 1742–45, 1842–45 and 1942–45.
Getting there *By air:* Toulouse is the closest airport.
By car: A62 runs down the Garonne valley from Bordeaux to Toulouse, and is the region's northern boundary. N124 cuts across Gascony from Toulouse to Auch. Main north—south roads are N134 (Pau to Aire) and N21 (Tarbes to Auch).
By rail: there are main-line trains from Paris to Toulouse; from Paris, Bordeaux and Dax to Pau and Tarbes.
By bus: Auch is the centre for local buses; routes radiate to Agen, Lannemezan, Tarbes, Mont-de-Marsan, Condom, Barbotan-les-Thermes and Montauban.
Where to stay: Pau and Tarbes border the Pyrenees; other options are Auch, Aire,

Condom, Mirande and Mont-de-Marsan.
Outdoor living: local tourist offices have lists of campsites.
Activities *Walking:* GR65 runs from Roncevaux in the Pyrenees to Eauze and La Romieu, the starting point for the tour of Cœur de Gascogne, to Auch and back. GR653 heads from Toulouse to Auch and Maubourguet. Tourist offices have details of local walks.
Cycling: rent bicycles at the stations of Auch and Tarbes.
Riding: information from Association Départementale de Tourisme Equestre du Gers, Chambre d'Agriculture, route de Mirande, Auch, T:62 63 16 55.
Further information *Tourist information:* Auch, pl Cathédrale, T:62 05 22 89; Condom, pl Boussuet, T:62 28 00 80; Mont-de-Marsan, av Victor-Hugo, T:58 46 40 40; Pau, pl Royale, T:59 27 27 08; Tarbes, pl Verdun, T:62 93 36 62; Toulouse, Donjon du Capitole, T:61 23 23 00.

Parc Naturel Régional du Haut-Languedoc

Surprisingly lush upland park (145,000ha/ 360,000 acres) forming southern rim of the Massif Central

\\ \\

I sat down to lunch in a hillside meadow of dandelions, on the edge of some woods overlooking a deep valley. Wild roses lined the woodland edge. The smell of wild thyme sweetened the air and the loudest sound was the chattering of the cicadas. This was rural bliss.

Haut-Languedoc has a distinct feel of Greece about it. The valley of the River Orb, which runs through the park, could be the river valley at the foot of Mount Olympus: the trees are stacked up the valley sides so steeply that when seen from far off it appears as if the roots of one are supported by the boughs of that beneath. The rock outcrops, too steep for soil to cling to, show through gaps in the vegetation.

Despite the poorish soil, the hills bristle with oaks, sweet chestnuts and mountain ash; firs crown many of the hilltops.

The local villages, too, have a Greek flavour. St-Pons-de-Thomières, located in the centre of the park, is a case in point. Whitewashed houses spread up the hillsides, their Mediterranean red-tiled roofs glinting in the sun. The streets wind upwards, twisting and turning. The local stone is reflected in the architecture; even the streets of St-Pons are paved with marble.

The Parc Naturel Régional du Haut-Languedoc lies in the southwestern extremity of the Massif Central. These hills create an opulent landscape of shaggy woodland, with oak, beech, chestnut and pine interspersed with pasture. The greenery is easy to explain; the area falls in the watershed between the Atlantic and the Mediterranean. The northern part of the park is a granite plateau, known as Sidobre, while the southern section holds a range of hills known as the Montagne Noire (Black Mountain). The valley of the River Thoré and the industrialized plain of Castres separate the two.

The plateau of Sidobre is divided by the gorges of the Agout. The climate is almost Mediterranean, although a good supply of ground water keeps the vegetation lush. The mountains of Lacaune, to the north and east of the park boundary, have some of the highest rainfall in France. This is a climate frontier, where the warm Mediterranean climate meets the moist westerlies off the Atlantic. The clouds float in on the westerly winds, rise up when they meet the hills, and promptly dump their cargo of rain.

The birdlife in Haut-Languedoc is not easy to spot because of the dense vegetation, but just occasionally a buzzard will rise above the treeline to survey its domain. For the most part, however, prey and predator alike stay hidden behind the dense foliage, only their songs betraying their presence.

The valleys are considerably less wild, and more inhabited. However, the drive west to St-Pons takes in some striking views of gorges along the route. The valley itself is highly agricultural; here on the valley floor, the sport is to spot a square foot of soil without a vine on it. Viticulture is an important part of the local economy.

The Haut-Languedoc area is popular among the caving fraternity. The many caves were first explored in modern times by Edouard-Alfred Martel; some had been inhabited 3,000 years ago, and then left empty until Martel and the other intrepid explorers rediscovered them. Ancient civilization left another mark on the area, with a series of sculptured menhirs and other megaliths.

BEFORE YOU GO
Maps: IGN 1:100,000 Nos. 64 and 65; IGN 1:25,000 Nos. 2244, 2343–44 and 2443–44.

GETTING THERE
By air: Toulouse is the nearest airport.
By car: the park lies 30km (18miles) north of the A61 *autoroute*. At Carcassonne, D620 branches off into the park as far as St-Pons (site of park headquarters). D907 from Lacaune to St-Pons crosses the heart of the park.
By rail: 6 daily trains link Toulouse-Matabiau with Castres and Mazamet, on the edge of the Montagne Noire.
By bus: St-Pons has connections with Toulouse, Montpellier, Bédarieux and La Salvetat.

WHERE TO STAY
The 1-star Hôtel Pastré in St-Pons (T:67 97 00 54) is delightfully eccentric. Other convenient centres include Lamalou-les-Bains, Olargues, Roquebrun, La Salvetat, Anglès and Brassac.
Outdoor living: local tourist offices have lists of campsites.

ACTIVITIES
Walking: long-distance footpaths GR7, GR36, GR71 and GR77 traverse the park. The park office (address below) has details of shorter tours, including the path of St-Jacques-de-Compostelle (from St-Gervais-sur-Mare to Sorèze).
Climbing: information from Base de Plein Air, Mons-la-Trivalle, Olargues, T:67 97 72 80.

Caving: for a full list, contact Maison du Parc de Roquebrun, Mairie de Roquebrun, Cessenon, T:67 89 64 54.
Archaeology: the park is rich in archaeological remains, notably megaliths. La Maison du Parc, at Rieu-Montagne by the lake of Laouzas, has an exhibition.

FURTHER INFORMATION
Tourist information: Castres, pl République, T:63 59 92 44; Mazamet, rue des Casernes, T:63 61 27 07; Revel, pl Philippe-VI-de-Valois, T:61 83 50 06; St-Pons, pl Foirail, T:67 97 06 65; Toulouse, Donjon du Capitole, T:61 23 23 00.

Park headquarters are at 13 rue du Cloître, St-Pons, T:67 97 02 10.

CHAPTER 5

The Loire and Burgundy

France's longest river, the Loire, nearly cuts the country in two. Some 950 kilometres (600 miles) of woods, vineyards and châteaux line its banks as the river grows from a swift-flowing stream to wind ever more slowly through the flood plain on its journey down to the Atlantic. The wide agricultural valley of the lower Loire is not the wildest part of France. But nature has kept back a few treats which are well worth seeking out.

Some treasures are buried behind the châteaux and the tourists, such as the wooded wetland of the Sologne. And east of the valley of the Loire, in Burgundy, lie the Morvan hills, a rural fastness where birds of prey such as merlin and buzzard still thrive.

For most of the time the Loire is deceptively placid and languid as it meanders shallowly between the *levées*, the raised embankments that attempt to contain its course. Herons poise on banks in the middle of the river while kingfishers dart up and down its length. But the river is capricious and in full flood an awesome sight. The waters, swollen by the melting snows of spring far upstream in the Massif Central, angrily swirl around the piers of Decize's medieval bridge. Downstream the river sometimes breaks its banks, swelling on to riverside pastures and forcing sheep and cattle (and people) to retreat to higher ground. Weeping willows stand proud in the midst of the thick floodwater, marking the line of the bank.

This clearing in the wetland woods of the Sologne district of the Loire valley shows the typical heathland character with heather, broom and gorse.

Local ecologists say the Loire is the last truly wild river in Europe. It remains, apart from the shorter rivers of Brittany, the country's last breeding place for salmon. However, it may not remain wild for much longer, since it's recently become the centre of political controversy. Because of its capricious nature, the French government wants to tame the river with a series of barrages and dams. The salmon spawning grounds hang in the balance.

Between Nevers and Orléans the river sweeps around to the west, crossing the limestone plateau of Berry and forming the border on two sides of a triangle of the Sologne. This sharp change in direction is unusual; geologists believe that the Loire did once flow north, joining up with the Seine.

For much of its length canals run parallel to the Loire. Once the arteries of commerce, these canals are discovering a new lease of life in the pleasure-cruise market. One in particular, the Canal de Briare (which joins the Loire at Briare with the Loing, a tributary of the Seine) is said to have colonies of the European beaver.

From a wildlife point of view, two marshes represent the most interesting segments of the valley of the Loire. The Brière marsh lies at the mouth of the Loire on the Atlantic, and for geographical reasons is covered in the chapter on Brittany and Normandy. Farther inland, south of Orléans, the Sologne is the remains of a freshwater swamp, ill-drained and relatively inaccessible—though a new *autoroute* is being extended through its middle, to the dismay of environmentalists.

Stretching out of the valley of the Loire are a series of sweet forests. The 5,000-hectare (12,000-acre) Forêt de Chinon and the hunting Forêt de Chambord lie on the left bank, while the forests of the Nivernais (the region of Nevers) and Orléans are on the right. The limestone plateau of the Nivernais stretches between the Loire and the Morvan hills. This is a country of hedgerows, and distinctive white cattle, known as *charolais*, are raised over much of the region.

South of the Loire and the Sologne is the country of Berry, the land at the centre of France. A string of forests follow the valley of the Claise, a tributary of the Creuse, from the confluence of these rivers to Châteauroux and onwards over the Berry plateau and up the valley of the River Cher. Among the more interesting woodlands here are the Forêt de Tronçais and the Forêt de Lancosme, near Châteauroux, the latter home to honey buzzards and hen harriers, which perform aerial courtship displays in spring; at night the forests resound with the haunting calls of tawny and long-eared owls.

The area around the River Claise, known as the Brenne, is a smaller version of the Sologne, with its lakes and waterlilies. However, the wildlife is just as rich: these lakes and rivers are renowned as the last French stronghold of the European pond terrapin, the only freshwater turtle found in France. They are also exceptionally rich in birdlife; marsh harriers are resident throughout the year, while migrating ospreys regularly stop by. There are numerous other waterfowl, and black and moustached terns are a summer speciality.

In former times Burgundy was an independent duchy, and a curious historical realm that drifted across the pages of history, occasionally becoming independent and then once again being reunited with France, gaining and losing possessions to the south and to the north. Modern Burgundy is the one stretch of land that was common to this migratory state. From Nevers on the Loire the region today stretches east to Dijon, south to Mâcon. Its northern boundary ends just short of Fontainebleau.

The Morvan plateau, a plateau with some 900-metre (3,000-foot) peaks at the heart of Burgundy, is linked geologically to the Massif Central. The rock is granite. This granite plateau is in marked contrast to the chalky earth of the Parisian basin farther to the north, and to the limestone around Nevers and to the east around Autun.

In western Burgundy, towards Dijon and the valley of the Saône, lies la Côte d'Or (the Gold Coast). With its roll-call of famous vineyards, such as Gevrey-Chambertin and Nuits-St-Georges, this is the land of the Burgundy reds.

Burgundy was on the historic trade route, north from Italy and the Mediterranean to Flanders. It still lies on the main north–south route, although these days journey's end is more likely to be Paris or the Riviera. The modern quest for speed has disrupted some of the quieter countryside in the east of the region. In the 1960s came the Autoroute du Soleil, carving a swathe across the land. Then came the *train à grande vitesse* (TGV), whistling past at more than 250km/hr (150mph). Fortunately, most of the people on these great routes go straight through Burgundy, without pausing, leaving much of the country undisturbed.

GETTING THERE
By air: Nantes airport serves the western end of the Loire, though travellers from North America will normally arrive at Paris and change on to an internal flight. There are no airports serving the eastern end of the Loire and Burgundy.
By sea: the western end of the Loire can be reached fairly easily from the cross-Channel ports of St-Malo and Roscoff. More details of sailings across the Channel are listed in the chapter on Brittany and Normandy.
By car: A10 runs from Paris to Orléans and downstream to Tours. Be warned: the drive down through Burgundy on A10 is appallingly overcrowded at the beginning of Aug. A right fork, south of Fontainebleau on to the N7, takes drivers down into the Loire valley to Nevers.
By rail: there are frequent trains from Paris (Gare d'Austerlitz) to Orléans; about 8 a day continue down the Loire to Tours. Gien and Nevers receive 8 trains daily from Paris's Gare de Lyon.

The main lines from Paris to Burgundy run from the Gare de Lyon to Avallon and Autun, with a branch line off to Corbigny. The TGV runs to Le Creusot, which has a bus connection to Autun.

For train information (in English), T:45 82 08 41.

WHEN TO GO
The Loire attracts tourists throughout the year, but most come for the châteaux and wine, leaving long stretches of the river undisturbed. Burgundy is less crowded, except in Aug, when some roads are packed with French families travelling south.

WHERE TO STAY
The best centres for exploring the area are listed in the individual exploring sections. Tourist information offices have lists of hotels, and the offices at Blois, Nevers, Orléans and Tours will make bookings.

For self-catering holidays contact Maison des Gîtes de France, 35 rue Godot-de-Mauroy, Paris, T:47 42 25 43.

ACTIVITIES
Walking: this is one of the best means of seeing the area, whether on a lengthy hike or a gentle amble. Apart from the marshes the terrain is easy, and there are no stiff climbs.

The royal fern is a rare species found in sheltered damp conditions.

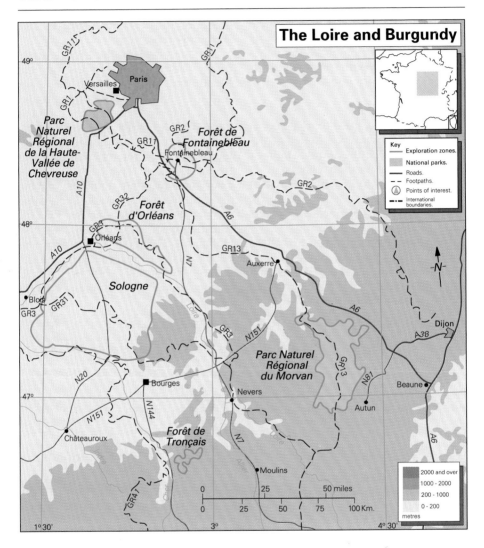

The Loire and Burgundy

49°

Versailles Paris

Parc Naturel Régional de la Haute-Vallée de Chevreuse

GR2 Forêt de Fontainebleau
Fontainebleau

GR11

GR2

A10

GR32

Forêt d'Orléans

A6

48°

Orléans

GR13

Auxerre

A10

Sologne

Loire

Blois

GR31

GR3

Dijon

GR3

N151

A38

A6

Parc Naturel Régional du Morvan

GR13

N81

Beaune

N20

Bourges

Nevers

Autun

47°

N151

N144

Châteauroux

Forêt de Tronçais

N7

Moulins

1°30'
3°
4°30'

Key
Exploration zones.
National parks.
Roads.
Footpaths.
Points of interest.
International boundaries.

-N-

0	25	50 miles
0	25	50	75	100 Km.

2000 and over
1000 - 2000
200 - 1000
0 - 200
metres

Riding: the UCPA (l'Union Nationale des Centres Sportifs de Plein Air) offers equestrian holidays at Sommet-en-Morvan; further information from UCPA, 62 rue de la Glacière, Paris. For shorter treks consult *Tourisme Equestre en France*, a free booklet available from Fédération Française d'Equitation at 15 rue de Bruxelles, Paris, T:42 81 42 82.

102

Boating: There are 6 canals and 3 navigable rivers in the area. Information is available from Bourgogne Voies Navigables, quai de la République, Auxerre, T:86 52 26 27. Canoë Découverte (Levée-des-Tuileries, La Chaussée-St-Victor, T:54 78 67 48) arranges canoeing trips on the Loire.
Fishing: for a map, *Pêche en France*, and information on

restrictions and licences contact Le Conseil Supérieur de la Pêche, 135 av Malakoff, Paris, T:45 01 20 20.

FURTHER INFORMATION
Tourist information: local tourist offices are listed under individual exploration zones.

The sun sets over the Etang de Combreux, one of many small lakes which make up the wetland wilderness of the Sologne.

Sologne

Marshlands, directly south of Orléans, covering 500,000ha (1.2 million acres); rich in water-loving flora and fauna

The European pond terrapin, a shy inhabitant of freshwater lakes and marshes, has declined due to pollution and discarded fishing tackle.

The smell of wood fires and the sound of gunfire characterize the Sologne. Vast areas of this flat, marshy woodland are sparsely populated, hugged by the arms of the Loire where the river turns west for the Atlantic. When you do stumble across some habitation, you are likely to smell the wood smoke before you see the house and its smoking chimney.

The Sologne is where the water meets the woods and they intermingle so thoroughly they almost cease to have any boundary. The lakes give way to trees, which in turn conceal still more ponds.

The Sologne is wilderness regained. First the Romans drained the swamps and developed agriculture; the region became the breadbasket of Roman Gaul. After the fall of the empire the drainage system became neglected, and agriculture became run down. The monks made an attempt to re-cultivate the area in the Middle Ages, but this attempt fell apart during the religious wars that convulsed France in the 16th and 17th centuries. By the 17th century the Sologne was almost deserted.

In the last century, under Emperor Napoléon III, a fresh attempt was made to control the area, with the plantings of Scotch pines and the digging of canals and drainage ditches. However, today only the western part of the Sologne is largely agricultural.

Hunting is common throughout the Sologne. Don't stray from the paths: signs warning of private property and hunting grounds spell danger not just for sundry wildlife—ramblers, too, are at risk. And here lies the irony. For although the hunters have exterminated whole species and threaten the continuation of others, it is hunting, mostly for rabbits, pheasants and waterfowl, that has preserved the Sologne

and created a refuge for wildlife.

The trees here are largely deciduous— silver birches growing out of a carpet of moss. Oaks, too, are common, though many Scotch pines were planted in the 19th century, and continue to be planted; for apart from hunting (and tourism) forestry is the main industry in the area.

There are about 2,000 lakes in all. In smaller quantities the dampness of the soil shows through on the forest floor, carpeted by a mixture of moss and ferns. Lakes cover 12,000 hectares (30,000 acres) of the Sologne. The region's eastern side tends to be drier than the west, where most of the area's lakes are found. The soil is a mixture of clay and sand and, together with the wet warmish climate at the border between Atlantic and continental influences, creates the conditions needed for the area's rich flora. The most rewarding places for botanists are the valleys and the lakes in the west, with their white waterlilies, orchids and rare ferns, including the tall royal fern. One particularly interesting plant found here is the rare bird's-nest orchid, the plant realm's equivalent of a scavenger. It has no chlorophyll (the pigment that makes leaves green) but instead feeds "saprophytically" on fungi in the soil.

The attraction of the Sologne for its teeming wildlife is the mosaic of habitats jumbled together in an intricate network of weed-covered ponds with reedy fringes;

these harbour rare aquatic flora and provide food for a wide variety of aquatic invertebrates, especially dragonflies—the hawks of the insect world. Bitterns and little bitterns lurk unseen in the reeds, perfectly camouflaged against the streaky background. The only signs of birdlife may be the constant scratchy chattering of reed and sedge warblers, and the occasional flypast of the majestic marsh harrier. The thousands of wintering ducks are best seen on the *étangs* of Grande Corbois, Courcelles, Bièvre and Marcilly; the latter is one of the principal sites for the huge breeding colonies of black-headed gulls, a feature of the Sologne.

The drier habitats add more variety to this impressive area and in the dense oak and hornbeam woods are many deer, most visible during the autumn rutting period.

Many clearings retain a heathland character, with heather, broom and gorse; this is the characteristic home for Dartford warblers, as well as a rich variety of uncommon plants typical of sandy, poor soils.

On the western border of the Sologne is the Forêt de Chambord. This 5,400-hectare (13,000-acre) forest, a former royal hunting preserve, once again became the property of the state in 1932. It's populated by a wide variety of animals, including deer and a thousand head of wild boar, while the most common of the smaller predatory mammals is the polecat, though its numbers have declined considerably due to trapping. About 1,500 hectares (3,700 acres) of the forest are open to the public, and there are a number of hides and vantage points where visitors can observe animals in their natural environment.

BEFORE YOU GO
Maps: IGN 1:100,000 Nos. 26 and 27, also 1:100,000 map of the Sologne. IGN 1:25,000, 2120–3, 2220–3, 2320–2323 and 2421–3.

GETTING THERE
By car: an *autoroute* is being extended straight through the Sologne, running due south of Orléans; the closest existing road is N20. To penetrate the Sologne take D923 (towards Blois) or quiet D15, just off N20 south of Orléans.
By rail: the line follows the roads south of Orléans, with about 7 local trains a day. From Salbris a branch line meanders around to Romorantin-Lanthenay (4 local trains daily). Bicycles are available at the following stations: Romorantin-Lanthenay, Salbris, Nouan-le-Fuzelier, La Ferté-St-Aubin, Lamotte-Beuvron, Gien, Orléans and Blois.
By bus: main routes from Blois operate to Chambord and Lamotte-Beuvron; to Nouan-le-Fuzelier and Salbris; and to Romorantin-Lanthenay

and Villefranche-sur-Cher.

WHERE TO STAY
Romorantin-Lanthenay and La Ferté-St-Aubin are the main centres in the Sologne. Romorantin-Lanthenay is on the expensive side, but the 2-star Le Colombier (10 pl du

Vieux-Marché, T:54 76 12 76) is a comfortable base.
Aubigny-sur-Nère, Bourges, Blois and Orléans are other convenient locations.
Outdoor living: there are about 30 campsites in the area; tourist offices have a list.

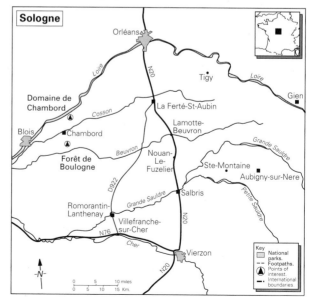

105

Extensive waterlily pads and dense reed beds illustrate the typical wetland vegetation found in the lakes of the Sologne.

ACTIVITIES
Walking: 2 long-distance paths run through the Sologne, GR41 (Chambord to Vierzon) and GR3 (Chambord to Gien); GR31 skirts the southern edge. There are also many smaller walks, all marked on the IGN 1:100,000 map of the Sologne.
Cycling: this is easy cycling country, as roads are flat and have little traffic.
Fishing: the lakes, river and canal provide an immense variety of angling. Tourists can buy day licences at the 60 towns or so in the area.
Riding: contact the Comité Départemental de Tourisme Equestre du Loir-et-Cher, 32 rue Alain-Gerbault, Blois, T:54 79 93 08.

FURTHER INFORMATION
Tourist information: Bourges, 14 pl Etienne-Dolet, T:48 24 75 33; Blois, 3 av du Dr Jean-Laigret, T:54 74 06 49; Orléans, pl Albert-1er, T:38 53 05 95; Romorantin-Lanthenay, pl de la Paix, T:54 76 43 89; Sully-sur-Loire, pl du Général-de-Gaulle, T:38 35 32 21; Vierzon, pl Gabriel-Péri, T:48 75 20 03.
Fondation Sologne, Le Ciran, Ménestreau-en-Villette, La Ferté-St-Aubin, T:38 76 90 93.
106

Forêt d'Orléans

Fabled forest, France's fifth largest, on the upper reaches of the Loire, 120km (70 miles) south of Paris

François Rabelais tells how the great forest above Orléans used to be 105 miles long and 51 miles wide "or thereabouts". His book *Gargantua* is an epic debunking of all that is scholarly and serious, but we can assume this estimate was about right.

Gargantua, "after drinking, as you will understand", was journeying to Paris through the forest on his giant mare. In order to ward off hornets the mare swished her tail vigorously, demolishing the trees as a scythe cuts grass. The Forêt d'Orléans, to follow this line of fiction, is the wood the mare's tail missed. It is the largest of a string of forests lining the banks of the Loire, and covers 35,000ha (86,000 acres) along the right bank of the Loire from Orléans to Gien.

The forest is mainly a mixture of oak and beech, with hornbeam and silver birch as well as more recently planted conifers, such as Scotch pine. Deer and wild boar still roam the forest. However, hunting and the number of roads that cross the forest cause considerable disturbance to the wildlife. The well-trodden paths are testimony that the forest attracts many visitors.

The lake of La Vallée, near Vitry-aux-Loges, is one of the more interesting sites, and a refuge has been created nearby for naturalists and ramblers who want to spend more time in the forest.
Before you go *Maps:* IGN 1:100,000 Nos. 20 and 27; IGN 1:25,000 2219, 2319 and 2320.
Getting there *By car:* Orléans is on A10; N60 runs up the right bank of the Loire as far as Châteauneuf-sur-Loire, D953 continues to Gien.
By rail: Orléans is at the forest's western end, Gien the southeastern.
By bus: there are buses from Orléans through the forest to Pithiviers; and from Orléans to Vitry-aux-Loges in the middle of the forest.
Where to stay: Orléans is boring and industrial; Châteauneuf, Gien and Pithiviers are better bets.
Outdoor living: tourist offices have a list of local campsites.
Activities *Walking:* GR3 from Orléans heads straight into the forest.
Riding: information from Association Départementale de Tourisme Equestre du Loiret, Ecurie de l'Orme, 314 rue des 3-Croix, Trainou, Loury, T:38 52 71 11.

Cycling: bicyles are available at railway stations of Gien and Orléans.

Arboretum: there is a 12-ha (30-acre) wood at Grande Bruyères, near the village of Ingrannes, just off D921.

Further information *Tourist information:* Châteauneuf-sur-Loire, 1 pl Aristide-Briand, T:38 58 44 79; Gien, rue Anne-de-Beaujeu, T:38 67 25 28; Orléans, pl Albert-1-er, T:38 53 05 95; Pithiviers, Mail-Ouest, Gare Routière, T:38 30 50 02.

Pink fox-gloves burst among the ferns of the Morvan hills.

Parc Naturel Régional du Morvan

Regional nature park of 173,000ha (427,000 acres) in the Burgundy hills, 270km (168 miles) southeast of Paris; varied terrain of hills, meadows, lakes and pine and mixed deciduous forest

The quickest way to the Morvan hills, at least from Paris, is to drive down the Autoroute du Soleil. But speed is not of the essence in appreciating these hills, so on my most recent visit I took the dawn train from Autun, up the eastern side of the park. The train is slow and the line winds its way up the best part of 300 metres (1,000 feet) above the valley on to the granite plateau of the Morvan. As the train approached the little station of Brazey-en-Morvan I saw my first kestrel some 50 metres or so away, sitting on top of a fruit tree.

Later that day, having cycled well inside the park, I stopped to pump up my tyre, which had developed a slow puncture. I looked up to see a buzzard with an enormous wingspan, flapping. The bird soared, taking advantage of some indiscernible thermal, and plummeted. Mercifully, the bird obscured my vision of the gory details.

It rose, flapped its wings a few times and settled a few feet away. It then noticed me and took off, prey in beak.

Hawks, buzzards and falcons all find sanctuary in the Morvan hills. These rural hills continue to resist the relentless advance of civilization, and are slow to

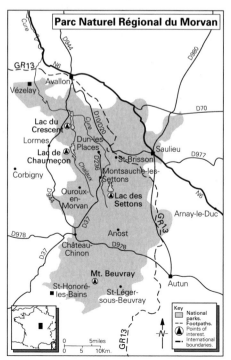

Parc Naturel Régional du Morvan

The pale and delicate silver birch makes a pleasing contrast when found among more sombre conifers.

villages and moorland farms. The age of these footpaths can been seen in their shape. The tramp of time has created U-shaped hollows with banks on either side.

There is groundwater throughout the Morvan. The lakes—some natural, some man-made—are a joy. Some, though, such as the Lac des Settons, now attract too many tourists. Anywhere with pedal-boats can scarcely be wild. One escape route is to do as I did and rent a bicycle; another is to take the long-distance footpath that does a tour of the lakes. But according to locals the best way to immerse yourself in the wild woods—and actually stand a chance of seeing some of the many wild animals inhabiting its depths—is to explore on horseback. In this way you may see red and roe deer, wild boar and badgers, and possibly catch sight in the half-light of dawn or dusk of the secretive genet, wildcat or beech marten.

Aside from the lakes there are also smaller meres worth seeking out, or you may chance upon a brook running across, or even along, a footpath. The area is also littered with dew ponds, small pools, natural or man-made, which provide drinking water for cattle and wild animals.

Spring is always slightly later in the Morvan than in the surrounding region. Enough snow falls for ski resorts to operate. The peaks, however, are no more than 900 metres (3,000 feet) high, and the snow disappears early in the year.

The hills around the charming town of Vézelay, in the north of the park, contain some of the most beautiful countryside in Burgundy. There are no dark overtones of the black mountains here; the wooded countryside clothed in its summer green gently rolls away into the distance. The broadleaf combination of beech and oak warms the woods and strikes a contrast with the gaunt hills of dark pines farther south.

In the southern end of the park the hill of Le Beuvray was the site of an old Gaulish fortress. Today the fort, originally called Bibracte, is buried beneath beech trees. A paved road enables motorists to drive to the top, but the walk produces a better appreciation of the view from this strategic site overlooking the valley of the Loire.

change. This is reflected in the wildlife, the countryside with its dry stone walls, and even in the place names. Very little is known about the language of the Gauls, the tongue spoken in France before the Romans invaded. A few words survive in place names. Morvan is one such; in Celtic it means "black mountain".

From afar the hills do indeed seem dark, even on sunny days. The rock underlying the mountains is granite, and the planting of conifers on many of the summits underscores the darkness of the distant summits. Forestry is one of the most important industries within the boundaries of the regional park, and unfortunately for the wildlife exotic conifers take precedence over the native deciduous forest.

The footpaths that cross the Morvan were once the main thoroughfares linking up

BEFORE YOU GO
Maps: IGN 1:100,000 Nos. 28, 36 and 306; also 1:25,000 2722–4 and 2822–4.

GETTING THERE
By car: the Autoroute du Soleil passes 20km (12 miles) to the east of the park. N6 goes to Avallon and Saulieu. From Auxerre N151 heads south to Clamecy, and D985 continues to Corbigny. D978 links Nevers to Autun by way of Château-Chinon.
For a tour of the park leave Avallon on D10 then take D211, D236 and D193 or D37.
By rail: on Fri and Sat there are 2 express trains from Paris to Avallon, Saulieu and Autun; Sun–Thurs you must change at Laroche Migennes and catch a local train (4 or 5 a day). Journey time from Laroche to Avallon is 1½hr. The line from Nevers to Autun skirts the south of the park, with 7 trains a day.
By bus: there is a daily service from Nevers to Château-Chinon, and from Autun to Château-Chinon; buses link Tamnay-Château to Nevers, Château-Chinon, Cercy-la-Tour, St-Honoré-les-Bains and Rémilly.

WHERE TO STAY
The following towns are good bases for the Morvan: Arnay-le-Duc, Autun, Avallon, Château-Chinon, Dun-les-Places, Lormes, Montsauche-les-Settons, St-Honoré-les-Bains and Vézelay.
The park leaflet *Tour du Morvan par les Grands Lacs* details *gîtes* along the route.

ACTIVITIES
Walking: the GR13 footpath from Ile de France to Burgundy passes through the park for more than 100km (60 miles). There is also a 220-km (130-mile) circular tour of the park and its lakes. The park

offices also have details of shorter strolls.
Riding: the following centres offer tours on horseback for beginners or experienced riders—Centre Equestre des Settons, Montsauche-les-Settons, T:86 84 50 11; Centre Equestre Ourouxois, Hôtel de la Poste, Ouroux-en-Morvan, T:86 78 21 86; Association Morvandelle du Croux, St-Léger-sous-Beuvray, T:85 82 56 07.
Climbing: there is good rock climbing at Anost and Dun-les-Places. Details from the Association Pleine Nature en Morvan, Montsauche-les-Settons, T:86 76 10 11.
Cycling: bicycles can be rented at the stations of Saulieu, Autun and Avallon.
Canoeing: on either the rivers Cure or Chalaux; details from the park office or the Comité Départemental du Tourisme, Hôtel du Département, Nevers, T:86 57 80 25. There are lessons for beginners on the Lac de Chamboux; contact Centre Social de Saulieu, T:80 64 20 43.
Skiing: there is downhill skiing in the south of the Morvan, around Arleuf, Glux-en-Glenne, St-Prix and Le Haut-Folin. There are 8 cross-country circuits around Haut-Folin.
Museum: an interesting geological museum is at St-Léger-sous-Beuvray, T:85 82 51 01.

FURTHER INFORMATION
Tourist information: Autun, 3 av Charles-de-Gaulle, T:85 52 20 34; Auxerre, quai République, T:86 52 06 19; Avallon, 24 pl Vauban, T:86 34 14 19; Nevers, 31 rue du Rempart, T:86 59 07 03; St-Honoré-les-Bains, pl Firmin-Bazot, T:86 30 71 70; Saulieu, rue d'Argentine, T:80 64 00 21; Vézelay, rue St-Pierre, T:86 33 23 69.

Forêt de Tronçais

Part of a chain of woodlands stretching across the geographical centre of France; located midway between Bourges and Montluçon

Through the mists of the forest, Le Grand Meaulnes discovers a magical château, full of music and dancing. When the hero of Alain-Fournier's novel next comes back to the château it is closed and shuttered. The book was made into a film— called *The Wanderer* or *The Lost Domain*, depending on whether you saw it in Britain or America. The novel is firmly based in the country to the south of Bourges. Meaulne is the name of a village barely 5km (3 miles) from the forest, while Fournier himself lived as a child in Epineuil, a couple of kilometres farther up the River Cher. You stand little chance of finding such a castle in the middle of this forest, but the wood is quiet enough to recreate the atmosphere of the film, which was shot in the region.
Even on the ditchwater dull day I visited the Forêt de Tronçais, it still had its quota of magic. The clouds glowered and threatened rain, soon making good the threat. It was a disheartening way to start the day. Then three black kites suddenly flew past, doubtless surprised to be disturbed on such a day. The quixotic April weather turned sunny and then back to rain again but not before it disclosed the new brown oak leaves.
The Forêt de Tronçais is

109

just one of a series of woods that stretch in a belt from east to west. The Forêt de Lancosme, on the edge of the Brenne lakes, is the western edge of this chain, which extends right to the Loire at Nevers. From the Forêt de Châteauroux, south of Châteauroux itself, through the Bois de Meillant (north of St-Amand-Montrond) is a limestone plateau known as the Champagne Berrichonne, where the woodland is sliced by rivers, roads and agriculture. This is the geographic centre of France, a distinction claimed by several communes in the area.

With its dense stands of oak and beech, the Forêt de Tronçais is particularly noteworthy as the westernmost outpost of the black woodpecker. Raptors, too, are a great speciality: in addition to typical arboreal species like goshawk and honey buzzard, the attentive observer can hope to find short-toed and booted eagles, both on the edge of their ranges here.

More than 5ha (12 acres) of this forest are a local biological reserve, set up to protect the oaks planted more than 300 years ago under the reign of the Sun King, Louis XIV.

110

Red deer browse undisturbed deep in the mixed deciduous forests.

Before you go *Maps:* IGN 1:100,000 Nos. 27 and 35; IGN 1:25,000 No. 2426.
Getting there *By car:* take N144 south from Bourges. Some 15km (9 miles) after passing through St-Amand-Montrond D978 takes you into the forest.
By rail: St-Amand-Montrond has 4 daily trains from Paris (Gare Austerlitz). Alternatively, get off at Ainay-le-Vieil or Urçay and walk into the forest.
By bus: there is 1 bus a day (except Sun) from St-Amand-Montrond to St-Bonnet-Tronçais, and another to St-Bonnet from the railway station at Moulins-sur-Allier.
Where to stay: Urçay has 2 pleasant hotels; the Etoile d'Or (T:70 06 92 66) is recommended. There are plenty of hotels in St-Amand and Montluçon.
Lakeside *gîtes* are open year-round at St-Bonnet; for lists and reservations contact the Office Bourbonnais du Tourisme et du Thermalisme, 35 rue de Bellecroix, Yzeure, T:70 44 41 57.
Outdoor living: summer only at St-Bonnet, Pirot, Ainay-le-Château, Cérilly, Hérisson,

Meaulne, Urçay and Vallon-en-Sully.
Activities *Cycling:* rent bicycles at St-Bonnet.
Riding: summer only at St-Bonnet.
Fishing: possible on the lakes and the rivers Aumance and Cher. Details from the Association du Pays Tronçais, Cérilly, T:70 67 55 89.
Ruins: Ainay-le-Vieil has a particularly fine medieval castle. Northwest, near Drevant, are ruins of Roman baths, a temple and an amphitheatre.
Further information *Tourist information:* Bourges, 21 rue Victor-Hugo, T:48 24 75 33; Montluçon, 1 av Marx-Dormoy, T:70 05 15 52; St-Amand-Montrond, pl République, T:48 96 16 86.
Le Centre Permanent d'Initiation à l'Environnement, Tronçais, T:70 06 14 69.

Forêt de Fontainebleau

Extensive forest (20,000ha/50,000 acres) surrounding Napoleon's favourite hunting lodge; located 65km (40 miles) southeast of Paris

One of Paul Cézanne's better-known landscapes is *Les Rochers de Fontainebleau* (*The Rocks at Fontainebleau*) which now hangs in New York's Metropolitan Museum of Art. Cézanne's painting dates from the early 1890s, but the rocks still hold

Sunlight struggles to penetrate the dense deciduous forest, home to deer and wild boar.

something of the same mystery as the painting: paths lead between them, with sudden turns revealing unanticipated glades. Nowadays, though, the element of surprise is likely to include stumbling over an apprentice rock climber.

The Forêt de Fontainebleau covers 170 sq km (65 sq miles), making it the sixth-largest forest in France. Like many hunting forests, Fontainebleau has been thinned out considerably, to load the dice in favour of the hunter rather than the hunted. More than four out of ten trees are oaks, and the southern end holds some magnificent oak copses. The other important deciduous tree is beech.

Thanks to its sandy sub-soil the forest is fairly dry, so you can leave your rubber boots behind. The other side of the coin is that the undergrowth tends to scrub: brambles and ferns abound. Since the 1830s Scotch pines have been planted on the more arid soils, to such an extent that these trees are now as common as oaks. Larger clearings have developed a heath-like vegetation, which helps to provide variety and balance to the ecology of the area.

It was during the mid-19th-century reigns of Louis-Philippe and Napoléon III

that the forest first became popular. Hunting, that sport of kings, is still widespread, which is one of the forest's more disappointing aspects. Even in spring, in many areas barely a bird breaks the silence. But this belies the actual wealth of birdlife and other animals which manage to live here. The forest hosts a full range of the typical forest birds of northern France, including five species of woodpecker, redstart and most notably pied flycatcher. Nesting raptors include honey buzzard and hobby.

The paths are well trodden, though the authorities have created zones of silence to minimize the effects of tourism.

Before you go *Maps:* IGN 1:100,000 No. 21, 1:25,000 No. 401.

Getting there *By car:* take either A10 (turning off on to N7) or N7 all the way. Parking is restricted on forest roads.

By rail: frequent local trains run from Paris's Gare de Lyon to Fontainebleau-Avon; journey time about 1hr. You can rent bicycles here, too.

By bus: town buses (*les cars verts*) run from outside the railway station. The walk to the town centre takes 20mins.

Where to stay: Fontainebleau and Avon are the twin local towns, and as good a starting point as any for touring the

forest. Barbizon, on the forest's western edge, is close to the zones of silence.

Outdoor living: there is camping on the edge of the forest, near Samois-sur-Seine, T:64 24 63 45.

Activities *Walking:* there are over 300km (180 miles) of forest paths, reserved for pedestrians, cyclists or riders.

Climbing: more than 130 climbs are listed by the tourist office in Fontainebleau.

Riding: equestrian weekends are organized by Le Club Hippique des Joncs Marins, 36 chemin du Bois-Badeau, Brétigny-sur-Orge, T:60 84 05 40; also Association de Tourisme Equestre Esterhazy, Ferme les Coudray, Etiolles, Soisy-sur-Seine, T:69 89 01 81.

Viewpoints: Croix-du-Calvaire has a good view over the forest; there are also several picturesque gorges and a ruined hermitage which in the C18th was a refuge for bandits.

Further information *Tourist information:* Fontainebleau, 31 pl Napoléon-Bonaparte, T:64 22 25 68.

Office National des Forêts, 217 bis rue Grande, Fontainebleau, T:64 22 20 45.

Parc Naturel Régional de la Haute-Vallée de Chevreuse

Wooded valley at the southern edge of the Parisian commuter belt; regional nature park of 25,600ha (63,300 acres)

On the train running through the Legoland of suburbs that

WILD BOAR—*SANGLIER*

The wild boar, which is the ancestor of the domestic pig, is not a rare creature, for it ranges over much of the country, inhabiting the vast forest areas and, in the south, the *maquis*, and may attain quite high population densities. But, widely hunted, it is a furtive and timid creature and, being nocturnal, it is a very rare sight. One's closest contact is more likely to be from signs on the ground. Wild boar are particularly fond of digging for bulbs and tubers, leaving large irregularly churned patches in the ground of woodland clearings.

has developed to the south of Paris over the last 30 years, it was hard to believe that anything remotely wild might lie at the end of the line. True, Jean Racine, who lived in the area, could write of the giant oaks and lindens with their ornate arms; but that was 1656, nearly 150 years prior to the French Revolution. I had left Paris armed with my 1930 guidebook that still wrote of the "beautiful Chevreuse valley", but 1930 fell a good half-century before the age of the *autoroute*. Could the valley have survived the southern sprawl?

As the train neared the end of the line the answer became clear. Trees began to intervene between the houses, then whole woods appeared on the hilltops. In the park proper the hills and valley sides are largely wooded; some are accessible, some reserved for hunting. In the valleys is a mixture of housing and agriculture.

Deciduous woods of beech and oak, as well as chestnut, hazel and silver birch, line the Chevreuse valley. These woods, mostly hunting domain, are heavily coppiced and surprisingly deserted given their proximity to Paris—provided you are prepared to hike out of the valley bottom away from the main roads.

Out of the river valley the landscape is gentle and agricultural, mostly small rolling hills and arable crops in the fields. There are banks of woodland, mostly deciduous but also some plantations of Scotch pine.

The park of the Haute Vallée de Chevreuse is one of the country's latest generation of regional nature parks, created in 1984. By designating this area a park

The wild boar, though rarely seen, leaves heavy footprints and large areas of disturbed ground.

the regional council of the Ile de France hopes to stave off the pressure of urbanization, and maintain Paris's green lung. The council talks of achieving this aim by creating a sustainable mixed economy of agriculture and, of course, tourism.

Before you go *Maps:* IGN 1:100,000 No. 20; IGN 1:25,000 Nos. 402 or 2215.
Getting there *By car:* N10 runs from Paris to Rambouillet; take the exit after Trappes. Another way is the A10 *autoroute*, taking the exit first for Dourdan and then for Saclay.
By train: local trains link Paris's Gare Montparnasse to Rambouillet. A better option, which lands you in the middle of the park, is to take the RER line B to the terminus of St-Rémy-ès-Chevreuse, or RER line C to St-Quentin-en-Yvelines.
By bus: local buses run (infrequently) from Versailles (Rive Gauche) to St-Rémy and from St-Rémy to Chevreuse, Cernay-la-Ville and Rambouillet.
Where to stay: apart from Paris and Versailles the best places to stay are in the park itself; Dampierre and Chevreuse are pleasant towns,

with a choice of hotels. Rambouillet, just outside the park boundary, is another option.
Outdoor living: lists of campsites are available from local tourist offices.
Activities *Walking:* 2 long-distance footpaths traverse the park—GR1 and GR11. There are a number of shorter trails, including the 15-km (9-mile) chemin Jean-Racine, from the RER station at St-Rémy to Port-Royal and back. Details from the park office.
Cycling: rent bicycles at the RER station at Rambouillet.
Riding: horseback tours of the Chevreuse are organized by Association Sportive d'Equitation des Molières, 13 rue de Cernay, Les Molières, T:60 12 08 49.
Further information *Tourist information:* Rambouillet, Hôtel de Ville, T:34 83 21 21; St-Rémy-ès-Chevreuse, opposite RER station, T:30 52 22 49 (open Wed and weekend only).
The park offices at Dampierre, 13 Grande Rue, T:30 52 54 65, are very helpful.

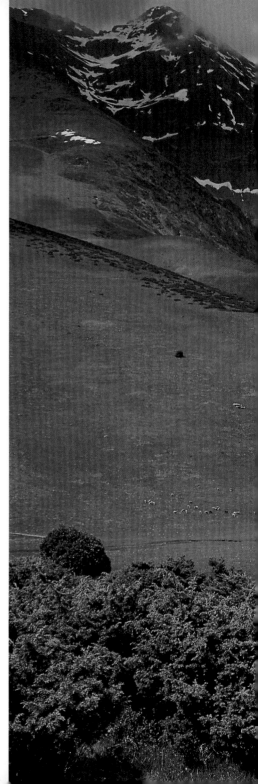

CHAPTER 6

The Pyrenees

The mountain range of the Pyrenees defies comparison, although it has often been described as a lesser cousin of the mighty Alps. Those who have been to the Pyrenees often prefer them because they are less developed, wilder and no less challenging than the Alpine peaks.

The Pyrenees run 400 kilometres (250 miles) northwest to southeast across the neck of land that bars France from Spain between the Atlantic and the Mediterranean. The range is actually divided in two by the cleft of the Val d'Aran, through which the infant River Garonne, called here the Garona, flows out of Spain on its long journey to the Bay of Biscay. The mountains have marked the French–Spanish frontier since the Treaty of the Pyrenees of 1659, but the separation is by no means absolute. The frontier doesn't always follow the crest of the mountains, and there are enclaves on the French side of the divide, most noticeably on the Cerdagne plateau. Quite apart from the co-principality of Andorra, where sovereignty is shared between France and Spain, there are strong cultural links at both ends of the range, where Basques and Catalans live on either side of the frontier.

The Pyrenees are not great mountains. There are only three peaks over the 3,000-metre (9,900-foot) mark, and the highest of these lies in Spain. Where the Pyrenees score is in the great variety and wildness of the terrain, which changes constantly from the green western country of the Basques as it moves east to reach the sun-scorched mountains above the

Sheep graze on the lush upland pastures of the Pyrenees near Arreau.

wine plains of Roussillon, with great valleys, high *cols* and snowfields coming up all along the way.

Oak forests dominate the foothills, with the common and white oak in the more maritime western areas and cork oaks and evergreen oaks in the drier Mediterranean east. At the 800-metre (2,600-foot) level, the true mountain forest begins, with beech and, eventually, fir dominating the higher ground. Seemingly silent at first, these forested areas are full of the high-pitched notes of the coal tits, crested tits, goldcrests, treecreepers and chaffinches. Then there is the urgent tapping of the real forest specialities—the black, white-backed and middle-spotted woodpeckers. Above 1,500 metres (5,000 feet), the forest gives way to an open zone of scattered pines and juniper shrubs, then to Alpine meadows beneath the bare rock faces and snow. These upper reaches provide a habitat for water pipits, Alpine accentors, rock thrushes, and in some places even the snow finch. Raptors such as golden eagles, lammergeiers and griffon vultures soar above the peaks on strong thermals.

For the sake of simplicity, it's best to divide the French Pyrenees into three main regions—the Pays Basque, the Hautes-Pyrénées and Roussillon. But within these three main areas fall Béarn, Bigorre, Foix, Andorra, Ariège, the Cerdagne and perhaps a score of smaller places. The western frontier of these mountains begins in the hill country of the Basques, which start on the Atlantic coast, south of Les Landes, and reaches up towards the mountains through the valley of the Bidassoa. The hills hereabouts are of no great height, although the great peak of La Rhune seems higher than its 900 metres (2,953 feet). There are green hills all the way east from here,

and two impressive valleys, through one of which (above St-Jean-Pied-de-Port) the pilgrim road to Compostela reaches into Spain through the famous pass of Roncesvalles where Roland fell fighting with Charlemagne's army against the Basques.

The pattern of rising mountains cut by valleys and passes is emphasized farther southeast in Béarn, the modern Hautes-Pyrénées. The wildlife, flora and fauna of the region is protected and preserved south of the spa at Cauterets by the Parc National des Pyrénées Occidentales, which abuts the Spanish Parque de Ordesa at its eastern end. The tallest peak hereabouts on the French side of the frontier is Pic du Midi d'Ossau at 2,884 metres (9,462 feet) and there are others almost as striking. The other notable feature of these central Pyrenees is the number of mountain lakes, which spatter the range with flecks of deep blue and feed the mountain streams; all the streams are full of trout, and some shelter the rare desman, a kind of aquatic mole similar to the platypus, but with a long tail and webbed hind feet.

Moving east, past the Réserve Naturelle de Néouvielle, one of several officially designated reserves in the region, the mountains stop briefly at the Val d'Aran before the pattern of mountain and valley begins again in Ariège, north of Andorra. East of here Roussillon begins on a spectacular note, with Pic Carlit rising 2,921 metres (9,587 feet) above the great plateau of the Cerdagne, which, at 1,600 metres (one mile) above the plain, is fresh and green even in the hottest months of summer. Still farther east Mont Canigou soars up to 2,784 metres (9,137 feet) before the Pyrenees fall away at last down the dwindling peaks of the Albères into the Mediterranean.

GETTING THERE

By air: the main airports are Toulouse (Blagnac) and Perpignan, serving the west-central Pyrenees and Roussillon respectively.

By sea: the port of Santander, on the Cantabrian coast of Spain, is the nearest maritime access-port to the French Pyrenees, via Hendaye or the pass of Roncesvalles. By either route it's a full day's drive from the port.

By car: the French Pyrenees are well served by the *autoroute* network either via the Rhône valley (Montpellier–Perpignan) or on the western side via Bordeaux–Toulouse or Bordeaux–Bayonne. The central Pyrenees are reached via Pau.

By rail: the fast trains, like the *autoroutes*, link up the main cities, usually via Paris, but an increasing number of services start at the Channel coast and terminate in Narbonne. From main-line stations at Bayonne, Pau, Toulouse, Foix, Narbonne and Perpignan, local trains probe many of the valleys, supplemented by mountain railways.

By bus: local buses tend to operate mainly as a supplement to rail travel.

WHEN TO GO

The climate varies considerably, being generally milder in the west and drier east of the Val d'Aran. Snow lies on the Pyrenees from Dec–early Apr and may be expected anywhere above 1,800m (5,900ft). The growth of tourism means that most of the mountain passes are kept open throughout the winter.

WHERE TO STAY

Recommended bases are listed in the individual exploration areas. Detailed lists for hotels and campsites can be obtained from tourist offices in all main towns and most villages. Backpackers and campers should know that wild camping is permitted anywhere over 1,500m (4,900ft) or more than 1hr walk from a campsite.

The fragile desman inhabits fast-flowing mountain streams.

ACTIVITIES

Walking/climbing: easier routes lie at either end of the range; harder, steeper and more exposed routes fall in the centre.

The main organizations for walkers and climbers are the Randonnées Pyrénéennes, 4 rue de Villefranche, St-Girons, T:61 66 02 19; and CIMES Pyrénées (Centre d'Information Montagne et Sentiers), 3 square Balague, St-Girons, T:61 66 40 10.

Cycling: this is superb cycling country. One mountain route, D118/D918 — the Raid Pyrénéen — stretches over 18 cols between the Atlantic and the Mediterranean and involves many thousands of feet of ascent and descent. Less strenuous routes are available.

Fishing: there is good trout fishing throughout the range and salmon fishing around Navarrenx in the Pays Basque.

Skiing: the ski season runs Dec–Apr. Resorts are smaller than those of the Alps, but offer good scope for off-piste skiing and ski mountaineering. Main resorts are Gourette, Barèges, La Mongie, Cauterets, St-Lary, Andorra at Pas-de-la-Casa and Soldeu, and on the Cerdagne plateau at Font-Romeu.

FURTHER INFORMATION

Tourist information: for regional information, contact Maison des Pyrénées, 24 rue du 4-Septembre, Paris, T:12 46 39 26; Comité Régional du Tourisme, 3 rue de l'Esquile, Toulouse, T:61 23 22 05; or Agence de Tourisme du Pays Basque, 1 rue Donzac, Bayonne, T:59 59 28 77.

FURTHER READING

R. Hunter, *Walking in France* (Oxford Illustrated Press); Neil Lands, *The French Pyrenees* (Spurbooks); John Sturrock, *The French Pyrenees* (Penguin); Arthur Battagel *Pyrenees East* and *Pyrenees West* (West Col); Kev Reynolds, *Walks and Climbs in the Pyrenees* (Cicerone Press); A. W. Taylor, *Wild Flowers of the Pyrenees* (London).

Pays Basque

The modern département *of Pyrénées-Atlantiques, redolent with Basque and Navarre associations, covers the area from the Atlantic to the first Pyrenees peaks*

This was the first part of the Pyrenees I ever visited, and the impact of that visit has never left me. It is a striking countryside, the hills a rich billiard-table green, seamed with deep valleys from which the mist rises thickly early in the morning, shredding up into the trees in the sunlight. In the valleys nestle villages of white-washed houses topped with slate roofs.

Walking is what attracted me to this area, although there are interesting caves and underground river systems, plus plenty of opportunities for birdwatching, plant-spotting and fishing. The hills around the peak of La Rhune make for excellent walking, full of open ridges, stunning views and

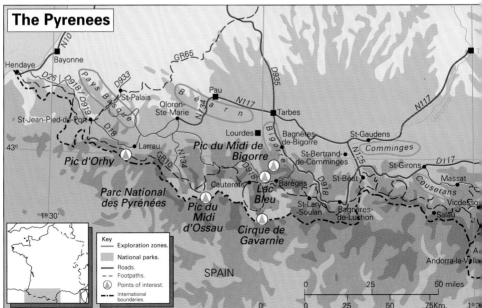

The Pyrenees

Key
— Exploration zones.
National parks.
— Roads.
- - Footpaths.
Ⓐ Points of interest.
- ▪ - International boundaries.

Brown bear and lynx still find refuge in the remoter forests and peaks of the Basque Pyrenees.

breezy paths through the meadows and copses. There is also some hilltrekking available on small, piebald local ponies known as *pottocks*. A ride into the hills on one of these shaggy mountain ponies is a real experience, but a little hard on the knees; after an hour you'll be more than ready to get off and walk.

The hills begin to rise as you move east, and you encounter a mixture of moorland and forest. The Forêt d'Iraty, at the heart of the Basque Pyrenees, is a vast terrain of beech and pines, a marvellous spot for birds, notably tits and woodpeckers. It is also said to be the last refuge of the Pyrenean brown bear. The forest also shelters the European lynx (*Lynx lynx*). The first major peak in the Pyrenees, the Pic d'Orhy (2,017 metres/6,620 feet), rises above the valley of the Gave de Larrau.

119

Around the peak, soaring on the summer thermals, you may see the griffon vulture, recognizable by its black wings and white neck. The largest bird in the Pyrenees is the bearded vulture, or lammergeier, a magnificent bird with a wingspan of up to $2\frac{1}{2}$ metres (eight feet), making it the largest of all the European raptors.

The Plateau d'Iraty is sheep pasture, good for walking, covered with sheep browsing on the bracken. North of Iraty lie two fine beech forests, at Ahusquy and Arbailles, the latter draping a limestone plateau seamed with sheer valleys, while just northeast of the Pic d'Orhy lie the forked valleys of the Haute-Soule, one of which, the Gave de Ste-Engrâce, leads to the Gorges de Kakouetta, the natural wonder of the Pays Basque. These gorges are a spectacular sight, narrowing to ten metres (33 feet) in width, dropping to 250 metres (800 feet) or more in places, and ending with a great waterfall. Air descending into the gorge cools and become clammy, thick with moisture, a complete change from the dry hot air in the hills outside. The change is so marked that a micro-climate exists, and in the humus created by the beech-leaves, orchids grow amid the rocky crevices.

BEFORE YOU GO
Maps: IGN 1:250,000 No. 113; IGN 1:100,000 No. 69; IGN (RP) 1:50,000 Nos. 1 and 2.

GETTING THERE
By car: take N10 south from Bordeaux, or D932/N124 south from the Lot via Bazas and Mont-de-Marsan.
By rail: the main line from Paris runs to Hendaye and across the Spanish frontier. Another line, south from Dax, terminates at St-Palais, and another via Sauveterre-de-Béarn stops at Mauléon.
By bus: there are bus services into the hills from Hendaye, Bayonne, Orthez and Pau.

WHERE TO STAY
Recommended hotels include the Hôtel de la Rhune in Ascain (T:59 54 00 04); Hôtel du Fronton in Itxassou (T:59 29 75 10); Hôtel Ramuntcho in St-Jean-Pied-de-Port (T:59 37 03 91).
Outdoor living: practically every town and village offers a good, if simple, campsite. Details from tourist offices.

ACTIVITIES
Walking: the 170km (103 miles) of GR10 from Hendaye to La Pierre-St-

...ld take a fit
· a harder walk
'onnée from
h. · shorter
walk. ·re,
Aïnhoa, .
Palais, Mau.
of the Haute So.
Tardets-Sorholus, ∟
Arette-la-Pierre-St-Ma.
Caving: there's a good cav. system—Oxocelhaya—near Isturits.
Fishing: there is good fishing in all the rivers of the Pays Basque, mostly for trout.

FURTHER INFORMATION
Tourist information: the best source of general tourist information is the Agence de Tourisme du Pays Basque, 1 rue Donzac, Bayonne, T:59 59 28 77. Outdoor information can be had from Randonnées Pyrénéennes, 4 rue de Villefranche, St-Girons, T:61 66 02 19. Weather information can be obtained from the Station Météo, Aéroport de Pau, T:59 62 17 34.

THE PYRENEAN BROWN BEAR
The last of the European big game, the brown bear is now reduced to relict populations in remote mountain forests across the Continent. In France bears were widespread in the Middle Ages, but by the end of World War II there were less than 100. Now there are less than 30, in the valleys of Ossau and Aspe, just outside national park boundaries. They are confined to the mountain forests between 900 and 1,500 metres (3,000 and 5,000 feet). Merely walking through such a "bear forest" generates a sense of excitement, although it's unlikely that the king of the Pyrenees will grant you an audience. But you may find signs of his presence—scratch marks on a tree or footprints in the mud.

The Pyrenean brown bear can grow to $2\frac{1}{2}$ metres (8 feet) in height, and weigh from 120–200kg (260–440lb). It is an extremely powerful animal: a single blow can despatch a donkey. The bear is also a tireless walker, covering 25km (15 miles) in a single nocturnal prowl. When the mood takes it, it can run at up to 40kph (25mph).

Béarn

Birthplace of Henri IV, France's most popular monarch, the region of Béarn stretches in a series of valleys southwest from Pau to the Spanish frontier

Outdoor lovers with only a limited amount of spare time in the Pyrenees should head directly for the city of Pau and its hinterland, the country of Béarn. The medieval *comté* of Béarn, birthplace of Henry of Navarre, *le grand Béarnais*, lies in the Hautes-Pyrénées, between the Pays Basque and the Bigorre. A ramble in the forests and Alpine meadows of these high hills will create lasting impressions. Indeed, it is fair to say that this region contains a lot of all that is best in the entire range: great mountains, rushing rivers, spas, excellent walking, good climbs on the higher peaks and a great variety of wildlife. This is the place to see izard scrambling on the rocks, and wild pig or boar rootling for forage in the undergrowth. Above great eagles and vultures wing their way about the peaks, while bitterns and herons fish in rocky ponds. Many of these species are summer residents only, but throughout the year you can expect to see many of the raptors for which the Pyrenees is most famous: black and red kites, goshawk, sparrowhawk, buzzards, booted eagles, and even the mighty golden eagle, as well as Egyptian vulture and bearded vulture.

Heading southwest from Pau, the first major valley is the Vallée d'Aspe; the road then follows the fast-flowing River Aspe towards its source in Spain. The dramatic pass at Col du Somport (1,632 metres/5,356 feet) forms the border with Spain. This road is a wild and rocky trail, usually blocked by snow from December to April, and cuts through the Parc National des Pyrénées Occidentales (see box). Unlike the harsh high-mountain country on either side, this valley is a place of grassy meadows, tinkling streams, shady trees and warm breezes. The rocky banks of the many trout streams are

In contrast to its ferocious reputation the brown bear, now extremely rare, is principally vegetarian.

the home of the elusive desman. Keep your eyes peeled for signs of his curious webbed tracks.

Between this valley and the Vallée d'Ossau, many tracks and footpaths cross the mountainous divide with paths set from 1,400 metres (4,600 feet) up to the 2,884-metre (9,465-foot) high Pic du Midi d'Ossau, which dominates the southern end of the Ossau valley, south of Pau. The valley is the site of the 82-hectare (200-acre) Réserve Naturelle de la Vallée d'Ossau, which was established to protect the griffon vulture, one of Europe's largest raptors. The sheer limestone cliffs support a number of these birds. Naturalists encourage them to stay by placing carrion at feeding places; this is a vulture that feeds exclusively on dead meat.

The D918 corniche road, one of the most spectacular routes in the Pyrenees, heads east out of the valley at Laruns, passing meadows, dramatic *cols* and ski resorts before descending to the ski resort of Argelès-Gazost, on the frontier of the Bigorre region. From here, a road leads up to Pont d'Espagne, the main entrance to the national park. Another, running more southeasterly, climbs through Luz-St-Sauveur to the fabulous Cirque de Gavarnie. This *cirque*, or mountain amphitheatre, together with the neighbouring Cirque de Troumouse, is a stunning sight when seen from the track that leads up from the village of Gavarnie to the foot of the *cirque* itself. At a distance it seems like a sheer wall, but as you draw closer, either on foot or taking the popular option of riding up from Gavarnie on a donkey or a horse, you'll see that the *cirque* rises up in a series of gigantic steps, each marked out, even in summer, by a wide belt of snow; from the top waterfalls plummet thousands of metres into the valley.

Gavarnie is widely noted as a migration point for butterflies, although birdwatching can be even more rewarding. You have to be up early and actually at the crossing point at the *col* to see these impressive movements, but it is well worth the climb. Raptors draw the most attention, for there are few sights more inspiring than large numbers of eagles, buzzards, hawks, kites, vultures, and falcons passing over this magnificent range.

BEFORE YOU GO
Maps: IGN 1:100.000 Nos. 69 and 70; IGN (RP) 1:50,000 No. 4.
Guidebook: A. T. Battage, *Pyrenees West of the Gavarnie Cirque* (West Col).

GETTING THERE
By air: via Tarbes, Toulouse-Blagnac or Pau-Uzein.
By car: the area can be approached from the south over the Somport pass, or, in summer only, over the Pourtalet. From the north good roads delve deep into the valleys from the main cities of the plain.
By rail: train services are declining, with Lourdes as the nearest railhead. Rent bicycles at Lourdes, Tarbes or Argelès-Gazost stations.
By bus: daily services from Pau, Oloron and Lourdes.

WHERE TO STAY
The following are recommended: Hôtel des Cimes in Gavarnie (T:62 92 48 13); Hôtel Bon Accueil in Luz-St-Sauveur (T:62 92 80 39); Hôtel Etche Ona in Cauterets (T:62 92 51 43).
Outdoor living: camping is not permitted within park boundaries.
Refuges: there are refuges by the Brèche de Roland on the Cirque de Gavarnie, and 5 Club Alpin Français (CAF) refuges in the park itself.

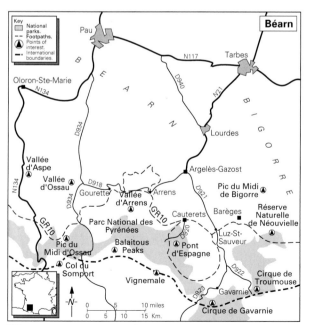

Snow melt-waters carve their way through the rich pastures below the Pic D'Anie. The wide variety of flora is characteristic of undisturbed upland areas.

ACTIVITIES
Walking and climbing:
climbers should head for the
Balaïtous peaks on the
frontier, or cross to climb in
the Vignemale south of
Cauterets. Good walks
include the one from the
village of Gavarnie to the
cleft of the Brèche de
Roland; and east from
Accous in the Vallée d'Aspe,
across the mountains to the
Gorges du Bitet in the Vallée
d'Ossau.
   Caution: this is high-
mountain country—boots,
maps, a compass and an eye

on the weather are essential.
Skiing: from Barèges,
Cauterets and inside the park.
Viewpoints: the best mountain
views are from boulevard des
Pyrénées in Pau; you can see
83 peaks if the weather is
clear. Cable cars at Gourette
lift walkers to Pic de Ger
(2,613m/8,576ft); at Cauterets
for the Cirque du Lys
(1,850m/6,000ft).

FURTHER INFORMATION
Tourist information:
Cauterets, pl de la Mairie,
T:62 92 48 26; Laruns (Vallée
d'Ossau), T:59 05 31 41; Luz-

The small yellow-faced Egyptian
vulture inhabits a wide variety of
terrain, but is particularly at home
on rocky escarpments.

St-Sauveur, 1 pl du 8-Mai,
T:62 92 81 60; Oloron-Ste-
Marie, pl de la Résistance,
T:59 39 01 96.
   Bureau de Guides at
Argelès-Gazost, T:62 97 02 63;
Cauterets, T:62 92 50 27; Luz-
St-Sauveur, T:62 92 80 58.
   Park headquarters is at
Tarbes, T:62 93 30 60.

Bigorre

*Dramatic mountainous region extending
south from Lourdes; much of it is
protected by national park or nature
reserve*

ᛏᛏᛏ

The region east of Béarn is Bigorre, which
continues and expands the high wild
country of Béarn and contains much of the

most spectacular scenery in the entire
Pyrenean range. The mountains are snow-
tipped even in summer, and the land below
the peaks is Alpine, a mixture of grassy
mountain meadows where sheep and cattle
are sent for summer pasture. These
pastures are well watered by snow-melt
from the heights above, and this steady
supply of moisture keeps the countryside
green, with the trees flourishing and the
streams filled even in the driest summer.
   Some of the best scenery is by the ski
resort of La Mongie, which stands at the
southern end of the Vallée de Gripp. There

is splendid wild country on either side of the D918, which leads here from Luz-St-Sauveur and over the Col du Tourmalet. To the north lies the rugged Pic du Midi de Bigorre (2,872 metres/9,422 feet), one of the great mountains of the French Pyrenees. The area contains some excellent walking trails, notably the one up to the Lac Bleu, which nestles in the fold of the hills as if an azure carpet had been spread across the rocky mountain slope. South of the road, the national park continues into the Réserve Naturelle de Néouvielle ("Old Snow" Nature Reserve), the third oldest nature reserve in the country, and this reserve is arguably the most impressive both for scenery and wildlife. It covers 2,313 hectares (5,715 acres), from 1,800 to 3,091 metres (5,910 to 10,145 feet) altitude. The reserve experiences a mixture of climatic influences, which account for the proximity of unlikely neighbours, such as the cross-leaved heath of Atlantic origins, the arctic marsh cinquefoil and several Mediterranean species. There are several bogs, which together support some 22 species of sphagnum moss. Altogether the reserve has 94 species of lichen and 1,238 high plant species. Over 250 types of beetle find nourishment on this varied feast.

The midwife toad is remarkable here, for at 2,400 metres (7,880 feet) altitude, its tadpoles take a good 20 years to complete their development. The most notable reptile is the rare Seoanei's viper. This thriving species comes as a surprise to those who associate reptiles with hot environ-

ments. A wide selection of typical Alpine birds can be found here, including the wall-creeper, ptarmigan, capercaillie and the rare Pyrenean race of common partridge. There are no longer thought to be any bears, but suitable areas of habitat do remain. However, otters, hares, foxes, and the unique desman are still present, even though you must be extremely lucky to see them.

The Vallée de Campan, further east, is one of the wider valleys of the central Pyrenees, running northwest to southeast and lined on either side by grassy mountain meadows. Make the spa of Bagnères-de-Bigorre your base; it is a good centre for day-walking, and the tourist office has marked many footpaths into the surrounding hills. Ramblers in springtime will be rewarded with sightings of the yellow turk's cap lily, one of the most extravagantly coloured plants in the Pyrenees.

To reach the next major valley of Bigorre, the Vallée d'Aure, take the southern road from Ste-Marie-de-Campan over the Col d'Aspin, and follow its zigzag pattern down to the valley floor near Arreau, where the main outdoor centre lies to the south at the resort and ski centre of St-Lary. There are plenty of trails and marked footpaths leading into the hills and mountains around St-Lary: east into the next valley, the Valleé du Louron, or west up to the Néouvielle massif. The Pic de Néouvielle itself gives great views over some of the wildest country in the entire range.

The midwife toad, though mainly a lowland species, is to be found at over 2,000 m. in the Pyrenees.

BEFORE YOU GO
Maps: IGN (RP) 1:50,000 No. 4; IGN 1:25,000 Nos. 1747–48 and 1847–48.

GETTING THERE
By car: the region's central towns are Lourdes and Tarbes. By car the best route is first up one of the main

A light dusting of snow (*overleaf*) adorns the impressive high peaks of the central Pyrenees.

125

valleys of Aure or Campan, then cut across the range on scenic D618.
By rail: an infrequent service runs from Tarbes to Bagnères-de-Bigorre, and into the Vallée d'Aure.
By bus: buses service all the valleys from Lourdes and Tarbes.

WHERE TO STAY
Good places to stay include:

Hôtel Trianon, pl des Thermes, Bagnères-de-Bigorre, T:62 95 09 34; La Montagne Fleurie, Centre Ville, Barèges, T:62 92 68 50; La Sapinière, Espiaule, St-Lary-Soulan, T:62 98 44 04.
Outdoor living: tourist offices have lists of campsites.

ACTIVITIES
Walking: the classic walk is from Fabian in the Vallée

d'Aure, up to the Massif de Néouvielle.
Cycling: a challenging route follows the Route des Cols along D618.

FURTHER INFORMATION
Tourist information: Arreau, pl du Monument, T:62 98 63 15; Bagnères-de-Bigorre, 21 rue des Thermes, T:62 95 50 71; St-Lary, T:62 39 50 81.

Comminges

Forested district in the southeast corner of the Hautes-Pyrénées département, where the Garonne enters France through a lush valley

I first made the journey up the valley from Bagnères-de-Luchon at the end of the 1950s, when the Pyrenees were distinctly wilder than they are today. It was late February or early March, and when I left Bagnères it was growing dark and starting to snow; by the time I got about a kilometre out of town I was wishing I had stayed overnight. I pressed on into the blizzard, however, which was now hurling snow across the mountains, got gloriously lost, and was just thinking of pitching my tent and waiting it out until morning when out of the dark loomed the Hospice de France, which was open to all comers in those days and positively crammed with people: French, Spanish, some English, a few Germans, walkers and climbers, even a few muleteers. They all shifted up on the benches, passed the jugs of wine and the mountain ham and rough rye bread, and in half a dozen languages we passed the night away.

Comminges is a curious part of the French Pyrenees, not least because it is here that the Val d'Aran thrusts north across the

mountains from Spain and places the Franco-Spanish frontier well north of the watershed. It is through this Val d'Aran that the infant River Garonne begins its long journey to the Atlantic. The Comminges countryside represents a change from its lofty and imposing neighbours; here the terrain is greener and more forested, and the mountains a jumble of lower peaks rather than majestic ranges.

The way in from the west comes over the Col de Peyresourde, a ski centre in winter, and down to the Luchon valley and the spa of Bagnères-de-Luchon. Southwest of here, in the country running up to the frontier, are high mountain lakes. Most notable is the Lac d'Oô, backed by a 271-metre (900-foot) high waterfall and a number of steep-sided valleys, like the Vallée du Lys, which holds yet another waterfall, the Cascade d'Enfer.

The great contrasts you can find in the French Pyrenees are never more obvious than here. South of Bagnères-de-Luchon, the country is in the main gentle, but if you walk out of Bagnères up the Vallée du Lys and on to the Hospice de France you leave civilization rapidly behind, as I found out all those years ago. This is a region of sharp peaks, small lakes, thickly wooded valleys and a distinct lack of footpaths and sign-posts. It's a frontier region, with no roads across save a few old smugglers' tracks, and there is nothing to stop you crossing the frontier to scramble on the lower slopes of the Pic d'Aneto through the Port de Vénasque.

128

North of Bagnères-de-Luchon, a branch of the Pyrenees juts up from the south, making the Spanish frontier east rather than south. Here the Vallée d'Oueil veers off northwest, while the main Luchon valley runs north past the little fortress town of St-Béat in the Garonne valley, and so up to one of the great pilgrim places in the entire range, the abbey-church of St-Bertrand-de-Comminges.

The main mass of the Comminges lies east of St-Bertrand and south of the Garonne, which bursts out of the Pyrenees at St-Bertrand and swings away east through the town of St-Gaudens, the present capital of the region. The main road along the foothills of the Pyrenees, N117, follows this valley, but outdoor lovers will prefer to return up N125, past St-Bertrand, and take the winding, spectacular D618 once again. A scenic route all the way, D618 winds into the hills from Fronsac and cuts here and there across the hills of Comminges, climbing steadily to the 1,069-metre (3,508-foot) pass of the Col de Portet d'Aspet.

BEFORE YOU GO
Maps: IGN 1:250,000 No. 113; IGN 1:25,000 1847 (east and west) and 1848 (east).

GETTING THERE
By air: airports at Toulouse, Tarbes and Perpignan.
By car: N125 through St-Bertrand runs up to Bagnères-de-Luchon; D26 crosses from the Garonne to the Luchon valley. N6180 turns out of the Luchon valley near St-Béat, and enters Spain via the Val d'Aran.
By rail: there is a train service to Bagnères-de-Luchon, and a good main-line service along the northern Garonne valley to St-Gaudens.
By bus: buses from St-Gaudens run up the 2 main valleys to St-Béat and Bagnères-de-Luchon.

WHERE TO STAY
The best centres are St-Béat for the Val d'Aran; St-Gaudens for the northern Comminges; and Bagnères-de-Luchon for expeditions into the mountains along the frontier.

ACTIVITIES
Walking: local trails abound but the most exciting walks are from Luchon up the road past the Hospice de France and then on footpaths into the Malditos, the Val d'Aran and Pic d'Aneto. Lac d'Oô can be reached via the Vallée du Lys, and there are more good walks east of St-Bertrand.
Climbing: information from the Club Alpin Français, 1 rue de la Charité, Toulouse, T:61 63 74 42.
Fishing: trout and salmon can be caught in the Garonne and in the high lakes of the Pyrenees beyond Luchon.
Skiing: Alpine skiing at Superbagnères and Peyresourde Dec–Apr.
Viewpoints: particularly rewarding views can be had from the cols on D618; from the grassy slopes below Superbagnères; and from Col du Portillon above the Val d'Aran.

FURTHER INFORMATION
Tourist information: Bagnères-de-Luchon, 18 allées d'Etigny, T:61 79 21 21; St-Gaudens, pl Mas-St-Pierre, T:61 89 15 99.

PARC NATIONAL DES PYRÉNÉES OCCIDENTALES

The Parc National des Pyrénées Occidentales was created in 1967 to join with the Spanish Parque de Ordesa on the other side of the frontier. It runs along the mountains for 100km (60 miles) and has a depth of between 3km (2 miles) and 15km (10 miles). Together with the smaller Réserve Naturelle de Néouvielle in its northeast corner, this park enfolds a superb mountain area of 45,700ha (113,000 acres), straddling the *départements* of Pyrénées-Atlantiques and Hautes-Pyrénées. Thanks to the varied altitudes and nature of the soil, the park is a zoologist's paradise, and contains many of the rarest Pyrenean species: izard, the Pyrenean chamois, marmots, aquatic desman, pine martin and red squirrel. However, unfortunately the most threatened species of the region, indeed the park's symbol—the brown bear—does not occur within its boundaries. The equally fragile mountain plantlife contains rare Alpine lilies and several varieties of orchid.

Ariège

*The rushing River Ariège gives its name
to the sparsely populated* département
on the borders of Andorra

The Ariège marks the point where the uplands of the central Pyrenees begin to assume a drier, more Mediterranean air. The change is noticeable as soon as you cross the border from the Comminges, in the Hautes-Pyrénées *département*, to the Couserans district of western Ariège. Here the air dries out and the soft grass gives way to short, tufty tussocks. Trout streams still course through the valleys, but move on to the upper slopes and the land becomes bleak, rocky and uncomfortably hot. In winter many of the villages are ski centres, and here the snow comes early and lies late. Even the geology is varied, a mixture of granite in the Barguillère, and limestone in the valley of the Ariège south of the city of Foix.

The Couserans region has suffered severely from emigration, and its largest town, St-Girons, has a population of only 7,000—less than half the 1850 figure. Wildlife, however, has thrived in direct proportion to the human exodus; keep your eyes open as you rove about and you will see marmots, mountain goats and larger-than-usual numbers of rabbits, prey for the ever-watchful eagles, buzzards and other raptors. The highest peak is Mont Valier (2,838 metres/9,314 feet), lying southwest of St-Girons.

Until Napoleon decreed that all *départements* created since the Revolution should, where possible, bear the name of the main local river, Ariège was known as the country of Foix, home to an ancient line of warlike nobles. Modern Ariège is hemmed in by Andorra to the south, the plain of

The Cascade d' Oô in the Montagnes de Luchon is one of the spectacular waterfalls which, together with the mountain lakes and torrents, are some of the best sights of Comminges.

Toulouse to the north, and the great plateau of the Cerdagne to the east. Some of the best scenery is in the small valleys between Foix and Andorra. The lush valley of the Vicdessos lies beneath a long east–west ridge, which shelters the valley and allows it a mild micro-climate. The valley runs up through mainly empty country to the bare peaks and ridges along the Franco–Spanish–Andorran frontier. The area has no towns, few villages and very few hamlets. This is hardly surprising as there are no roads, only a few tracks to take the walkers and campers deeper into the hills in the wild, barren frontier before Andorra. The great joy of this part of the region is its large number of lakes, many created by glaciation and feeding mountain streams full of rainbow trout and char.

East of a north–south line between the towns of Foix and Tarascon-sur-Ariège, the country is green, open and studded with half-deserted villages, such as famous Montaillou, in the Cathar country. Walkers and backpackers can explore the fascinating places once inhabited by the heretical Cathars. This sect, whose believers were also known as Albigensians, viewed the world as the creation of the Devil and set about purifying themselves without the intercession of clergy or the Church. An anti-Cathar crusade in the early 13th century dealt cruelly and mercilessly with this proto-Reformation, which at one point had converted much of southwest France. Many of the Cathars withdrew to remote hilltop castles, such as Montségur, Puivert and Puilaurens, before being burned at the stake and their last outposts razed to the ground. Nature has begun to reclaim these former citadels, and ravens, choughs and crows nest among the ruins.

Within the wide confines of the Ariège, the natural features include the Pic de St-Barthélemy (2,348 metres/7,706 feet) in the Monts d'Olmes, and the hills west and south of Ax-les-Thermes, an area virtually without roads now that the villagers' homes have been abandoned and the byways which lead into the hills have crumbled into tracks. East of a line between Ax and the road into Andorra, the country is open, but the hills are steep, ideal for skiing in winter and walking along the ridge in summer.

NATURE RESERVES OF THE EASTERN PYRENEES

Le Massif de la Carança nature reserve is located between the valleys of the Têt and the Tech. Landscape and vegetation is typically Pyrenean, including a selection of endemic plants in the high Alpine zone—saxifrages and the Isard parsley. Another local botanical speciality is the tall herbaceous community known as "megaphorbiae", among which grows the Pyrenean lily, *Eryngium bourgatii*, mountain delphinium and a mountain form of angelica of more Mediterranean origin, *Molopospermum peloponnesianum*.

Such a varied flora naturally hosts an abundance of insects and beetles, moths and butterflies are particularly well represented. Notable among the latter are the distinctive and large Apollo, while for specialists there is the challenge of distinguishing two small, brown species, Lefebre's ringlet and the Gavarnie ringlet, which both inhabit the high alpine meadows above 1,800m (5,900ft).

The three adjoining reserves of the Massif de Madres and the Mont Coronat cover 3,160ha (7,810 acres) north of the Têt valley. The vegetation is typical of limestone mountains but with a strong Mediterranean influence from the warm air blown up the Têt valley. On the plateaus of red limestone are great carpets of bearberry, a spreading, mat-forming shrub with shiny, leathery oval leaves. Naturalists can enjoy the area for its reptiles, which in turn attract the short-toed, or snake eagle; there are also a couple of pairs of golden eagles and a pair of eagle owls. Invertebrates are abundant, including marbled skipper and mountain small white butterflies, and most notably the blind scorpion *Belisarius xambui*. Perhaps most notable, though, are the mammals, with wildcat, genet, izard, wild boar, red deer and recently reported sightings of lynx.

BEFORE YOU GO
Maps: IGN 1:250,000 Nos. 113 and 114; IGN (RP) 1:50,000 No. 7; IGN 1:25,000 Nos. 1947 (east), 2047 (west), 2048 (east and west), 2148 and 2248 (east and west).

GETTING THERE
By air: the nearest airports are Toulouse-Blagnac and Perpignan.
By car: the most direct route into Ariège is via N20, which leads through Foix, Tarascon-sur-Ariège and Ax-les-Thermes; minor roads branch off the Vicdessos and other valleys.
By rail: a service links Foix to Ax-les-Thermes and St-Girons.
By bus: bus services run in summer between Foix and Ax-les-Thermes and into some of the main valleys.

WHERE TO STAY
There are plenty of hotels in Foix, Ax, Tarascon, St-Girons and the larger villages and main valleys. Some of the better ones include Hôtel Audoye Lons, 6 pl G-Duthil, Foix, T:61 65 52 44; Hostellerie de la Poste, 16 av Victor-Pilhes, Tarascon-sur-Ariège, T:61 05 60 41; Hôtel des Pyrénées, 3 av Delcassé, Ax-les-Thermes, T:61 64 21 01.

Outdoor living: lists of campsites available from local tourist offices.

ACTIVITIES
Walking: an excellent trek heads south from Laramade in the Vicdessos, to the Peyregrand campsite near the Pic du Pas de Bouc (2,602m/8,539ft) on the Spanish frontier. Ax-les-Thermes has many local trails up to the Tute de l'Ours (2,255m/7,400ft); others extend to the west of this peak. Several disused mule tracks lead up to the Spanish frontier from Mont Valier.
Caves: the grotto and caves of Mas d'Azil, northeast of St-Girons, are justly famous —

Honey buzzards feed on honey from the nests of wasps and bees.

their soaring height rivals that of some of the country's cathedrals. The caves at Niaux are full of prehistoric paintings, while those at Bédeilhac and Lombrives sheltered Cathars.

FURTHER INFORMATION
Tourist information: Ax-les-Thermes, av Delcassé, T:61 65 12 12; Foix, 14 rue de Lazéma, T:61 65 29 00; St-Girons, pl A-Sentein, T:61 66 14 11; Tarascon-sur-Ariège, av V-Pilhes, T:61 05 63 46.

Andorra

Tiny co-principality (27km/ 17 miles by 30km/19 miles) in the French Pyrenees; haven for botanists

Andorra is a barren, desolate, mountainous country with only two roads. Avoid the busy main one, which runs across the country from France to Spain and take the much smaller road north from the capital, Andorra-la-Vella, to the ski resort at El Serrat. You pass outcrops of alkaline rocks along this route, and it is among these rocks that you will find the widest variety of Andorra's famous flora. Over 1,000 species of flowering plants have been identified in Andorra, making it one of the best areas in the Pyrenees for

the botanist.

Andorra lies in the French Pyrenees, but it is not French. Its frontier independence was guaranteed by a treaty of 1278 between the Spanish Bishop of Urgel and the Counts of Foix, although the latter's responsibilities have long since been assumed by the President of France. The co-principality of Andorra is the only country in the world where Catalan is the official tongue.

Getting there *By air:* the nearest airports are at Barcelona, Toulouse or Perpignan.
By car: the main road across Andorra is N1/N2, which runs from Pas de la Case in the north to the old cathedral city of Seo de Urgel in Spain.
By rail: from Barcelona there are trains to Puigcerdà on the Spanish–Andorran border, and buses from there to Andorra-la-Vella. From Toulouse there are trains to Ax-les-Thermes, and buses from there to Andorra.
Activities *Walking:* Andorra is wild, tough country, suitable only for well-equipped walkers. You can make a circuit up the Valira d'Ordino to El Serrat and then up to the Pic de l'Estanyo (2,912m/9,557ft).
Skiing: at Soldeu, Canillo, Arinsal, Pas de la Case and Massana.
Further information *Tourist information:* Andorra-la-Vella, calle Dr-Vila-Nova, T:62 82 02 14.

FOOTPATHS OF THE PYRENEES

The *Grande Randonnée 10*, which spans the Pyrenees from Hendaye in the west to Banyuls on the Mediterranean, is one of the great footpaths of France. The 400-km (250-mile) long-range footpath is covered by five well-illustrated *topo-guides* published by the organization responsible for the *grande randonnée* network, which break the journey into sections. The GR10 is certainly a challenge, but the rewards for taking it up are considerable. The trail across the Hautes-Pyrénées is wildly beautiful and alert walkers will see a considerable amount of wildlife: Egyptian vultures, booted eagles, the Pyrenean chamois, a host of Alpine plants and, in the meadows below the bare upper slopes, a riot of flowers and butterflies.

Higher and even harder than the GR10 is the Haute Randonnée Pyrénéenne, much of which follows a route over the 1,800-m (6,000-ft) level. To complete the whole of this splendid challenge will take at least five weeks. For long sections the walks are far from any habitation, so thorough planning is essential as is a knowledge of weather lore and map and compass work. There is no real climbing involved but plenty of scrambling, with the trail running along knife-edged ridges and over 2,400-m (8,000-ft) high *cols*—not places for the inexperienced walker. The best guide to the route is *Pyrenees High Level Route* by Georges Véron, published by West Col.

Cerdagne and Capcir

Lush, cool plateau and valley nestling between Andorra and the dusty plain of Roussillon

If I were pressed to declare one part of the Pyrenees I prefer above the rest, I would put forward the Cerdagne and the area which abuts it, the Capcir. Perhaps the main reason for this is that when you enter the Cerdagne from the west, you leave France proper behind, and come into the country of the Catalans—Roussillon. Yet the Cerdagne is a complete contrast to the hot, dusty, vine-draped plains of Roussillon far below. The vast rolling plateau is a place of farms and meadows, surrounded by snow-capped mountains; the air is cool and sweet and cattle graze on rich, belly-high meadow grass.

The road in from the west and Andorra climbs up to the plateau over the Col de Puymorens (1,915 metres/6,285 feet), from which there are good views across to the highest peak of the Cerdagne, the Pic Carlit (2,921 metres/9,587 feet). Once past the *col*, the road climbs on for 25 kilometres (15 miles) or so, rising steadily, and comes into the Cerdagne by the enclave of Llivia, which by an accident of history is a Spanish town within the frontiers of France.

The Giro footpath in the Vallée d' Aspe is one of many such paths with stunning views of this ever-changing landscape.

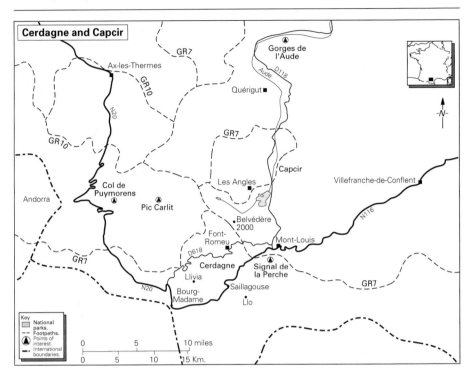

A road circles the Cerdagne, and the simplest way to explore the region is to follow it east from Bourg-Madame, past Hix and along the meadows and valleys leading up to the Spanish frontier; it continues through Saillagouse, over the Col de la Perche and past the viewpoint at the Signal de la Perche to Mont-Louis, a fortified town at the point where the Cerdagne tips down into the steep, narrow valley of the Conflent gorge. Along this southern road to Mont-Louis are marvellous views on either side up to the Pic Carlit to the north or south across the meadows to the line of peaks and *cols* which mark the Spanish frontier.

This part of the Cerdagne is meadowland for the most part, seamed with half-hidden streams tucked away amid the grassy tussocks. Arriving at Mont-Louis, we turn back on our tracks and head west to the spa and ski-centre of Font-Romeu. Nearby lies Odeillo, famous for the vast, many-mirrored solar oven that stands in the centre of the village. It is some indication of the good

weather you can enjoy on the Cerdagne plateau that the French chose to build this experimental oven up here. The road skirts the foothills of the Pic Carlit on its way to Bourg-Madame. North of this road, the countryside is steeper, glorious short grass country with springy turf. There are small lakes and ponds, and lots of streams for fishing and bathing. There is wildlife here, too, and plenty of it: izard on the slopes of Carlit, goats browsing in the meadows, otters splashing in the streams, and a wealth of birdlife, particularly in summer when the songbirds flourish in the tall grasses. Butterflies are another feature of the Cerdagne; look out for the black-veined white, swallowtails and purple emperors, the fritillaries and blues.

The second wild area up here is the Capcir valley, which runs off the Cerdagne to the north, descending to the gorges of the River Aude. Botanists find the Capcir fascinating because of its profusion of wildflowers and orchids. Follow some of the

136

marked trails up the steep valley to see the full range of plant life, with certain species thriving only in the narrowest of altitude bands—prolific in one meadow and non-existent 10 minutes along your climb.

You can descend from the plateau by taking the *petit train jaune*, the "little yellow train" that runs from Villefranche-de-Conflent all the way up to Bourg-Madame, one of the most scenic railways in Europe.

BEFORE YOU GO
Maps: IGN 1:250,000 No. 114; IGN (RP) 1:50,000 No. 8; IGN 1:25,000 Nos. 2249 (east and west), 2349 (west) and 2250 (east).

GETTING THERE
By air: the nearest airport is at Perpignan.
By car: take N116 west up the Têt valley to Villefranche-de-Conflent and on to the Cerdagne. The Capcir is served by D118 between Mont-Louis and Quérigut.
By rail: from Perpignan a train runs along the Têt to Villefranche from where the *petit train jaune* climbs to the Cerdagne.

By bus: the region's erratic services originate in Perpignan.

WHERE TO STAY
Accommodation is not a problem anywhere in the Cerdagne–Capcir region, even in winter, for the villages operate as summer centres and as ski resorts. Try Le Coq Hardi in Font-Romeu (T:68 30 11 02).

ACTIVITIES
Walking: marked trails cover the area, but 3 of the most rewarding walks extend from Lac des Bouillouses to the Pic Carlit; across the Pyrenees from Llo to Nuria; and across

the Cerdagne from Carlit to Canigou (allow 5 days).
Skiing: 3 established resorts are at Font-Romeu, Belvédère 2000 and Les Angles.
Viewpoints: there are remarkable views from the Pic Carlit, Belvédère 2000 and the Signal de la Perche.

FURTHER INFORMATION
Tourist information: Les Angles, La Matte, T:68 04 42 04; Font-Romeu, av Emmanuel-Brousse, T:68 30 02 74; Mont-Louis, T:68 04 21 97.

In spite of its name, the scarce swallowtail is common in southern France and is frequently seen feeding beside footpaths.

(*Overleaf*) Dense pine forest is mirrored in the still waters of the Lac des Bouillouses on the Cerdagne plateau.

Conflent and Vallespir

Two dramatic valleys of the easternmost Pyrenees; a varied countryside of waterfalls, narrow valleys and orchards

The Conflent and the Vallespir are the two major valleys of the Pyrénées-Orientales *département*, the first to the north, the second to the south. Between them they cradle the last rocky thrust of the Pyrenees and the mighty bulk of the Pic du Canigou (2,784 metres/9,137 feet), the highest mountain of the Catalans. Down these valleys rush two rivers, the Têt and the Tech. Both valleys support vineyards and orchards, groaning in springtime with the weight of cherry, apple and almond blossom; and both look up to the soaring peaks on either side.

I shall take the Vallespir last, for this valley is barred to the south by the descending range of the Chaine des Albères, which reach out and dip their rocky fingers into the Mediterranean Sea near Port-Vendres, while the Conflent stops some way short of this, and carries the River Tet out onto the flat plain of Roussillon, and so out of the confines of this chapter.

The entrance to the steep Conflent valley lies off the Cerdagne from Mont-Louis, where the road and railway for the *petit train jaune* plunge down a steep gorge. Waterfalls burst from the rocky sides and send their spray tumbling down the face for hundreds of metres, and there is at least one remarkable feat of engineering to see at the bridge of the Pont Séjourné. Below here, a mule track leads into the hills, and steep though the gorge is, there are tracks up and off it to either side, giving access to the Capcir valley and the Vallée de Rotja, which skirts the eastern slopes of Canigou. The main town hereabouts is Villefranche-de-Conflent, from which a network of minor roads leads into the southern mountains to the spa at Vernet-les-Bains and the monastery of St-Martin-du-Canigou, below the massif itself. Canigou is the dominant

feature of the landscape; a footpath runs up to the top, where it joins others coming in from the Cerdagne. I have done this walk from the Cerdagne one wild October, and it is not a trip to undertake lightly.

I went with a companion to walk from the Pic Carlit in the Cerdagne, along the Spanish frontier and up to the top of Canigou, an expedition we calculated would take about five days of slow, pleasant walking. Instead, the snows started early, and our uncomfortable progress was slowed even more by sleet and white-outs. Inevitably, when we got to the bottom, the skies cleared and we camped that night by a small mountain lake in a dream-like setting of rocks and mountains and blue lakes, with a dramatic sunset to round it off. It took three more days of hard climbing to get to the top of Canigou. When we finally crawled exhausted on to the summit we were greeted by two sprightly gentlemen in their eighties who had climbed the mountain from its northern side and led us down to the car park like a couple of spring lambs.

Around the Massif of Canigou are several nature reserves: Py and Mantet to the west (accessible on GR10) with typical evergreen woodland of the higher Roussillon Pyrenees; Conat and Nohèdes (both near Prades) and Jujols (near Olette), all just off N116, with typical vegetation of the warmer, lower Roussillon Pyrenees.

Moving on down the valley, past Prades, the road reaches the valley of the Têt, one of those rushing, stony, mountain rivers, and you can follow this as far as Ille-sur-Têt, where the valley widens and mountain lovers must turn south, up into the Aspres, the last outpost of the main range. Trails and footpaths lead off this minor road, which enters the Tech valley at the spa town of Amélie-les-Bains.

There is no road into the Haut-Vallespir from the west, only a track along the spine of the Pyrenees, where peak follows peak at about the 2,500-metre (8,205-foot) mark, descending into the Vallespir by La Preste, where the track gradually broadens into a road to meet the main route coming in from Spain at Prats-de-Mollo. This valley of the Haut-Vallespir is nothing if not spectacular, full of trails and small hamlets, with the Gorges de la Fou in the Tech alone making the visit worth while; to the north the path runs up past Corsavy towards the central point of Canigou. The road runs along beside the Tech to Amélie-les-Bains, and out onto the Roussillon plain by the town of Céret.

Here we might end, but the hills of the Albères do provide a wilderness route to the Mediterranean. Only minor roads, little more than tracks, run into the Albères, because this area was left deliberately deserted as a bastion against invasion. The main roads and the *autoroute* run into Spain by the Col du Perthus, but the peaks are already down to the 1,000–1,200-metre (3,300–3,900-foot) mark, and the best way through is to follow the GR10 down to the sea at Banyuls.

BEFORE YOU GO
Maps: IGN 1:250,000 No. 114; IGN (RP) 1:50,000 Nos. 10 and 11; IGN 1:25,000 Nos. 2449 (east and west), 2549 (west), 2350 and 2450.

GETTING THERE
By air: the nearest airport is Perpignan-Rivesaltes.
By car: from Toulouse D118 runs past Carcassonne, south to Quillan and then into the Capcir and Cerdagne-Conflent. N116 and D115 run up the Têt and Tech valleys respectively, giving good access to the Conflent and the Vallespir.

By rail: a train from Perpignan runs up the Têt valley to Villefranche-de-Conflent and another via Elne serves the Tech as far as Céret.
By bus: buses offer an infrequent service to Prats-de-Mollo.

WHERE TO STAY
Recommended hotels include Hôtel Central in Amélie-les-Bains (T:68 39 05 49); Les Glycines in Arles-sur-Tech (T:68 39 10 09); Hôtel Princess in Vernet-les-Bains (T:68 05 56 22); Hostellerie Le Relais in Prats-de-Mollo (T:68 39 71 30).

ACTIVITY
Walking: one of the most exhilarating walks is that from St-Martin-de-Canigou to the summit. There are marked trails around all the main centres, and particularly good trails from Prats-de-Mollo.

FURTHER INFORMATION
Tourist information: Céret, av G-Clemenceau, T:68 87 00 53; Prats-de-Mollo, pl Le Firal, T:68 39 70 83; Villefranche-Conflent, pl de la Mairie, T:68 96 10 78.

The Iberian lynx hunts at dusk for rabbits and other small mammals which form its staple diet.

CHAPTER 7

The Atlantic Coast

The giant arc of coastline which is the French Atlantic coast splits conveniently, like Gaul in Caesar's description, into three parts, divided from one another by two of France's greatest rivers. First comes the indented coast of southern Brittany, cut by dozens of estuaries and creeks. To the south lies the wide estuary of the Loire; its northern bank is fringed by the heavy industries of St-Nazaire and Donges, its southern side by gently rolling vineyards.

Beyond the Loire, the landscape changes gradually from a northern to a southern character. The grey slate roofs of Brittany give way to the orange-red pantiles of the south, more and more of the countryside is given over to vineyards, and the crops are further advanced. This is a favourite part of the coast for French holidaymakers and day-trippers, who trail out nose-to-tail on fine weekends to Pornic, Noirmoutier, St-Jean-de-Monts and dozens of smaller seaside resorts. It is also famous for its oysters, which flourish in the sheltered waters of the bays north and south of La Rochelle, and in any number of smaller estuary creeks.

Travellers from abroad, however, tend to rush through the region of the Loire estuary and the Vendée on their way south to Biarritz or Spain. This is a great pity, because the area is full of unexpected delights. Only a few miles out of Nantes is the bird-haunted Lac de Grand-Lieu, where eel-fishermen

The open coast of the Bassin d' Arcachon is exposed to the fierce attrition of wind and wave from the Atlantic Ocean. Daily, new pools, riverlets and channels are formed in the shifting sands.

still make a precarious living. Between the Grand-Lieu and the coast stretches the wide expanse of the *marais* of Machecoul and Challans: drained salt marshes where cattle browse under an immense canopy of sky, with hardly a tree to lessen the force of the west winds blowing off the Atlantic. Here the wide Bay of Bourgneuf, sheltered along much of its western side by the long finger of the Noirmoutier peninsula, is a great haunt of wading birds, among them plovers, stilts and avocets. Being situated at the junction of two major migration routes down from Greenland and Siberia, these coastal flats see some of the major concentrations of birds in Europe.

South of the Noirmoutier peninsula, a narrow fringe of forest stretches between the coast road and the sea almost as far as La Rochelle, where it is broken by the tidal flats of the Anse (bay) de l'Aiguillon, and the drained Marais Poitevin (marshland of Poitou) stretching far inland. Between La Rochelle and Royan, forest takes over again in the Forêt de la Coubre.

South of Royan, the Atlantic coast's second great water barrier, the Gironde, cuts into the shoreline like a giant downward-slanting axe-stroke. Unlike the Loire, which runs almost east–west between Nantes and the sea, the Gironde's estuary is virtually north–south. On either side lies a gently rolling landscape of vineyards producing the classic red wines of Bordeaux.

The Médoc area lies at the northern tip of Les Landes, a seemingly endless forest of pine trees. This million-hectare (2½-million-acre) expanse, shaped like a huge isosceles triangle, with its base along the foothills of the Pyrenees and its sides bounded by the Atlantic and the Garonne, is Europe's largest forest. From the map it looks as though it would be monotonous to explore, but in spite of its flatness, the sameness of its long straight roads and the constant vistas of conifers stretching into the distance, Les Landes has a fascination unlike any other part of France, combined with that quality of stillness the French call *le calme*.

If you follow any of the minor roads from one village to the next, you will pass sprawling half-timbered farmhouses, with low-pitched red-tiled roofs, surrounded by outhouses and wood-stores built in the same harmonious style. Down some narrow lane you may find a time-worn church among the trees, on the medieval pilgrim route to the shrine of Santiago de Compostela in northern Spain. The Landes these pilgrims trudged through was very different from the forest the traveller sees today.

Les Landes did not assume its modern, tree-covered appearance until the 19th century, when enormous tracts of flat land were planted with conifers to stabilize the sandy soil and hold back the encroaching dunes.

As you head west across Les Landes towards the sea, the sand takes over completely. The pines vanish as the coastal dunes approach, and are gradually engulfed as the wind blows the sands inland. You can see this phenomenon at its most dramatic at the huge Dune du Pilat at the entrance to the Bassin d'Arcachon. This Sahara-like mountain of sand, at 117 metres (384 feet) the highest dune in Europe, is advancing relentlessly inland at the rate of a metre a year. Though its surroundings are hardly wild—on either side are some of the most civilized summer resorts along the Atlantic coast—it is worth seeing for itself, and worth struggling to the top for the marvellous view north across the Bassin d'Arcachon and inland over the treetops of Les Landes.

The lover of wildlife will not find any great variety on the sandy coast of Les Landes, or in the tree-filled hinterland. Between beach and woodland, though, about six kilometres (four miles) inland, an irregular chain of lakes runs along the whole length of the coast. Together with the Bassin d'Arcachon they provide ideal conditions for water-birds and swamp-loving plants. The other natural jewels of Les Landes are the numerous winding rivers bedecked on either side with a luxuriant gallery of forest, which, experienced from a canoe or barge, can easily evoke the feeling of some tropical jungle.

It is this quality of infinite scenic variety that makes the French Atlantic coast a fascinating area to explore.

GETTING THERE

By air: the region is well served by airports at Nantes, La Rochelle, Bordeaux and Biarritz.

By sea: the most direct routes are by Brittany Ferries, with car ferries sailing Portsmouth–St-Malo or Plymouth–Roscoff.

By car: from St-Malo, the most direct route to the Atlantic coast is via N137 through Rennes to Nantes, from which roads radiate southwards. Rennes has an excellent bypass (*rocade*), but Nantes can be a nightmare to negotiate. Alternatively, go to Rennes, then cross-country on D roads via Redon and Pontchâteau to the St-Nazaire toll bridge.

By rail: Nantes, Bordeaux and Bayonne are all important rail centres, with connections to places along the coast. Railways tend to radiate from the capital, however, which means cross-country journeys can be time-consuming. Les Landes has a single north–south line between Bordeaux and Bayonne, via Morcenx and Dax. This runs 25–30km (15–20 miles) inland, with only a single coastal spur, to Arcachon.

By bus: local timetables are available from tourist offices in each area.

WHEN TO GO

As this is an excellent area for watching migrating and overwintering birds, bird-lovers are recommended to visit between Oct and Mar. Temperatures are moderate, though in Les Landes it can be blisteringly hot and sultry even in May. It's sensible to avoid the Atlantic coast area between mid-June and end-Aug, when roads become crowded and it's difficult to find accommodation.

WHERE TO STAY

Most inland towns and large villages have at least 1 hotel of Logis de France 2-star standard, or equivalent. Seaside hotels are packed in summer, but out of season may be virtually empty; however, many do not open until May or even June. For country hotels, refer to the *Guide des Auberges et Hôtels de Campagne (Editions Rivage)*.

Campsites are abundant throughout the region.

FURTHER INFORMATION

This chapter takes in the western parts of 3 regions—the Pays de la Loire, Poitou-Charentes and Aquitaine. The relevant information services are: western Loire, Comité Régional de Tourisme, Maison du Tourisme, pl de Commerce, Nantes, T:40 48 24 20; Poitou-Charentes, Comité Régional de Tourisme, 2 rue Ste-Opportune, Poitiers, T:49 88 38 94; and Aquitaine, Comité Régional de Tourisme, 24 allée de Tourny, Bordeaux, T:56 44 48 02.

FURTHER READING

Blue Guide to France (A. and C. Black); *Côte de l'Atlantique* (Michelin, Les Guides Verts); John Gooders, *Where to Watch Birds in Britain and Europe* (Christopher Helm).

The rare butterfly iris from the Marais Poitevin.

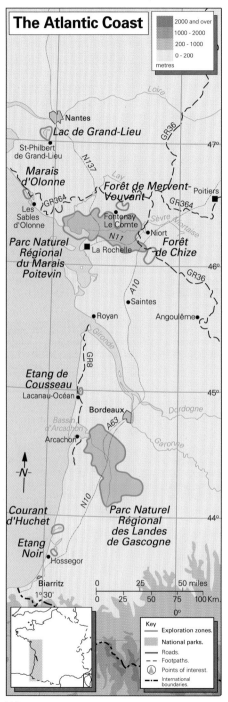

The Atlantic Coast

2000 and over
1000 - 2000
200 - 1000
0 - 200
metres

Loire
Nantes
Lac de Grand-Lieu
GR36
47°
St-Philbert
de Grand-Lieu
N137
Marais
d'Olonne
Lay
Forêt de Mervent-
Vouvant
Poitiers
GR364
Les
Sables
d'Olonne
GR364
Fontenay
Le Comte
Sèvre
Niortaise
Niort
Parc Naturel
Régional
du Marais
Poitevin
N11
La Rochelle
Forêt
de Chize
46°
GR36
A10
Saintes
Royan
Angoulême
Gironde
GR8
Etang de
Cousseau
Lacanau-Océan
45°
Bordeaux
Dordogne
Bassin
d'Arcachon
A63
Arcachon
Garonne
-N-
Courant
d'Huchet
N10
Parc Naturel
Régional
des Landes
de Gascogne
44°
Etang
Noir
Hossegor
Biarritz
0   25   50 miles
1°30'
0   25   50   75   100 Km.
0°

Key
— Exploration zones.
▨ National parks.
— Roads.
-- Footpaths.
Ⓐ Points of interest.
-∎- International
boundaries.

Lac de Grand-Lieu

Inland lake and nature reserve 15km (9 miles) southwest of Nantes

Long, conical black-tarred fish-traps fringe the edge of this inland lake. With a summer surface area of 4,000 hectares (9,900 acres), it is the fourth-largest lake in France; but when swollen by winter rains it expands to more than 6,000 hectares (14,800 acres), thus becoming the largest. Though Nantes is so close by, you feel yourself a thousand miles away from civilization, as a cold wind ruffles the water and herons pick their way through the shallows, stabbing their bills downwards as they hunt for the lake's abundant fish.

According to legend, the lake came into being to swallow up a town notorious for its evil ways; and on Christmas night Grand-Lieu fishermen have been known to hear the ghostly chimes of its underwater bells. More prosaically, it is on one of the main European migratory routes for huge numbers of wintering wildfowl, waders and raptors.

A simple glance at the figures indicates the richness and importance of this vibrant aquatic ecosystem; it supports the largest heronry in France, some years attaining 1,300 breeding pairs. Their numbers have prospered since the arrival of catfish in the lake, of which the local fishermen capture some 700 tonnes a year! Fortunately, there are some left for the local otters, although some otters fail to run the gauntlet of nets placed around the lake and become trapped. Other fish hunters commonly found here are purple herons, little bitterns, bitterns and little egret. Altogether some 226 bird species have been recorded, along with 43 species of mammals, 19 reptiles and amphibians and 19 fish.

With such a rich natural community it is hard to appreciate that the lake is slowly dying, but each year the marsh vegetation reaches out a little farther into the open water, while in turn the damp margins give

The Lac de Grand-Lieu supports an exceptional range of wildlife, including numerous waterfowl.

way to scrub and then woodland. Currently herons nest in sallows, which grow as floating forests on former reed beds, while in the drier forest the specialities are genet, honey buzzard and hobby. But once the open water disappears, choked under a blanket of waterlilies, reedmace and sedges, there will be nowhere for the specialized aquatic fauna to go.

As the reserve is so near Nantes, and thus more vulnerable than remoter places, general public access is not allowed. Fortunately, the local wildlife can be enjoyed from close to at the village of Passay, north of the lake's small 'metropolis' of St-Philbert. Passay is the home of the few remaining fishermen who eke out a living from the lake, and its small museum, the Maison du Pêcheur, gives the visitor a fascinating insight into how they lived in former years.

Behind the museum is an observatory equipped with powerful binoculars for studying the lake's birdlife; while television cameras connected to screens inside the observatory allow visitors to birdwatch in indoor comfort.

BEFORE YOU GO
Maps: Michelin 1:200,000 No. 67; IGN 1:100,000 No. 32.

GETTING THERE
By car: St-Philbert is on D117 halfway between Nantes and Machecoul. For Passay, head north on D65, then turn left on D62 in La Chevrolière. It is possible to drive around the periphery of the reserve on a series of minor roads. Clockwise from St-Philbert, these are: D61, D64, D264, D85 and D65.
By rail: nearest station is at Nantes.

By bus: buses from from Nantes to St-Philbert.

WHERE TO STAY
Auberge la Riviéra, St-Philbert-de-Grand-Lieu, T:40 78 70 32.
Outdoor living: La Boulogne, St-Philbert, T:40 78 88 79.

ACTIVITIES

Museum: St-Philbert's Musée Avifaune holds a varied collection of stuffed birds; open Apr–Sept 10–12 and 3–6.30.

Observatory: the observatory at Passay is open all year 10–12 and 3–6.30.

Riding: an equestrian centre at St-Philbert (T:40 31 07 62) organizes guided tours.

Sightseeing: lovers of ancient architecture should visit St-Philbert's magnificent C9th abbey church, in the town centre; regular concerts are held in summer.

FURTHER INFORMATION

Tourist information: St-Philbert-de-Grand-Lieu, pl de l'Abbatiale, T:40 78 73 88.

THE OTTER

At the turn of the century otters inhabited every *département* in mainland France outside Paris, and their numbers reached some 30–50,000. The latest full survey, published in 1986 by the French otter group, found this secretive mammal still common in only ten *départements*, mostly along the Atlantic coast. They consider that the 1986 population was between 500 and 1,000 animals, a more than 95% decrease since 1900.

To describe the habitat of the otter would be to list virtually all aquatic environments from mountain lakes to salt marsh, but today they are not necessarily found in their most favoured environment—slow-moving rivers—but rather in areas that have been least disturbed by modern development. For the otter is above all a shy creature, and many naturalists have done detailed research on the species without ever having seen one in the wild. Bearing in mind the otters' huge territorial areas—a male may patrol a 20–40-kilometre (15–25-mile) stretch of river—you can appreciate how fortunate you must be to see one.

Marais d'Olonne

Inland lake and bird sanctuary north of Les Sables-d'Olonne

In summer the roads radiating from the popular seaside resort of Les Sables-d'Olonne are choked with traffic; but few drivers take time out to relax in the bird sanctuary of L'Ileau, 7km (4 miles) north of town. The sanctuary has a small bird observatory beside the Marais d'Olonne, which ranks as one of the Atlantic coast's most important sites for watching both migrant and resident species.

The Marais is a long, narrow stretch of drained salt marsh, about 5km long by 1km (3 miles by half a mile) wide, separated from the sea by the pine woods of the Forêt d'Olonne. On hot summer afternoons you can stroll down to the dune-lined beach along any number of shady, resin-scented paths leading off the main coast road (D80). During the Middle Ages the "capital" of the area was at Olonne-sur-Mer, which then stood on the edge of a bay but is now a small village stranded 5km (3 miles) inland. As the sea retreated, the bay dried out, leaving behind a salt marsh lake, now in part neatly embanked, elsewhere choked with reeds and undergrowth.

The observatory, hardly more than a very large hide, is just outside the village of L'Ile-d'Olonne. From it you can look across the Marais and see an amazing variety of wetland birds, including France's largest colony of avocets. Other birds you can watch from the observatory include cormorants, egrets, herons, black-winged stilts, shelducks and, in autumn, large numbers of passage waders. August–September is a time of great avian activity, but the most impressive spectacle can be witnessed a little farther down the coast in summer when several thousand Manx shearwaters assemble offshore at the Plage de Sauveterre.

Before you go *Maps:* Michelin 1:200,000 No. 67; IGN 1:100,000 No. 32.

Getting there *By car:* take D32 north from Olonne-sur-Mer; after 2km (1 mile) turn left along D38 towards L'Ile-d'Olonne. The bird observatory (*Observatoire d'Oiseaux d'Eau*) is on the left before the village.

By rail: Les Sables-d'Olonne is a French Railways terminus; bicycle rental is available.

By bus: service from Les Sables-d'Olonne.

Where to stay: As a major seaside resort, Les Sables-d'Olonne has hotels and guesthouses of every category. They include the Chêne Vert (5 rue de la Bauduère, T:51 32 09 47) and Les Pins (43 av Briand, T:51 21 03 18).

Further information *Tourist information:* rue Général-Leclerc, Les Sables-d'Olonne, T:51 32 03 28.

Parc Naturel Régional du Marais Poitevin

Regional nature park covering 206,000ha (510,000 acres) of reclaimed estuary marsh, together with surrounding forested hills, inland from La Rochelle

The otter is an extremely rare sight in France, having disappeared from nearly all lowland rivers.

Off the windswept promontory of the Pointe d'Arçay the gulls wheel and scream, while far inland, on the tree-shaded canals of France's "Green Venice", flat-bottomed punts glide silently between fields yellow with buttercups. As great an environmental contrast as can be imagined—yet both coast and canals come under the protective umbrella of the Parc Naturel Régional du Marais Poitevin, which covers almost 2,000 square kilometres (800 square miles) of widely varied terrain. The park takes its name from the Marais Poitevin (literally "Marshland of Poitou"), in former centuries a huge bay stretching 50 kilometres (30 miles) inland, almost to the town of Niort. Since the Middle Ages the bay has been gradually reclaimed for agriculture.

The Marais has three main divisions: the eastern part, known as the *Venise Verte* or *Marais Mouillé* ("Wet Marshland"), which covers about 16,000 hectares (40,000 acres); the western part, mainly agricultural, known as the *Marais Desséché* ("Dried-out Marshland"); and the coast of the Anse de l'Aiguillon (bay of l'Aiguillon), which runs south from the small resort of La Faute-sur-Mer around to Esnandes, about seven kilometres (four miles) north of La Rochelle.

At the heart of the Marais is the "Green Venice", lying roughly between the villages of Coulon in the east and Maille in the west. Here the lower courses of the Autise, the Sèvre-Niortaise and a tangle of lesser streams are linked by canals large and small, dating back to the days when all transport in the Marais was waterborne.

As with Venice proper, the only way to see the Venise Verte is from the water—though here you do not glide past crumbling palaces and churches, but beneath a canopy of ash trees, willows and poplars, between fields where cream-coloured Charolais cattle graze among the buttercups. As you drift along, your punt (*plate*) brushes past reeds and yellow flag irises, and over a carpet of waterlilies. Fishermen line the banks, waiting patiently for a bite from the pike, tench, eels and carp that thrive in the muddy waters, while countless dragonflies dart and hover over the calm surface. The changeover from farming to tourism is highlighted by the abandoned condition of the smallest canals, which are largely silted up and overgrown now that they no longer have any practical purpose. These undisturbed backwaters are hiding places for polecats and beech martens, both highly secretive creatures.

I went out in a punt from the jetty—flatteringly called the Grand Port—below the pretty little town of Maillezais, within sight of one of the most beautiful ruined medieval abbeys in the whole of France. Our boatman was one of the last of the older generation still working on the canals of the Venise Verte, where vacationing students have largely taken over. He handled his punt-pole (*pigouille*) like a virtuoso. Apart from the swishing of the punt through the water, all we could hear was the sound of birdsong in the trees overhead, interrupted from time to time by the clanking of pedal-boats, the only form of mechanical trans-

149

port allowed on the canals.

Though I did not see a single wild mammal in the hour or so I spent on the water, the Marais Poitevin, and the Venise Verte in particular, is one of Europe's last strongholds for the otter, whose tracks can be seen from time to time in the mud. Though a protected species, otters here as elsewhere tend to fall victim to the traps and poisons put out for the ecologically far more harmful coypus and muskrats.

The Marais Desséché is at least three times as large as the Venise Verte; but since it is mainly agricultural, it is much less interesting from the wildlife and scenic point of view. You can cross it and never even realize you are in the *parc naturel*, as all you see are wide fields planted with wheat, fruit trees and *mojettes*, the local type of green bean.

The area has one small nature reserve, beside D25 just east of the village of St-Denis-du-Payré. Set up in 1976 on 200 hectares (500 acres) of pastureland, it has been allowed to revert to its natural condition, and all shooting is forbidden. The birdlife is nevertheless extremely vulnerable to hunting, however, even though there is a *réserve de chasse* that effectively extends the protected area to the south. Unfortunately, these two parcels are divided by a canal and dyke, the Chenal Vieux, along which hunting is still allowed, making it a real trap for any bird passing along the supposedly green corridor.

Despite this the site maintains an excellent flora and fauna. The wetter marshland is enlivened by several rare and spectacular flowers, such as the thrumwort, a floating annual with whorls of white flowers on leafless stalks, and the largest remaining colony in the region of the rare butterfly iris; in more brackish places are marsh mallows. In summer the pastures are dotted with the delicate pink spikes of pyramidal orchid and the unusual grey flowers of the lizard orchid. Among this botanical paradise is an

The marshland of the Venise Verte comprises a labyrinth of canals and streams which create a romantic world of dappled green light and lush waterways.

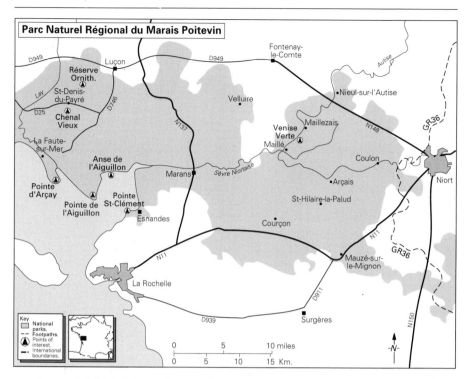

Parc Naturel Régional du Marais Poitevin

Key
- National parks.
- Footpaths.
- Points of interest.
- International boundaries.

0   5   10 miles
0   5   10   15 Km.

-N-

equally special bird fauna: the marshes resound to the reedy cries of some 50 pairs of black terns and the shriller notes of the rarer whiskered tern in summer, while on the pastures one can marvel at the intricate courtships of three of the most elegant wading birds — black-winged stilts, black-tailed godwit and ruff, the latter in its only site south of Brittany.

The third main subdivision of the Marais Poitevin consists of the coastline, which runs south from the resort of La Faute-sur-Mer, around the horseshoe of the Anse de l'Aiguillon (L'Aiguillon bay), to the Pointe St-Clément, a few kilometres north of La Rochelle. The sandbars and silt of the bay, fed by the rivers Lay and Sèvre-Niortaise, are a paradise for aquatic birds of all kinds — and an ideal environment for growing the mussels served in the local restaurants.

The best place to get away from everything except wildlife is along the eight-kilometre (five-mile) beach of the Pointe d'Arçay, south of La Faute-sur-Mer. The 152

whole of the tree-covered peninsula has been designated as a *réserve nationale de chasse*, which means that hunting is forbidden. Once you have walked a kilometre or so south of La Faute, you will find the magnificent beach deserted. Stranded cuttlefish, razor-shells, seaweed and the inevitable plastic bottles mark the tideline. Flocks of sandpipers scuttle busily about the sand in search of food, while buzzards float lazily above the pine woods.

L'Aiguillon bay forms a large "C" between two prominent headlands, the Pointe de l'Aiguillon and the Pointe St-Clément. At low tide it is almost empty of water, and its muddy expanse attracts almost every kind of wading bird. Species that winter here in their thousands include knots, dunlins, redshanks, black-tailed godwits and Brent geese. Indeed, it is claimed to be the most important site in France in terms of wading birds, and the 5,000 wintering avocets is the second-largest concentration in Europe.

South of the bay, beyond Esnandes, the

coast road runs below a low cliff that marks the ancient shoreline of the *Lacus Duorum Corvorum* "Lake of the Two Ravens", as the Romans called L'Aiguillon bay. In Esnandes itself it is well worth visiting the Musée de la Mytiliculture (Museum of Mussel-growing), where you can find out about the natural history and cultivation of this coast's main edible product. Out at the Pointe St-Clément you can see where mussel cultivation is carried out. Off the headland itself and far out into the shallows are acres of black stakes (*bouchots*) driven into the mud, which are festooned with ropes and on which the mussels grow coiled spirally around.

BEFORE YOU GO
Maps: Michelin 1:200,000 Nos. 67 and 71; IGN 1:100,000 Nos. 33, 39 and 40. The *parc naturel* also publishes its own 1:135,000 map that marks places of interest (not always accurately), and gives addresses and phone numbers of local tourist offices.
Guidebook: J.-L. Eulin and E. Rousseaux, *La Nature dans le Marais Poitevin* (Ouest-France).

GETTING THERE
By car: the *parc naturel* is roughly bounded on the north by D949/N148 from Les Sables-d'Olonne to Niort; east by N150 from Niort to St-Jean-d'Angély; and south by D939 from St-Jean-d'Angély via Surgères to La Rochelle. N11 cuts across its centre.
By rail: main stations are at Luçon, Fontenay-le-Comte, Niort, Surgères and La Rochelle. Car rental is available at Niort, Surgères and La Rochelle, bicycle rental at Niort and La Rochelle.
By bus: regular bus services run between main towns, but between villages and on minor roads are non-existent or erratic.

WHERE TO STAY
Most people visiting the Marais Poitevin want to stay in the Venise Verte, but there are not many hotels here, apart from 2 Logis de France, in Maillezais (St-Nicolas, rue

du Dr-Daroux, T:51 00 74 45) and Coulon (Au Marais, 48 quai Tardy, T:49 35 90 43). Surrounding towns (Luçon, Fontenay, Niort, Surgères) offer a wider choice, as do L'Aiguillon-sur-Mer and other seaside resorts. During summer, book in advance; if you arrive without a booking go to La Rochelle, which has numerous hotels and *pensions*.

ACTIVITIES
The Club du Marais Sauvage, at St-Hilaire-le-Palud (T:49 35 33 09), runs a horse-riding scheme called *Rencontres de l'Eau et du Cheval* ("Where Horse and Water Meet"). The club also rents out bicycles, boats and canoes. From Apr–Sept you can rent horse-drawn gypsy-style caravans (*roulottes*) to explore the park.
Guided tours: minibus tours of the Venise Verte are available from La Répentie de Magne, Coulon, T:49 35 02 29. Canal trips are organized from Coulon (the main centre), Arçais, Maillezais, St-Hilaire-le-Palud and several other villages.
Museums: at Nieul-sur-l'Autise, the old village watermill has been restored as the centrepiece of the Maison de la Meunerie (Milling Museum), open July–Aug, daily exc Sun and Mon mornings 10.30–6.30; May–June and Sept–Oct, Sat 10.30–6.30, Sun 2.30–6.30. The Musée de la Mytiliculture (Museum of Mussel-growing)

in Esnandes is open mid-June–mid-Sept, Tues–Sat 10–12.30 and 2.30–7, Sun 2.30–7; mid-Sept–mid-June Mon–Fri 2–6.
Walking: La Faute-sur-Mer has a 13-km (8-mile) waymarked forest walk.

FURTHER INFORMATION
Tourist information: L'Aiguillon-sur-Mer, T:51 56 43 87; Coulon, pl de l'Eglise, T:49 35 99 29; Esnandes, T:46 01 34 64; La Rochelle, 10 rue Fleuriau, T:46 41 14 68.
Parc Naturel Régional du Marais Poitevin, Maison du Parc, La Ronde, Courçon, T:46 27 82 44.

The rare lizard orchid (left) and more common bee orchid (right) are both found amongst the sand dunes of the Atlantic coast.

Forêt de Mervent-Vouvant

Small forest north of Fontenay-le-Comte, included in the Parc Naturel Régional du Marais Poitevin

Apart from its three main habitat types—the Venise Verte, the Marais Desséché and the coastline—the Parc Naturel Régional du Marais Poitevin includes its peripheral forested hills (*massifs forestiers*). In spite of its small size, the Forêt de Mervent-Vouvant is easily the most varied.

This crescent of forest, on a granite plateau, is hardly more than 16km (10 miles) across, yet in its limited area you will find deep tree-covered ravines, a reservoir and wide clearings that in spring are full of spiky pink asphodel and yellow-flowered broom. Its trees include beech, oak, hornbeam and chestnut. In summer the ground below the trees is rich in edible fungi, much prized by local gourmets.

In the 1950s a dam (the Barrage de Mervent) was built across the River Vendée to provide fresh water for the nearby town of Fontenay-le-Comte. The reservoir and the streams that drain into it are full of carp, pike, eel and bream; while frogs (including the edible variety) and toads breed in the shallows. Birds include kingfishers, black kites, two rare varieties of

magpie, and the even rarer short-toed eagle, which feeds on mostly snakes and lizards. Among the mammals are badgers, roe deer and pine martens; and a few wild boar are said to lurk in its depths.
Before you go *Maps:* Michelin 1:200,000 No. 71; IGN 1:100,000 No. 33.
Getting there *By car:* from Nantes, take N137 as far as Ste-Hermine, then turn left on N148 to Fontenay-le-Comte. The forest begins 6km (4 miles) north of Fontenay, on D938.
By rail: Fontenay is at the end of a branch line from Niort.
By bus: local services run from Fontenay to the small town of Mervent in the middle of the forest, and Vouvant at its northern end.
Where to stay: Ermitage de Pierre-Brune, Mervent, T:51 00 25 53;
Activities: cycling in the forest is for the fit, as roads are mainly very steep. Horse-riding excursions are available from main centres.
Further information *Tourist information:* Fontenay-le-Comte, quai Poey-d'Avant, T:51 69 44 99.
Parc Naturel Régional du Marais Poitevin, Maison du Parc, La Ronde, Courçon, T:46 27 82 44.

Forêt de Chizé

Forest park of 10,000ha (25,000 acres), run by the Parc Naturel Régional du Marais Poitevin

Lying southeast of the Marais Poitevin, this magnificent stretch of woodland, mainly

oak and beech, is the remnant of the vast Forêt d'Argenson that once covered the whole region. It is dotted with small villages, while frequent open glades among the trees make it a delightfully varied place for the walker. In the northern section is a large fenced-off *réserve nationale de chasse*, where all hunting is forbidden.

The Chizé forest marks the transition between northern and Mediterranean tree types, with beech growing alongside Montpellier maple. Among its tree curiosities is an extraordinary oak tree down a track just north of the village of Chizé. Known as *Les Sept Chênes* ("Seven Oaks"), it is not in fact seven trees, but a single oak with seven trunks growing from a single base.

The mammals that breed in the reserve include roe deer, badger, marten, wild boar and dormouse. But what most people come to Chizé to see is not wild but captive—the *baudet de Poitou* (Poitou donkey). This animal, much taller and hairier than an ordinary donkey, has a shaggy, dark brown coat and a large and lugubrious head that would make the ideal model for Bottom in Shakespeare's *A Midsummer Night's Dream*. Male *baudets* are crossed with Poitou mares to produce a large and powerful type of mule. From the Middle Ages until tractors took over in the 1950s the Poitou mules were used on farms in the region, but with the coming of total mechanization the breed was in danger of extinction.

Outside the village of Dampierre-sur-Boutonne, on the fringe of Chizé forest, a remote and peaceful farm (La Tillauderie) is now run as the Asinerie Nationale (National Donkey Centre). Here *baudet*

The wooded slopes and deep ravines of the Forêt de Mervent-Vouvant harbour an outstanding range of animals, birds and plants.

stallions are kept for stud in their stable, while offspring of all shapes, sizes and degrees of hairiness frisk about in a large open meadow.
Before you go *Maps:* Michelin 1:200,000 No. 71; IGN 1:100,000 No. 39.
Getting there *By car:* from Niort, head south along N150 for 17km (10 miles) to Beauvoir-sur-Niort, then turn east into the forest along D1. For long-distance travellers, the Paris–Bordeaux A10 skirts the forest's western edge.
By rail: Niort is on the Poitiers–La Rochelle line, and has facilities for car and bicycle rental.
By bus: local buses run from Niort to Virollet, Chizé and the other main forest villages.
Where to stay: Hôtel Terminus, Niort, T:49 24 00 38. Auberge des Cèdres, Villiers-en-Bois, Beauvoir-sur-Niort, T:49 09 60 53.
Activities: Horse-riding in the forest, walking on waymarked tracks. The National Donkey Centre is open all year.
Further information: Parc Naturel Régional du Marais Poitevin, Maison du Parc, La Ronde, Courçon, T:46 27 82 44.

Etang de Cousseau

A secluded lake and nature reserve, between the larger lakes of Hourtin and Lacanau

The small resort of Lacanau-Océan is less than 65km (40 miles) from the centre of Bordeaux, and on fine summer weekends cars crawl bumper-to-bumper out of the city to get to the sea here.
156

Yet hardly more than 8km (5 miles) away is one of the most peaceful and remote nature reserves on the entire Atlantic coast—the Etang de Cousseau, a small link in the chain of lakes that runs down the length of Les Landes a few miles inland.
   The lake is reached along a forest path easy to follow as it consists of a narrow strip of concrete laid for cyclists. It runs first below tall pine trees, some of which are scarred with the long gashes cut in their bark by resin collectors. Beyond the trees it crosses a clear-felled expanse, where plants that have colonized the ground in succession to the pines include seedling oaks,

heather, gorse, rock-rose and scabious.
   After about half an hour's walking you reach the reserve proper, where ground cover is mainly dead leaves and sand beneath an arching canopy of holly, pine and evergreen oak. The path drops down to a clearing beside the *étang* where you can look across the water to the reeds and sedges of the Marais de Talaris on the other side.
   The reserve itself, which covers some 600ha (1,480 acres), comprises three principal habitats: the mixed oak woods on the former dunes to the west; the open waters of the shallow *étang*; and, most importantly, the extensive reed beds of the

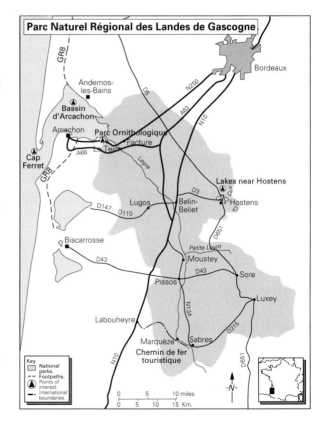

Parc Naturel Régional des Landes de Gascogne

Marais de Talaris, which includes a strong colony of the great fen sedge and some giant specimens of the imposing royal fern. A large part of the water surface of the *étang* in summer becomes speckled with the white and yellow flowers of waterlilies, while underneath grow a couple of species of the delicate and now quite rare bladderwort. Among this verdant growth live several pond terrapins and a few otters, the latter dieting sumptuously on some of the uncommon fish which inhabit the lake.

Before you go *Maps:* Michelin 1:200,000 No. 71; IGN 1:100,000 No. 46.
Getting there *By car:* take D6 from Lacanau to Lacanau-Océan. In the hamlet of Le Huga, 1km (½ mile) east of Lacanau-Océan, take D6E, which runs north to D207. The path to Cousseau begins at a verge beside D6E.
By rail: the nearest station is at Bordeaux.
By bus: buses connecting with the train at Bordeaux run between Lacanau-Océan and Lacanau.
Where to stay: Etoile d'Argent, Lacanau-Océan,

T:56 03 21 07. Hôtel de l'Océan, Carcans-Océan, T:56 60 31 13.
Outdoor living: there are numerous campsites on the coast and around the Etang de Lacanau.
Activities *Walking and cycling:* the Lacanau-Océan tourist office (see below) will supply a map showing the footpaths and cycle-tracks in and around the Lac de Lacanau. Guided walks to the Cousseau reserve start at 10am on Wed in summer.
Further information *Tourist information:* Lacanau-Océan, T:56 03 21 01.

Parc Naturel Régional des Landes de Gascogne

Regional nature park southwest of Bordeaux, covering 206,000ha (half a million acres) of pine forest

Although this huge park is almost exactly the same size as the Marais Poitevin, it would be hard to imagine two similar-sized areas with greater differences. While the latter is infinitely varied, the Landes de Gascogne park is virtually homogeneous. Apart from a short stretch of coast on the Bay of Arcachon, it consists of seemingly endless forest, broken here and there by large agricultural clearings where crops such as asparagus are grown. Villages are often as much as 16 kilometres (10 miles) apart, which is unusual in France, where three or four kilometres is the average. Except for a small man-made lake at Hostens it does not include any of the wide stretches of water that break the monotony of the rest of Les Landes.

For centuries this was a region of large-scale sheep-farming, where shepherds on

stilts followed their flocks over the flat, treeless grazing lands. All this changed in the 19th century, with the extensive planting of maritime pines, exploited for the products made from their resin. By the 1950s the resin industry had virtually disappeared, though you will still see trees with resin oozing slowly from gashes in their bark.

Through the centre of the park runs the River Leyre, whose two branches—the Grande and Petite Leyre—meet at the village of Moustey. Fringed by alders, oaks and chestnuts, it was formerly the region's main transport artery, though nowadays it

The Aleppo and stone pines (left and right) are the principal pine species of the region, each creating its own distinct vegetation community.

157

is used only by canoeists and fishermen. Most of the villages are built along its banks, like water-cooled oases in the hot monotony of the countryside. Largest of these is the double village of Belin-Béliet, where park authorities have their headquarters in the old town hall opposite the southernmost church.

For the wildlife enthusiast, the park has only one centre of outstanding interest, the magnificent bird reserve on the coast of Le Teich, east of Arcachon. Elsewhere the variety of environment is as limited as you would expect from hundreds of square kilometres of conifers planted on soil that is little more than sand, with virtually no undergrowth to provide food and shelter for mammals and birds. Despite this apparent sparsity of life and the unnatural origins of the forest, nature has managed to reassert itself and there are a good number of wild creatures such as boar, hare, fox and introduced deer somewhere out there in the vastness of the forest. Keep to the edges, where sunlight penetrates to the ground and allows the natural flora to develop, much to the benefit of the huge variety of insects for which this area is noted.

The Le Teich bird reserve, on the southern side of Arcachon bay, is easy to find, signposted by the church in the middle of Le Teich, Arcachon's easternmost

The white stork is one of the most conspicuous birds of the Le Teich reserve, with its habit of building large nests on man-made structures.

suburb. Completely protected on all sides, with a single narrow entrance guarded by the arm of Cap Ferret, the tidal mud flats of the triangular bay attract some 280 bird species each year; about 200 are migratory, while 80 nest and breed here.

Set up in 1972, the reserve covers 120 hectares (300 acres), and is laid out to cater for different degrees of birdwatching enthusiasm. Nearest the entrance are enclosures for such exotic species as emus and golden pheasants, together with a "hospital" aviary where birds of prey, wounded by hunters outside the reserve, are looked after before being returned to the wild. Just beyond, nesting platforms at treetop level have been set up for families of storks.

Beyond the storks is the reserve proper, which extends out into the bay via a broad causeway, protected on either side by hedges. Spaced along it are ten hides; from the first you can look across a narrow stretch

The dense canopy of the planted forest of Les Landes prohibits luxuriant undergrowth, but numerous insects thrive in the flora of the forest margins.

of water to a massive heronry, with dozens of nests in the trees, and herons and egrets probing the shallows for food. Other hides give similar views of spoonbills, cormorants, swans, geese, teal, mallard and dozens of other species. Fish such as eels and bass are bred and reared in the brackish water that covers much of the reserve.

BEFORE YOU GO
Maps: Michelin 1:200,000 No. 78; IGN 1:100,000 Nos. 46, 55 and 62.

GETTING THERE
By car: the park covers too large an area to have a single access point. From Bordeaux, you can reach its headquarters at Belin-Béliet either by A63 or N10, the latter allowing a far better view of the Landes countryside.
By rail: main-line stations are at Bordeaux and Arcachon. There is also a ruler-straight branch line from Facture on the Arcachon line down to Dax, passing the western side of the park. Car and bicycle rental is available at Bordeaux and Arcachon.
By bus: there are infrequent bus services throughout the park, but the places to see do not necessarily have bus connections and are so scattered that bus travel between them is not a practical proposition.

WHERE TO STAY
Auberge des Pins, Sabres, T:58 07 50 47; La Bonne Auberge, Lugos, Belin-Béliet, T:56 88 02 05. Further afield, there are hotels and *pensions* of every grade in the resorts around Arcachon Bay (Cap Ferret, Andernos, Arcachon) and down the coast at Biscarosse.
Outdoor living: at Le Teich, Camping du Parc, T:56 22 62 36.

ACTIVITIES
Cycling: tourist offices supply a leaflet (*Landes Itinéraires Cyclo*) with 25 recommended

circuits covering the whole of the Landes, including a 329-km (205-mile) circuit of the park.
Riding: there are 6 equestrian centres scattered throughout the park; addresses and phone numbers in *Guide Pratique* available from park headquarters at Belin-Béliet
Walking: there is a marked nature trail by the village of Hostens that winds through landscape ranging from open heath to mangrove swamp.
Watersports: canoeing and fishing on the Leyre.

FURTHER INFORMATION
Tourist information:
Préfecture des Landes, Mont-de-Marsan, T:58 46 40 40.
Vallée de la Leyre, for main park villages (Sabres and Pissos), T:58 07 70 23.
Information on the park and its activities from: Parc Naturel Régional des Landes de Gascogne, pl de l'Eglise, Belin-Béliet, T:56 88 06 06. Le Teich Bird Reserve, T:56 22 84 89. Office National des Forêts, Secteur d'Hostens, Maison Départementale, Hostens, T:56 88 54 85.

Courant d'Huchet

An 8-km (5-mile) watercourse and nature reserve of great scenic diversity between Lac de Léon and the sea

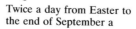

Twice a day from Easter to the end of September a

flotilla of small rowing boats sets out across the wide Lac de Léon for a trip down one of the natural wonders of the Atlantic coast. As they glide down the Huchet Current—not a proper river but a channel for the overflow water from the lake—they pass through several different *biotopes*, or types of environment, marked by striking changes in terrain and vegetation.

The Courant begins its seaward journey at a stretch of reed-covered marshland, fringed by willows and alders, on the southern side of the lake. Known as the Cout de Mountagne, it covers about 140ha (350 acres). Until the 1960s the marsh vegetation was kept in check by the cattle which browsed around its edges, but since their disappearance the reeds have grown unchecked, though areas have been cleared to provide open water for ducks, moorhens, herons and other waterbirds.

Beyond the marsh, the Courant runs under an arcade of willows and alders, past the giant fronds of royal ferns, lady ferns and a host of exotic plants such as the Brazilian water-milfoil and the rosy hibiscus. Strangest of all are the bulbous pneumatophores (aerial roots) of the rough-barked Arizona cypress growing in the shallows. Downstream, near the little seaside resort of Huchet-Plage, the tree canopy opens out into a small lake (Marais de la Pipe), where young eels that have swum thousands of miles across the Atlantic from the Sargasso Sea feed on the rich growth of plankton.

The fauna would also be impressive were it not for the prevalence of hunting. Both otter and genet occur here, but do not receive any formal protection which, on top of their natural shyness, means they are only rarely sighted. Members of the heron family are not hunted, and both night heron and bitterns are found in the marshy areas; but much the most likely encounter for the waterborne visitor will be the vivid flash of azure blue as a kingfisher darts along the river.

From the Marais the Courant meanders south, protected from the Atlantic by a wide sand bar, and reaches the sea near Moliets-Plage. The dunes at Moliets were stabilized as long ago as 1832 by dumping loads of clay on the shifting sand, which was then planted with marram grass. The feet of today's holidaymakers, however, are now endangering this fragile ground cover.

Before you go *Maps:* Michelin 1:200,000 No. 78; IGN 1:100,000 No. 62.

Getting there *By car:* take N10 to Castets, then D142 to Léon, following signposts to Lac de Léon. Boat trips down the Courant d'Huchet start from the beach.

By rail: the nearest station is at Dax, 30km (18 miles) away.

By bus: an infrequent service operates to Léon from Soustons.

Where to stay: Côte d'Argent, Vieux-Boucau, T:58 48 13 17. Hôtel du Centre, Messanges, T:58 48 12 08.

Outdoor living: there are campsites beside the lake (Lou Puntanou) and at Moliets-Plage (Les Cigales).

Further information *Tourist information:* Castets, T:58 89 40 09; Vieux-Boucau, T:58 48 13 47.

A New World exotic, the swamp cypress has now adapted to wet woodland habitats in Europe.

To book boat trips, normally done in advance, contact Bureau des Bateliers, Lac de Léon, Léon, T:58 48 75 39.

Etang Noir

Tiny marshland and lakeside nature reserve

This magical little reserve, in parts like a miniature humid jungle, forms a small tailpiece to the larger and more spectacular wildlife centres of the Atlantic coast. Just outside the village of Seignosse, it consists of a wooden walkway over a tract of marshland that seems like a primeval swamp—though you can hear the occasional car passing only a few hundred yards away. The walkway, which runs about a metre above the ground, leads first to a viewing platform looking across a small lake, then over a tangle of roots, decaying vegetation, yellow irises and reeds, where frogs croak and tadpoles flicker and bubble in the stagnant pools between the trees.

For all the botanical interest of this reserve (it has over 430 plant species listed, including many rare sorts of mosses, ferns, algae and aquatic microflora) the actual reason for the site being classified is its population of "monster" frogs. The resident edible frogs of this *étang* suffer from a genetic mutation, whose effects range from an extra toe to a complete realignment of the skeletal system in both pairs of limbs.

Before you go *Maps:* Michelin 1:200,000 No. 78; IGN 1:100,000 No. 62.

Getting there *By car:* leave N10 at St-Vincent-de-Tyrosse, 22km (14 miles) west of Dax and take D112 to Seignosse. The Etang Noir is just north of the village.

By rail: the nearest station is at St-Vincent-de-Tyrosse.

By bus: there is a service to Seignosse from Hossegor.

Where to stay: Les Hélianthes, Hossegor, T:58 43 52 19. L'Océan, Capbreton, T:58 72 10 22.

Further information *Tourist information:* Seignosse, T:58 43 32 15.

The Eastern Mediterranean and Corsica

My first day in Provence was memorable. I arrived at the Natural History Museum in the quaint old part of Aix, expecting to stretch my basic French to the limit in interrogating the country's leading expert on the natural ways of tortoises. He had other plans, however, and no sooner had we said *bonjour* than I was whisked off on a hair-raising car dash to catch a ferry for the island of Porquerolles, just off the coast near Toulon. By mid-afternoon he was trying to teach me the art of lassoing wall lizards by creeping up slowly behind them on all fours and dangling a noose of cotton thread around their necks, so they could be yanked clear from cover. Having laboured a good few hours in the heat to capture some specimens, my colleague measured each one with great precision and then took a photograph of their undersides, explaining that he was studying variations in island populations on the basis of differences in size and belly patterns.

Of course, I had no right to think this bizarre. Why should it only be English naturalists who get involved with minute studies on some rather esoteric subject? It was simply that I had not expected Provence to be such a hotbed of ecological research, and it felt even more out of place as we returned to base past shoals of bronzing tourists, baring as much as they dared, along one of the island's fine sandy beaches.

Rugged massifs and low oak scrub dominate the Provençal landscape above the Gorges du Verdon. This spectacular limestone canyon marks the meeting-point of Mediterranean France and the Alps.

I did eventually get taken to see the tortoise area in the Massif des Maures my colleague had promised me. The countryside was incredibly lush and green, and there on a damp, drizzly, and very un-Mediterranean Sunday afternoon, I saw my first wild French tortoise, resting motionless underneath a tree heather shrub. At this my colleague felt he had done his job so he took his leave. I did not feel up to negotiating accommodation in the nearby village so I camped out in an old stone barn on the edge of a vineyard. As darkness fell the sombre forest came to life. The nightingales became more obviously vocal, a background chorus of tree frogs took up their cue and in the dim distance a nightjar commenced its churring call. A bit nearer, another low but penetrating sound became noticeable — a scops owl calling from a telegraph pole along the roadside; I felt a million miles from home.

My original purpose in going to the Massif des Maures was not simply to see tortoises but to study them as part of a research project for the University of Kent. All this was incomprehensible to the local people of the tiny village I chose as my base; but they were admirable hosts and although I arrived unannounced they quickly resolved my accommodation problems. The mayor said I could live in the château! It was a large, abandoned house with few amenities but, set apart from the village among its own olive groves and flanked by three enormous stone pines, my new home was a naturalist's paradise.

Early every morning a flock of golden orioles would do a tour of the village and visit my pine trees. I shared the château with swifts, swallows and martins, and in the evenings I often had a Moorish gecko for company; sometimes skulking furtively in some nook or cranny, other times out in the open clinging to the ceiling. I could sit on the balcony and admire a nuthatch despatching another pine kernel, or across the olive grove I might spy a redbacked shrike, or even a hoopoe.

But I had to track down some tortoises. After a week of stomping through dense, thorny scrub I had only found a dozen or so animals — hardly the stuff of great research. Once again the locals came to my rescue, and herein lies a cautionary message about putting too much store in the experts.

An old lady who had spent her whole life working in the fields and orchards around the village advised me to take a walk beyond the back of the village — exactly the opposite direction from that advised in the scientific literature. Following her directions I climbed through a dense forest of sweet chestnuts, slipping frequently and wondering how on earth tortoises were supposed to cope with such gradients. Eventually the slope levelled off and I emerged from the forest into a small clearing where I stood transfixed. In front of me was a neatly tended olive grove, set out on terraces carved from the forested hillside and retained by dry stone walls. Beyond, the hills stretched for miles, covered with an uninterrupted expanse of dense evergreen forest. Surely this was ancient Provence.

A rustling sound caught my attention. Only an arm's length away, yet hidden under the tall herbage, two creatures were in earnest pursuit, oblivious to my presence. A sudden, dull and twice-repeated thudding sound followed by a thin, desperate squeaking confirmed it was a pair of tortoises in frantic courtship, well before they came into view in a more open patch of the clearing. The image of a tortoise as a free-living wild animal does not come easily to people used to them simply as sluggish garden pets. But here they were in their natural element re-enacting a ritual evolved over tens of millions of years, and showing a turn of speed and vitality unimaginable to anyone who has never witnessed them in the wild.

A slight movement in the corner of my eye made me look up. At the same instant a large Montpellier snake, all of two metres (6½ feet) long and thick as an arm, froze rigid and fixed me with its penetrating gaze. It was halfway down the terrace wall, a couple of metres in front of me. The head was arched up slightly, pointing in my direction, its heavy brow ridges emphasizing its menacing expression. Remaining motionless, I studied its minutest details, but it was those large yellow eyes holding my gaze that focused my attention; the stare of a truly wild animal alert to all dangers. Strange as it may seem, I was the threat, not the snake, a true denizen of this ancient world into which I had stepped uninvited.

Reptiles are not the only exciting creatures of the Mediterranean forest, but for me they represent that special element of primitive wildness and the exotic which gives this area such a feeling of being untamed and remote while

The liquid call of bee-eaters, high in the Provençal sky, is one of the memorable sounds of summer.

at the same time being civilization that you sense its vulnerability. The fact that such wilderness might so easily be lost reinforces one's appreciation of its existence and admiration for its flora and fauna, which have survived unaided for so long.

The last wild lands of Mediterranean France, with their mantle of thorny *maquis* and evergreen forest, their abundance of wildflowers, large insects in all shapes and livid hues, birds and reptiles, are an essential part of Europe's natural heritage. It is a wildlife that has coexisted with generations of Provençal man for thousands of years, and to enter these forests is to encounter a living history book of one of Europe's oldest landscapes.

GETTING THERE
By air: the region's main airport is Nice-Côte d'Azur (T:93 21 30 30), which is France's 2nd busiest, with direct flights from 35 countries. Corsica receives daily internal flights from Paris to Ajaccio, Bastia, Calvi and Figari.
By car: the A8 *autoroute*, La Provençale, crosses the Riviera from Aix-en-Provence to the Italian border at

Menton. A52 branches off at Aix for Toulon. A50 runs along the coast from Marseille to Toulon, as does N559, which then continues as N98 through all the coastal resorts to the Italian border. This is a very scenic drive but extremely busy June–Sept. On Corsica, there are 2 main north–south roads: the east coast D81 is flatter and easier than the central route (N197/ 193 and D69), which offers

exceptionally dramatic views but is often torturously steep and twisting.
By rail: SCNF (French Railways) operate regular services from Paris to the Riviera coast, including the high-speed TGV which takes 5hrs to Marseille or 7hrs to Nice. Year-round Motorail services run daily from Paris and Calais to Nice and Toulon overnight, and to Marseille by day, with

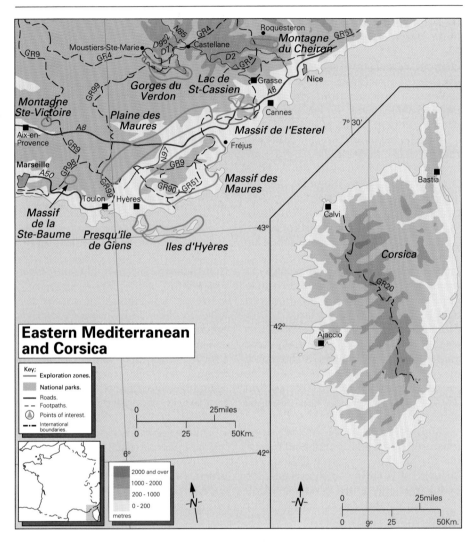

Eastern Mediterranean and Corsica

Key;
— Exploration zones.
▨ National parks.
— Roads.
-- Footpaths.
ⓐ Points of interest.
-·- International boundaries.

2000 and over
1000 - 2000
200 - 1000
0 - 200
metres

-N-

-N-

0   25miles
0   25   50Km.

additional services from the Channel ports to Fréjus and St-Raphaël May–Sept. All major towns are well served by coastal train services. On Corsica, a train links Ajaccio and Bastia.
By bus: long-distance services operate to Nice from Geneva, Madrid, Brussels and London. Most towns have local services. Timetables are available from the main bus station in Nice, or, in Corsica, 166

from local tourist offices.
By sea: there are ferries to Corsica from Marseille (5–10hrs), Nice and Toulon; these operate daily in summer, twice-weekly at other times.

WHERE TO STAY
As you'd expect, the French Riviera has no shortage of hotels, inns, hostels, *gîtes ruraux*, apartments and campsites. Reservations are

essential in the peak summer season, and expect to pay top prices since the area ranks as the most expensive in France. For a small fee, you can book accommodation through Accueil de France tourist offices in Cannes (T:93 99 19 77), Marseille (T:91 48 34 64), Nice (T:93 87 07 07), Toulon (T:94 22 08 22), and Ajaccio, 24 blvd Dominique-Paoli, T:95 22 70 79.

Outdoor living: many towns have a municipal campsite, though facilities may not be as sophisticated as at privately owned ones. During July–Aug it is advisable to reserve in advance.

ACTIVITIES

Walking and climbing: walking and mountaineering are both rewarding, as the hills behind the coast are spectacular, if strenuous. They are best tackled in the cooler months or in the early morning or evening during summer. An increasing number of footpaths and walking itineraries are being developed in Corsica; local tourist offices have details. The Parc Naturel Régional de la Corse, based at 4 rue Fioella, Ajaccio, also has brochures with marked trails.

Cycling: bicycles are available at railway stations, campsites and cycle shops, though most routes are hilly and the roads by the coast are often crowded.

Watersports: sailing and windsurfing are popular sports on the Mediterranean and the lakes, and windsurfers are easily obtainable at beaches all along the coast. Yachts and motorboats can be rented, with or without crew, at main harbours, including Cannes, Nice, Toulon; on Corsica at Ajaccio, Calvi and Bonifacio. Corsica also has numerous diving clubs.

FURTHER INFORMATION

Tourist information: every town and many villages have *syndicats d'initiative* (tourist information centres). Major regional offices are: Comité Régional du Tourisme Riviera-Côte d'Azur, 55 promenade des Anglais, Nice, T:93 44 50 59; Agence Régionale Tourisme et Loisirs (ARTL), rue Henri-Barbusse, Marseille, T:91 08 62 90; ARTL, 22 cours Grandval, Ajaccio, T:95 51 00 22.

FURTHER READING

Corsica: a Traveller's Guide (Lowe/Murray); Michel Fabrikant, *Guide des Montagnes Corses* (published in Ste-Lucie-de-Porto-Vecchio); Cathérine & Bernard Desieux, *Les Parcs Naturels Régionaux de France* (Créer); *Guide de la Nature en France* (Bordas); *Footpaths of Europe Series: Walks in Provence* (Robertson McCarta).

A dense layer of bracken carpets the cork oak forest on the slopes of the Massif des Maures.

Massif des Maures and the Maures Plain

Imposing headlands and rugged openland dominating the coast between Toulon and Fréjus

To my mind, the best examples of wilderness in Mediterranean France are the Massif des Maures and the Maures Plain. The Massif des Maures is particularly impressive. Although not attaining great altitudes (La Sauvette at 779 metres/2,557 feet marks the highest point), it presents a formidable dark wall to anyone approaching across the open plain on the northern side, or glancing across from the A8 *autoroute* or main rail line between Toulon and Fréjus. On the seaward side the massif appears equally steep and imposing and provides an impressive backdrop to some of the most attractive of the Riviera towns:

Hermann's tortoise, the most famous reptile of the Massif des Maures, can measure up to 20cm and rarely weighs more than one kilo.

Bormes-les Mimosas, Le Lavandou, Cavalaire-sur-Mer and St-Maxime. Around the edge are many small towns, but in the interior you would think yourself many miles from civilization among some of the country's most rugged hills and dense evergreen forest and *maquis*.

The Maures owe their name to this dark mantle of evergreen forest; the name is derived from an old Provençal word meaning "the dark massif". This sombre landscape bursts into colour for a few weeks in spring, first with the delicate blossoms of the tree heather, which are soon followed by masses of white, yellow, and blue from rock-roses, broom and lavender.

By midsummer the daytime heat becomes debilitating and the rolling expanse of *maquis* can seem empty, save for the incessant chirping of innumerable grasshoppers and crickets, the most notable being the famous *cigale* (cicada), a large beast reaching a good $7\frac{1}{2}$ centimetres (three inches) in length and capable of a strong and sustained rasping noise as it calls from a perch high up a maritime pine.

There are innumerable narrow tracks which head off into the bush. Many are made by hunters and are therefore only ever used during the autumn and winter. Others, though, are made by the hunters' usual quarry, the wild boar. These are truly wild creatures and extremely wary of approaching danger. To glimpse one would be a real red-letter day.

The Maures and its sister massif, the Esterel, are composed of siliceous rocks, and as such they possess a very distinctive vegetation in complete contrast to the limestone flora of the massifs to the west. The most characteristic feature of these massifs is the cork oak, which forms extensive forests on the lower slopes, generally from below the 300-metre (1,000-foot) level. The forest provides shade from the intense summer heat, and here, too, much of the area's wildlife makes its home. This is the last stronghold for Hermann's tortoise in France.

Some of the most rewarding places for birdwatching are on the low slopes near villages, such as Collobrières, Plan-de-la-Tour or La Môle, where the cork oak forests merge with great stands of ancient sweet chestnuts, and small vegetable plots and olive groves have been maintained in woodland clearings. Serins, cirl buntings and golden orioles are constantly calling from their treetop perches and the forests hold green, great and lesser spotted woodpeckers as well as nuthatches and jays. The old olive groves and the grassy clearings are the best hunting grounds for botanists and butterfly enthusiasts. For those with less stamina, the chestnuts offer even cooler shade than the oaks, though their dense foliage blocks out more light, so the undergrowth is less well developed. Still this is a good place to look for the delicate flowers of the Provence orchid (*Orchis provincialis*), and wall lizards thrive here.

Exploring the Massif des Maures is simple. There are no sites of special note, the whole range of hills is consistently good. For most people their closest and most impressive encounter with the Maures is the high, red cliff face known as the Rocher de Roquebrune, which overlooks the Fréjus Plain. Roquebrune-sur-Argens is also a good starting point for one of the most scenic routes, with views across the Golfe de Fréjus as the narrow road winds up through the hills to Plan-de-la-Tour and on to La Garde-Freinet. On the southern edge, the route from Canadel-sur-Mer over Col du Canadel to La Môle passes through some excellent cork oak forests and affords fine views back to the coast along the Corniche des Maures. The routes from Gonfaron to Bormes and Collobrières to Grimaud are among the best examples of typical rugged Maures scenery, but expect hard driving along some of the most winding roads. Even more spectacular views can be gained farther inland, along the Route des Crêtes between Notre-Dame-des-Anges, above Pignans and La Garde-Freinet. Just west of the latter is a superb viewing area by the Roches Blanches; on a clear day you can see down into the Golfe de St-Tropez, across miles of *maquis*-clad hills, while to the north stretches the vast Maures Plain and the snow-capped peaks of the Alpes d'Haute-Provence beyond.

There is a similar absence of human activity on the Maures Plain which lies between the Massif des Maures and the foothills of the high Var. This sedimentary plain represents an immensely important reservoir for the natural and wild flora and fauna of Mediterranean France, and is the

---

VILLAGE DES TORTUES

In 1988 the world's first ever "Tortoise Village" opened near Gonfaron in the Var. The Village's role is to breed and rear tortoises for release back into the wild as part of a project to restore the natural populations of Hermann's tortoise in the Massif des Maures. Visitors will find a nursery for juvenile tortoises, a special nesting pen, breeding enclosures, a diorama featuring the natural life cycle of tortoises, and a lecture theatre where videos and slide shows are shown regularly. Sick and injured animals are tended in the Tortoise Clinic.

FOREST FIRES

Forest fires are an ever-present danger in the Mediterranean countryside, especially during the hot summer months. The worst blazes occur when the strong *Mistral* winds fan the flames and push the fire forward at frightening speed. Some fierce fires have devastated thousands of acres in the space of a few days, and the scars endure for many years; one such fire was in 1979. At this time of year many of the remote forest tracks are marked *Route barrée* ("no thoroughfare"). For your own safety, as well as for the sake of the forest, do not use these routes.

---

largest remaining single area of the region's prime lowland *maquis* and open cork oak and pine forests.

The eastern plain is dominated by a majestic forest of stone pines, while on the western side the vegetation features Aleppo pines over a dense undergrowth of *maquis*. But it is the central area, with its open cork oak forest and mixed *maquis* and *garrigue*, still recovering from the great fire of 1979, that is the main attraction for naturalists. Few other areas of France have such an array of vibrant bird species: the gaudy bee-eater, golden oriole, hoopoe and roller, plus woodchat shrike, woodlark, nightjar, ortolan and melodious warbler.

Dirt tracks lead down into the wilds of the plain, to spots where the rock lies near the surface and the vegetation is no more than a short turf. These are just the places to admire the swathes of orchids, particularly the delicate green-winged orchids and mixed patches of two or more species of Seraphias orchids. Butterflies abound here, as do dragonflies and damselflies, and the air is always full of the sound of crickets and cicadas. The most striking insect, though, is like a large lacewing with black and yellow patterning on its wings.

The plain is also important for wild tortoises, and there are terrapins in the streams, but since the great fire, these animals have been slow to recolonize.

The wild flowers of the *maquis* provide a riot of colour against the dark forest backdrop of the Massif des Maures.

BEFORE YOU GO
Maps: IGN 1:100,000 No. 68;
Michelin 1:200,000 No. 84.

GETTING THERE
By air: the nearest airport is
Toulon-Hyères.
By car: leave the A8
autoroute at the Le Cannet-
des-Maures exit between
Brignoles and Fréjus; from
here, D588 to Grimaud leads
across the massif.
By rail: the nearest stations
are Hyères, which has regular
services from Toulon and
Marseille; and St-Raphaël,
with direct services from
Paris.
By bus: local services operate
around Fréjus, Hyères and
other towns along the coast.

WHERE TO STAY
The coastal resorts have a
large choice of hotels, but this
is a very busy area, and from
June–Sept reservations are
advised. There is less pressure
on accommodation inland.
Outdoor living: campsites
abound along the coast.

ACTIVITIES
Walking: from the highest
spots of the footpaths across
the Massif des Maures are
spectacular views, as well as

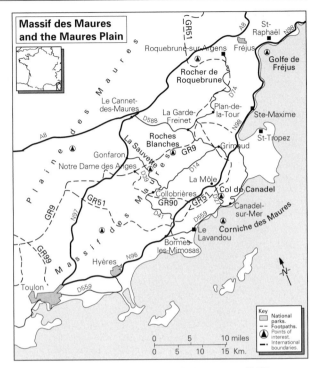

Massif des Maures and the Maures Plain

Key
National parks.
Footpaths.
Points of interest.
International boundaries.

0   5   10 miles
0   5   10   15 Km.

numerous old villages to
explore such as Grimaud and
Collobrières. The wooded
slopes around the Rocher de
Roquebrune, and the valleys
of the rivers Argens and Aille
to the west, are among the
best spots for searching out

typical Maures wildlife.

FURTHER INFORMATION
Tourist information: Fréjus/
St-Raphaël, pl Calvini,
T:94 51 53 87; Le Lavandou,
quai Gabriel-Péri,
T:94 71 00 61.

Presqu'île de Giens and Iles d'Hyères

*Sunny peninsula and secluded islands in
waters off Toulon; breeding grounds for
many bird species*

The salt pans and lagoons of the Salins des
Pesquiers form one of the principal
wild-life attractions of the small spit of land
known as the Presqu'île de Giens (Giens

peninsula), which projects into the
Mediterranean south of the ancient town of
Hyères, near Toulon. Indeed, this small
peninsula is one of the most important sites
for naturalists in eastern Provence.
    There are several other habitats in addi-
tion to the salt pans. On the extreme tip of
the Ile de Giens are some low sea cliffs
topped by a forest of Aleppo pines. This is
the best vantage point for observing sea
birds: both the Mediterranean Manx shearwater and Cory's shearwater are found
here. On the cliffs themselves both the blue
rock thrush and pallid swift nest.
    At the opposite end of the peninsula,

around the airport, are some freshwater marshes which host a good population of amphibians, including the western spadefoot toad. There are also several secluded pools with different depths of water in winter, providing a range of conditions suitable for egrets and herons. In summer they are mostly dried out and covered with the typical salt marsh plant, glasswort. This is the nesting area for avocets and stilts.

The main attractions, though, are the big lagoons, which at Pesquiers reach up to a metre (40 inches) deep. A submerged plant, *Ruppia maritima*, covers the base of the lagoon and harbours vast numbers of fish, particularly eels and mullet. This is, therefore, the ideal location for observing flamingos, ducks, coots and cormorants. During the migration season there is always a good variety of waders passing through.

The Presqu'île de Giens is equally remarkable for its flora. Despite the pressures of tourism all along the beach front, the visitor in August can still expect to see swathes of the bright white sea lily, and this is the only place in France for finding the delicate pink flowers of the three-horned stock. But above all come in spring to admire some of the 30 species of orchid (a third of the entire French orchid flora).

The peninsula also abounds in reptiles. Terrapins gather in the freshwater pools, Moorish geckos on the old salt works buildings, and numerous three-toed skinks in the grassy areas. At night above the din of croaking marsh frogs and tree frogs, listen out for the plaintive tones of the scops owl.

Just off the coast, and reached by a 20-minute ferry ride, are the Iles d'Hyères.

Although belonging to the same small archipelago, the three main Iles d'Hyères are remarkably different in character. The largest, Porquerolles, is the most varied, with a patchwork of cultivated fields in the lower-lying areas, surrounded by a dense forest of Aleppo pines and a *maquis* vegetation on the higher and rockier parts of the island. To the east, the smallest of the three islands, Port-Cros (which is a *parc national*), is almost entirely covered by an evergreen forest of holm oak and Aleppo pine. The easternmost island, Levant, is

The haunting call of the diminutive scops owl may be heard over long distances on still nights.

almost entirely covered with *maquis*, interrupted only by a few fire breaks.

A particular treat of the islands are the geckos, with all three species present. The Moorish and Turkish geckos are the commonest and inhabit buildings. The much rarer leaf-toed gecko, which is only found on Port-Cros and La Gabinière (a small islet off Port-Cros), only inhabits natural situations, principally crevices in juniper bark.

Birdwatchers, too, come to these islands, and for good reason. In spring they are about as good a place as any in southern France to find the elusive great spotted cuckoo, and breeding birds include peregrine and all three species of swift.

BEFORE YOU GO
Maps: IGN 1:100,000 No. 68; Michelin 1:200,000 No. 84.

GETTING THERE
By air: the nearest airport is Toulon-Hyères, which has flights from Paris and Lille.
By car: from Marseille, take A50 to Toulon and then either D559 through Carqueiranne or N98 to Hyères, turning on to D97 to travel along the narrow Giens peninsula.
By rail: the nearest station is Hyères, with regular services from Toulon and Marseille.
By bus: there are regular services from Hyères that serve the coast and the

Presqu'île de Giens.
By sea: ferries operate to the islands of Porquerolles, Port-Cros and Le Levant from La Tour-Fondue at the end of the Presqu'île de Giens, taking respectively 20, 30 and 40mins. La Tour-Fondue is the nearest point, but boats also run from Toulon, Le Lavandou, Cavalaire, Hyères-Plage and La Londe (the last 2 only to Port-Cros and Le Levant).

WHERE TO STAY
The best choice of hotels is in Hyères, where 2-star choices include Du Parc (7 blvd Pasteur, T:94 65 06 65) and Thalassa (6 av Jean-d'Agrève,

T:94 57 24 85). Porquerolles and Port-Cros have limited options.
Outdoor living: campsites abound in the area, particularly all along the east side of the Presqu'île de Giens; most are crowded in summer when reservations are recommended. A 3-star site is La Presqu'île de Giens, T:94 58 22 86. There are 3 sites on Le Levant, including La Pinède, T:94 05 90 47.

FURTHER INFORMATION
Tourist information: Toulon, av Colbert, T:94 22 08 22; Hyères, av de Belgique, T:94 65 18 55; Carqueiranne, Hôtel de Ville, T:94 58 60 78.

Massif de l'Esterel and Lac de St-Cassien

Charred coastal massif overlooking Cannes and extending to the budding nature reserve and man-made Lac de St-Cassien

A few years ago I would have written about the Esterel in the same glowing terms as its sister massif, the Maures. Today, however, the Esterel presents a very desolate scene, a landscape ravaged by fire. Whole hillsides and valleys are now a charred ruin of what was once magnificent countryside.

The fires have raged so much and so often, that even the *maquis* no longer grows, let alone any trees. Flights into Nice from the north frequently turn past the Esterel for the final approach, and looking down you can make out a parched brown land, reminiscent of the denuded hills of southern Greece or some parched North African desert.

These frightening glimpses from on high

only partly prepared me for my latest visit. Driving into the massif proper, I was, as ever, struck by the poignant beauty of the rock formations and the clear profile of the landscape as I looked back across the Golfe de Napoule to Cannes. The coastal plain was littered with houses, villas and urban developments of one form or another, all the way up to Grasse. But in the Esterel all was space and tranquillity. A lone raven circling overhead, and later a peregrine flying along a valley ridge, added a certain poignancy to the scene. It was hard to imagine what was left for them to eat, so little was there left of the once vibrant natural community of plants and animals.

Small pockets remain unburnt. I found a rough forest track, the Piste de Belvédères, that passed through some typical *maquis* of tree heather, spiny broom and strawberry tree, with small clusters of cork oaks and the typical assortment of aromatic herbs like rock-rose and lavender. Nightingales and Sardinian warblers called from the undergrowth and a Montpellier snake cruised across the path in front of me. Cleopatra

The rugged beauty of the Massif del' Esterel can not conceal the appalling devastation brought by recurrent forest fires in recent years.

and false ilex hairstreak butterflies were on the wing, as were a couple of the gaudy two-tailed pasha. But I only had to look across the charred valley to see the stunted strawberry trees gamely beginning the slow regeneration process, to remind myself that this small oasis of life was a mere remnant.

If the charred desolation of the Esterel becomes too much for you, there is always Lac de St-Cassien for respite. Located just north of the Esterel, this artificially created lake stretches for six kilometres (3½ miles) end to end, and provides nearly 30 kilometres (20 miles) of shoreline. The lake is a popular tourist spot, and the main road down the east side gives on to many restaurants and windsurfing points.

At the northwestern arm of the lake is the proposed site for the Réserve Biologique de Fondurane, part of a Provence-wide scheme to establish nature reserves in key sites. This covers 43 hectares (100 acres) of the lake's area, including the largest reed bed in the Var *département*, where over 150 species of birds have been recorded. There are plans for nature trails and observation hides around the lake edge and overlooking the reeds, but when I was last there I had to fight through a dense fringe of the very attractive but fiercely spiny Christ's thorn (*Paliurus spina-christi*), only to land knee-deep in a marshy field.

On the opposite side of this arm of the lake a dense, typically Mediterranean forest of white oak, maritime pine, tree heather and rock-rose grows right down to the shore. A track through this habitat follows around the entire western side of the lake, until the visitor is brought back to reality in the heart of a building site by the southern end, where yet another tourist complex is under way.

BEFORE YOU GO
Maps: IGN 1:100,000 No. 68; Michelin 1:200,000 No. 84.

GETTING THERE
By car: leave the A8 *autoroute* at Fréjus, Les Adrets or Mandelieu to join N7, which crosses the Massif de l'Esterel. For the Lac de St-Cassien, take D37. The N98 coast road skirts the massif to the south, passing through several small resorts west of Cannes.
By rail: the nearest station is St-Raphaël, which has regular direct services to Paris and overnight Motorails to Dieppe, Boulogne and Lille from May–Sept.
By bus: local services from Fréjus and Cannes.

WHERE TO STAY
One of France's most famous seaside resorts, Cannes has everything from top-class hotels to small *pensions*. St-Raphaël is another good coastal choice. A 3-star hotel at Valescure, near

REPTILES OF MEDITERRANEAN FRANCE
Perhaps the most striking aspect of Mediterranean wildlife is the abundance and variety of reptiles. Lizards are most abundant in Corsica, where the walker almost fears to tread for want of stepping on one of the local species, the Tyrrhenian wall lizard *Podarcis tiliguerta*.

Green lizards are very common on the mainland in rough scrubby areas, field margins and along forest edges. The most spectacular and rarest lizard, though, is the large ocellated lizard, which can reach over half a metre (20in) in length.

Even more exclusive to the Mediterranean region are three species of gecko; the most abundant, Moorish gecko, less commonly the Turkish gecko and most restricted and special of all the European leaf-toed gecko, which is only found on the Iles d'Hyères and a few smaller islets off the French coast and also in Corsica.

Snakes are a common sight, although the average visitor is more likely to encounter them as road victims than alive. The most abundant and obvious species is the impressive Montpellier snake, whose adults often attain sizes in excess of 1.5m (5ft). Other common reptiles are the natracine snakes—the grass (*Natrix natrix*) and the viperine (*Natrix maura*)—which commonly occur along streams and by other bodies of water. A walk into the *maquis* is a must if one wants any chance of seeing the southern smooth snake or the ladder snake, while the dense oak forests are home to the Aesculapian snake.

Undoubtedly the most famous of all the reptiles of the region is Hermann's tortoise, which is restricted to the Massif des Maures and its environs.

St-Raphaël, is La Cheneraie, blvd des Gondins, T:94 83 65 03. The 1-star Le Vieux Manège at Adrets-de-l'Esterel (T:76 71 09 91) is also recommended.
Outdoor living: of the area's numerous campsites, visitors may want to try Les Philippons (Les Adrets-de-l'Esterel, T:94 40 90 67), which has 150 *emplacements* and also tents and campers for rent.

FURTHER INFORMATION
Tourist information: the Cannes tourist office is at the railway station and offers an accommodation service, T:93 99 19 77; Fréjus/St-Raphaël, pl Calvini, T:94 51 53 87.

Gorges du Verdon

A spectacular canyon, located 100km (60 miles) northwest of Cannes; one of Europe's great wonders

Describing the wonders of the Gorges du Verdon in 1928, the French explorer E. A. Martel wrote: "You have to visit the Canyon at least twenty times before you can dare say that you have seen it. It is a marvel without equal in Europe, the largest, the wildest and the most varied of all the great faults in the Old World." Today you can drive along the top road with relative ease and peer over the sometimes less than substantial safety barriers, into the gaping chasm beneath. Even better for exploring the gorge is the footpath along the bottom. Beware, though: once committed there is no way out until you reach the end (about 25km/15 miles) unless you retrace your steps.

The gorge is composed of Jurassic and Cretaceous limestone, dating back 100 million to 200 million years. With the sheer sides of the narrow gorge 600m (2,000ft) high, there are times of the year when the sun does not penetrate directly to the valley floor. The dramatic range of heights and exposure, and the rugged topography, provide an entire range of micro-climatic conditions. It is also very much a frontier site, not simply because it marks the northern edge of the *département* of the Var, but because it represents the point where Mediterranean France meets the foothills of the Alps. There are all sorts of odd combinations of semi-montane, temperate and Mediterranean vegetation, creating an absolute paradise for the discerning botanist. And, given the isolating effects of such extreme relief, there are several very rare and in some cases endemic plants, such as the fern *Asplenium jahandiezi* and a species of sandwort, *Moehringia dosyphylla*.

Birdlife is an equally varied mix. Species include golden eagle, buzzard, peregrine, black woodpecker, rock thrush, wallcreeper and citril finch. The wood warbler also flourishes, well removed from its more temperate habitat in the beech forests of western France.
Before you go *Maps:* IGN 1:100,000 No. 68; Michelin 1:200,000 No. 84.
Getting there *By car:* leave A8 at Brignoles and head north on D554 to Barjols; then follow signs for Montmeyan and Aups. If you are coming from the east,

Wallcreepers with their brilliant crimson wings, are secretive birds of high mountain cliffs.

N85 north from Grasse leads to D21 for Comps-sur-Artuby and Castellane. From Moustiers, on D952 north of the Gorges du Verdon, a circuit is possible from either direction.
Where to stay: Castellane has 2 inns: the Bon Accueil (T:92 83 62 01) and the Teillon (T:92 83 60 88). Details of mountain shelters and hostels from the Comité Départemental de Randonnée Pédestre, 2 rue Deloye, Nice. *Outdoor living:* there are several campsites in the Castellane area, including the Camp du Verdon, Domaine de la Salaou, T:92 83 61 29.
Activities *Walking:* a 25-km (15-mile) footpath runs along the bottom of the canyon.

The Gorges du Verdon (*overleaf*), with their great variety of vegetation, are a paradise for botanists.

Climbing: experienced mountaineers can climb with a qualified guide. Mountaineering courses are available through the Club Alpin Français, 14 av Mirabeau, Nice, T:93 62 59 99. *White-water rafting:* 3-day raft excursions along the Verdon are organized by Plein Air Nature, 42 rue Victor-Hugo, Digne, T:92 31 51 09.
Further information *Tourist information:* Nice, 55 promenade des Anglais, T:93 44 50 59; Castellane, rue Nationale, T:92 83 61 14.

The large Montpellier snake is extremely nervous and flees at the first hint of human approach.

Montagne du Cheiron

A curious east–west massif supporting varied flora and fauna; often overlooked by visitors in nearby Nice

The Montagne du Cheiron, situated between the valleys of the Loup and the Var, and centred on the village of Roquesteron, is relatively unexplored and ideal for anyone who values a sense of discovery off the beaten track. Unlike most of the other massifs around Nice, the Cheiron is orientated east–west, so its series of north- and south-facing slopes support contrasting vegetation types, resulting in a varied flora and fauna. The vegetation passes through a series of stages from the low-altitude evergreen oak forest, up to beech and fir woods with hop hornbeam at higher altitudes (the summit of Cheiron is 1,780m/5,840ft) and on north-facing slopes. There are also vast areas of
180

open scrub country carpeted with a form of *maquis* consisting of box, lavender, and broom, interspersed with dry grasslands full of interesting and aromatic herbs and orchids.

Many elements of the Mediterranean reptile fauna occur, such as the Montpellier snake, green and ocellated lizards and southern smooth snake. These are found together with more northern species such as asp viper, and on higher ground are a few colonies of the rare and strictly protected Orsini's viper.

One of the most encouraging signs of the wealth of wildlife here is the fact that it forms the hunting zone for five pairs of golden eagle, three of which actually nest within the area. As in the case of the reptiles, there is a *mélange* of northern, montane and Mediterranean bird species. Few areas can match the Cheiron's motley assortment of birds: chough, black grouse, black woodpecker, Tengmalm's owl, blue rock thrush, black-eared wheatear and up to six warblers of the genus *Sylvia*.
Before you go *Maps:* IGN 1:100,000 No. 61; Michelin

1:200,000 Nos. 81 and 84.
Getting there *By car:* from Nice, drive north through Vence along the spectacular D2 over the Col de Vence to Coursegoules; the road skirts the Montagne du Cheiron. There are equally scenic routes from Grasse via D3 and D5. From the north, join D2 from N89, the famous Route Napoléon between Digne and Cannes.
By rail: the nearest station is at Nice.
By bus: there are local services around Nice.
Where to stay: Nice is one of the country's largest resorts, with everything from top-class hotels to small *pensions*, as well as apartments and villas. Inland are smaller towns and villages with interesting small inns such as the Auberge de la Clue at St-Auban, T:93 60 43 12. Details of mountain shelters and hostels from the Comité Départemental de Randonnée Pédestre, 2 rue Deloye, Nice. *Outdoor living:* there are numerous coastal campsites, fewer inland. St-Antoine is a 2-star site at Coursegoules, T:93 59 12 36.
Activities *Walking:* the GR4 long-distance footpath, which crosses the Montagne du

Cheiron from Grasse to Entrevaux in the Var valley, is accessible Mar–Nov.
Further information *Tourist information:* Nice, 55 promenade des Anglais, T:93 44 50 59; Vence, pl Gd-Jardin, T:93 58 06 38.

Massif de la Ste-Baume and Montagne Ste-Victoire

Rocky escarpments overlooking the entrance to Aix and Marseille

Anyone entering Provence via Aix or Marseille cannot fail to be impressed by the brilliant white massifs surrounding these towns. But for all their obvious allure and proximity to main population centres, these wild places remain largely ignored in the great rush for the Riviera beaches. This is a great mistake, for they contain some truly wild and exciting scenery. Both massifs are formed of limestone and in addition to vast bare rock faces, their southern aspects harbour pockets of typical Mediterranean vegetation of evergreen oak, Aleppo pine and a dense *maquis* undergrowth of spiny shrubs, lentisk and strawberry tree. The less arid northern slopes look completely different, combining elements of both Mediterranean and alpine influence. The more humid forests of the Ste-Baume are composed of beech, white oak, lime and maple, and offer a great harmony of colour in autumn. The massif

is dominated by a forest of deciduous white oak, which lends the impression of being somewhere further north in a more temperate climate; this is accentuated by the huge sizes of both yew and holly growing in the shadow of the great northern cliff face. The rich humus of the forest floor supports a wide array of herbs, including Solomon's seal and the saprophytic bird's-nest. The Ste-Victoire offers a similar contrast between a more parched and open southern face and a lush northern slope.

The most striking features of both massifs are the great rocky escarpments, which form the principal refuges for the larger rare birds of the area, notably Bonelli's eagle, short-toed eagle and eagle owl.

Before you go *Maps:* IGN 1:100,000 No. 67; Michelin 1:200,000 No. 84.
Getting there *By car:* Montagne Ste-Victoire is a short drive east from Aix-en-Provence. For the Massif de la Ste-Baume, take A8 from Aix and then A52, leaving it at Aubagne; this is a complicated interchange, however, so some drivers will prefer to take the main N96, which runs parallel.
By rail: Aix-en-Provence has frequent services from Marseille.
By bus: there are local services around Aix, including ones every 15mins from Marseille, and regular services from Nice.
Where to stay: Aix ia a charming spa town with a selection of 1–4-star hotels. The 3-star Relais Ste-Victoire (T:21 90 32 22) is just outside at Beaurecueil. There is also a youth hostel, Chemin de Valcros. The 2-star Lou Pebre d'Ai (T:42 04 50 42) lies at the foot of the Massif de la

Lavender, origano, marjoram and mint are some of the herbs which produce the heady aroma of the maquis.

Ste-Baume in the village of Plan-d'Aups.
Outdoor living: Aix has 3 campsites, including the Chantecier, av du Val St-André, T:42 26 12 98. Near the massif is Le Clos, Gémenos, T:42 82 06 29.
Activities *Walking and mountaineering:* there are marked footpaths in both areas. GR9 crosses the Montagne Ste-Victoire; GR98 crosses the Massif de la Ste-Baume.
Cycling: bicycles can be rented from railway stations, campsites and cycle shops. Side roads are pleasantly quiet.
Further information *Tourist information:* Aix-en-Provence, pl du Général-de-Gaulle, T:42 26 02 93.

The russet hues of the fertile plain give way to the dramatic white escarpments of Montagne Ste-Victoire (above), home to many of the larger raptors.

The olive, considered by many to be the definitive tree of the Mediterranean region, has been extensively cultivated over the centuries.

BUTTERFLIES OF PROVENCE

The abundance of butterflies along the country lanes and in the *garrigue* and forest clearings is especially gratifying to any naturalist visiting from areas where agriculture is more intensive. There are scores of species in the region; in one commune area in the Massif des Maures, over 60 species have been noted.

The largest and strongest flying butterly is the two-tailed pasha (*Charaxes jasius*), which has a brightly and intricately patterned underside contrasting with a more uniform dark upperside with orange bands along the tips. Even more complicated is the patterning on the festoon butterflies (*Zerynthia* species), two species of which appear in early spring on wooded slopes. Two species of swallowtail are also easy to find in a wide range of situations but ironically it is the scarce swallowtail (*Iphiclides podalirius*) that is the more abundant.

Corsica

France's important Mediterranean island, 160km (100 miles) offshore; last refuge for certain plant and animal species

ໄໄໄ

Islands are fascinating places. They hold a special character of their own, no matter how close they are to the mainland. It is not only the customs and traditions, or the more relaxed pace of life that sets them apart. For the naturalist an island can be a Pandora's box of unique treasures and Corsica certainly has plenty of these.

For such a small island, measuring a mere 75 kilometres (45 miles) at its widest by 180 kilometres (110 miles) long, Corsica is a kaleidoscope of landscapes and images. It has twenty peaks greater than 2,000 metres (6,600 feet), 900 kilometres (560 miles) of tortuous rocky coastline and miles of sandy beaches marking the edge of the long ribbon of the eastern plain. This coastal plain merges into the forests and *maquis* cloaking the roughly angled hills and precipitous valleys of the island's interior, up to the bare rocks and alpine grasslands of the great mountains with their continuously snow-capped summits.

Originally Corsica and Sardinia, its closest neighbour, were thought to be remaining fragments of a former sunken continent, Tyrrhenia. Now it is believed more likely that the Corso-Sardinian land mass broke away from France at the beginning of the Tertiary period and rotated southeast to its present-day location, 160 kilometres (100 miles) off the French coast. Corsica supports 2,000 species of plant, of which eight per cent are endemic to the island. Nearly half of all the known species in the mountain zones are endemic, and there are precious few species in common with the Alps. Some of these Corsican specialities therefore have a world distribution of only a handful of square kilometres, yet within their restricted niches they are often very abundant.

Apart from its own home-grown specialities, Corsica is host to many plants that occur in Spain, or Italy, or even North Africa, but which do not reach mainland France. The island also boasts some 1,200 species of lichen, hundreds of species of moss and over a thousand sorts of fungi.

The island's birdlife has also deservedly attracted the attention of ornithologists, both for its variety (nearly 130 breeding species) and quality. Like the flora, the fauna has a rich supply of endemics, some being full species, others merely special island races of commoner mainland forms. My visit certainly started well. As we drew into Bastia harbour, I was casually focusing my binoculars on some sea-gulls, when I realized that one of the group flying past the harbour wall was an Audouin's gull, one of the rarest gulls in the world, confined to a few Mediterranean islands.

Corsica's largely unexploited coastline and wealth of surrounding islets account for its fair share of seabirds. Most of the coast is impressive rocky cliff, but three spectacular sections stand out: the northern and western sides of Cap Corse in the extreme north; the coastal stretch within the Parc Régional de Corse on the west side between Calvi and Capo Rosso; and the breathtaking limestone cliffs upon which the ancient fortress town of Bonifacio is precariously lodged. The old ramparts provide a perfect vantage point to admire the flying skills of all three species of swift—common, alpine and pallid.

For sheer variety, though, the most important section of coast is in the Réserve Naturelle de Scandola, north of Porto on the western side of the island. Shags and herring gulls nest on the cliff faces, also frequented by the wild rock doves that make up the major part of the diet of the now rare peregrine falcon. Scandola is also one of the last Mediterranean stations for the magnificent osprey.

Winter can also be a worthwhile time to visit, with cormorants, gannets and various sea ducks offshore at either end of the island, and for the lucky observers there's always a chance of seeing wall creepers and alpine accentors along the cliffs, having come down from their summer retreats in the mountains to escape the winter freeze.

In total contrast, much of the eastern seaboard is open and sandy, backed in places by large, brackish, reed-fringed lagoons, such as the *étangs* of Biguglia near Bastia, and Diane, Urbino and Palo on the Plaine d'Aléria. In winter and during the passage seasons these lagoons are alive with waterfowl and waders, and in the breeding season birdwatchers can hope to find red-crested pochard, purple heron, moustached warbler and little ringed plovers. When I was there on a glorious mid-June morning, I followed the deserted coast from Etang d'Urbino to Ghisonaccia. In all the hours it took me to progress slowly along the upper beach and through the flanking forest of tall pines, I saw only two people: one a fisherman, the other a wood cutter. My only company along the route were a couple of Dartford warblers in the scrub, a Kentish plover flitting along the beach in short runs, and a woodlark and red-backed shrike.

The coastal scrub fringe is a form of littoral *maquis* and the co-dominant junipers, *Juniperus oxycedrus* and *J. phoenicia*, provide a natural home for the extremely scarce leaf-toed gecko. Much more abundant and easy to find is the Italian wall lizard which is in fact perfectly at home on the hot sand dunes, where it shows a turn of speed probably greater than any other lizard in the region. Throughout the Mediterranean it is the remaining natural coastal areas that are under some of the most serious threats of development, and Corsica is no exception. For nearly 30 years conservationists have been actively lobbying for greater protection of the remaining wetlands and their maritime fringes. Visit one of these lagoons on a day when the birdlife is active and you will appreciate the worthiness of their efforts.

For most people the epitome of Corsica is its expanse of *maquis*-covered hills, refuge for Corsican shepherds and bandits as well as endemic floral species. The *maquis* evokes countless stories and legends, and has played an important role in the island's rural economy—as an abundant source of fire wood, browsing for goats and provider

The Corsican nuthatch is found in the pine forests of the central and western mountains.

of numerous fruits and berries. Junipers come into their own for a potent liqueur, and at Asco there is a tradition for the priest to place a bucket made from juniper wood on the head of the bridegroom during the marriage ceremony.

You don't have to get married to appreciate the ambience of the Corsican *maquis*. There are many small warblers of the *Sylvia* genus; Dartford and Sardinian warblers are perhaps the most common, but the most eagerly sought by birdwatching visitors is the Marmora's warbler. The *maquis* is also home to Hermann's tortoise, ostensibly the same race as that on the French mainland, but with subtle differences in coloration and shell morphology. Sadly for the tortoise, and all the other wildlife associated with this classic habitat, vast areas have been denuded by burning, while the lowland Plaine d'Aléria has been converted to agricultural use. Much of the southeastern quarter of Corsica now presents a desolate fire-torn landscape, all the more forlorn for the innumerable wrecked cars dumped haphazardly throughout the countryside. It has at times the look of a dying country, and the beauty of still pristine areas, such as

185

The famous cliffs of Bonifacio, on Corsica's southern tip, are a favourite haunt of the swifts.

near Porto-Vecchio, only serve to emphasize the loss.

Moving on into the interior of the island means entering a world of high jagged mountains clothed in pine and fir forests and traversed by great torrents that have carved magnificent deep gorges through the ancient rocks. Much of central Corsica is uninhabited and lies within the large Parc Régional de Corse. The only town of any consequence inside the park is Corte, nearly 400 metres (1,313 feet) up. While in the interior I was determined to spot the endemic Corsican nuthatch, known to favour the inland conifer forests. I began my search in the pine forest of Asco since this also promised to be one of the most spectacular roads on the island. It winds up through a steep, rugged gorge to the small mountainside village of Asco, and then on another 15 kilometres (nine miles) to Haut-Asco, a small ski station at the base of some of the island's most formidable peaks, including 2,710-metre (8,894-foot) Mont Cinto, Corsica's highest point. Walking through the ancient forest was sheer joy, though somewhat disappointingly I had to

186

be content with coal tits, goldcrest and spotted flycatcher. Lizards were the real highlight though. Every step sent them scurrying, and when I sat down for a few minutes, all around they began to reappear from their hideaways and at any one time there would be at least a dozen of these brightly patterned creatures furtively patrolling the forest floor.

Further downhill I searched again along one of the many foaming torrents, tumbling down the mountainside. A dipper and grey wagtail, both looking so delicate and powerless against the incessant surge of white water, were indeed perfectly at home. The stream drowned out any other sounds from the surrounding forest, so I moved away and up through the steep valley sides. Shafts of sunlight poured through the

The cool mountain forests in north-west Corsica provide a distinct contrast to the lowland plains on the eastern side of the island.

canopy, emphasizing the height of the tall, straight pine trunks, leaving me dwarfed at the base of this army of giant pillars. Even the ground flora seemed somehow out of scale. The dominant herb, with its characteristic robust tufts, was the Corsican hellebore (*Helleborus lividus corsicus*), an impressive, primitive-looking plant, all the more menacing for its poisonous properties. Stretched out across the stony path I came across a melanistic whip snake (*Coluber viridflavus*), which slithered easily into cover as I approached.

My final attempt for the elusive nuthatch was in the Forêt de Valdo-Niello, at a spot just over 1000 metres (3,300 feet) altitude. The forest looked just perfect with many well-spaced, old mature pines covered in craggy bark, a scatter of dead trunks still standing, and plenty of young pines and

birches coming through. There seemed to be a wide variety of birdlife around—serin, chaffinch, coal tit, goldcrest and tree creeper, and in a clearing within a section of fir woodland was a flock of citril finches. But still my quarry eluded me as I retired for lunch by a small rivulet crossing the forest track.

Nature always has a habit of springing surprises. You go in search of one creature and more than likely something else equally interesting turns up instead. This day was one such occasion. I had tossed a peach stone into the stream when I noticed something move in the water. I peered into the pebbly stream bed to find a small, brown, superbly camouflaged newt-like creature—a Corsican brook salamander, another of the island's elusive endemics.

My few days on the island were but a fleeting visit and in no way could I have expected to see all local wildlife specialities. The fact that I had seen so many was a testimony to relatively short distances and quiet roads, and the great variety of habitats that are relatively easily accessible. One of the most striking aspects was the general lack of birdlife in the wider countryside, in contrast to the super-abundance of small lizards. But, unfortunately, the strongest impression of all was that given by the countless vistas of burned and degraded forest, particularly in the island's southeastern quarter, and the careless abandon of vehicles and other rubbish along almost every country road, no matter how remote.

Thank goodness for the mountains; it would take some effort to destroy these, too.

The Corsican hellebore, which grows profusely in scattered clumps, is one of the most striking flowers on the forest floor of the Gorges de Lasco.

BEFORE YOU GO
Maps: IGN 1:100,000 Nos. 73 and 74; Michelin 1:200,000 No. 90.
Guidebooks: *Corsica, a Traveller's Guide* (Lowe/ Murray); *La Nature en Corse* (Brun-Gamisans/Horizons de France).

GETTING THERE
By air: Ajaccio, Bastia, Calvi and Figari have airports with direct flights daily from Paris (90mins), Nice (30mins) and Marseille (40mins).
By sea: car ferries are operated by SNCM (Ajaccio, quai l'Herminier, T:94 41 25 76) at least twice

daily from Marseille, Nice and Toulon to Ajaccio, Bastia, Calvi, L'Ile-Rousse and Propriano; journey-time is 5–10hrs. There are regular car ferries to Bastia from Italy: from Genoa (7hrs) and Livorno (4hrs).
By car: driving presents the best means of making the

most of Corsica's scenery and exploring off the beaten track; car rental is available in all main towns.

By rail: Corsican Railways operate a scenic route through the mountains between Ajaccio, Corte and Bastia as well as along the coast between L'Ile-Rousse and Calvi.

By bus: most towns are served by at least 1 bus a day. The principal routes along the island leave from Ajaccio, Bastia, Calvi, L'Ile-Rousse, Corte, Sartène and Porto-Vecchio.

WHERE TO STAY

There is no shortage of hotels, apartments or *gîtes*. A guide is published by ARTL, 22 cours Grandval, Ajaccio, available at tourist offices.

Outdoor living: there are 116 recognized sites; it is dangerous, if tempting, to camp elsewhere. Beach camping is forbidden.

ACTIVITIES

Cycling: bicycle tours, with luggage transported and accommodation arranged, are organized by Vivre la Corse en Vélo, Résidence Napoléon, 23 cours Général-Leclerc, Ajaccio, T:95 22 70 79.

Riding: there are 15 reputable centres with about 100km (60 miles) of riding tracks. Three- to 10-day trips can be arranged.

Walking and mountaineering: an increasing number of footpaths and walking itineraries are being developed, particularly in the *parc régional*, which is crossed by the GR20 long-distance footpath. Two- and 3-day walks are organized by the I Muntagnoli Corsi association, quartier Santa-Maria, Quenza, T:95 74 62 28.

Watersports: sailing and

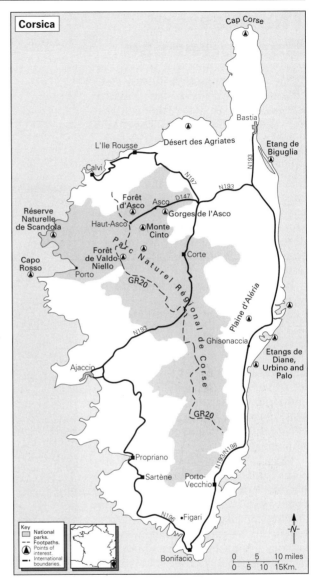

windsurfing equipment is easily available at coastal centres, and there are many diving clubs. White-water rafting on the River Tavignano is possible Mar–Oct from Corte; details from Base du Tavignano, Piedicorte-di-Gaggio, T:95 48 83 59.

FURTHER INFORMATION

Tourist information: Ajaccio, Hôtel de Ville, T:95 21 40 87; Bastia, 35 blvd Paoli, T:95 31 02 44; Bonifacio, rue des Moulins, T:78 73 11 88; and Calvi, Port de Plaisance, T:95 65 16 67.

189

CHAPTER 9

The Western Mediterranean

The warm, tranquil, brilliantly sunlit land that follows the Mediterranean around from the Rhône delta to the Spanish border has long been tamed and civilized. So long, indeed, it is surprising just how much wilderness survives at the uncultivable margins of this silent, forceful landscape. A sea of ancient vineyards covers the flatter country, and laps against the edges of unruly limestone hills cloaked with dense, evergreen forest. Overhead a blue silk sky is smoothed by bone-dry northern winds.

Behind the coast, stretching to the hazy Cévennes, lies the basking Languedoc plain, a land which has seen much turmoil in history, movements of peoples and of armies, but which now is utterly tranquil. Remarkably few tourists come this far from the coast, except to a handful of interesting old towns and cities which do indeed deserve a visit. In most of the rural back-country, village life continues unaffected by summer visitors.

Most of the region's visitors stay within sight of the coast resorts, the majority of which were not here twenty-five years ago. Despite this massive upsurge in coastal tourism, Languedoc's *étangs*, shallow saline lagoons strung along the seashore from the Camargue to the Pyrenees, retain a strange, inscrutable and remote character, totally out of keeping with the life of the holidaymakers. Sometimes hard to approach except on foot because of the enclosing grasses and succulents, these tideless expanses of

Dawn steals over the reed beds of the Camargue, Europe's most famous wetland and a great inspiration for modern conservationists.

water do not attract a great deal of tourist attention. Because of this, they provide a fine breeding environment for numerous species of wildfowl, both resident and migratory, particularly waders. Most striking is the extraordinary pink flamingo. These colourful birds can be spotted standing one-legged in the shallows, great groups of them together.

Languedoc's rustic interior is characterized by an almost total monoculture of vines. The myriad haphazard patterns of fields—some large, some tiny, each striped with neat rows of grapevines—are one of Languedoc's most distinctive and appealing features. Stand on a hillside in the evening and watch the sinking sun illuminating the pearly heat haze over these countless fields, changing the sky into a gigantic kaleidoscope of colour. For most residents of the region's small, unpretentious villages, these vines are the very basis of life. Most communities have their *cave co-opérative*, where the local wine is made, and all work revolves around the annual cycle of the vineyard. The harvest, *les vendanges*, is the high point of the year. All hands are employed to help bring in the grape harvest—post offices and shops will close if necessary—and roads are clogged with tractors hauling overflowing trailers. At harvest time, the grapevines are a spectacular sight, their green leaves turning an astonishingly brilliant crimson red and vivid yellow. Spectacular or not, however, these low-lying vineyards are, from a wildlife point of view, practically desert-like, with small insect populations and very sparse animal and birdlife.

In contrast to the relative lack of flora and fauna in the vineyards, inland Languedoc's wild *garrigue*, or dry, aromatic forestland, is extremely rich in Mediterranean flora and harbours numerous insects, reptiles and small mammals. The densest, wildest *garrigue* flourishes on the rocky slopes that mark the limits of the Languedoc plain, and in the hilly, limestone landscapes spanning the northern halves of the Hérault and Gard *départements*.

Throughout the region, whether in *garrigue*, vineyard or village square, insectivores are in their element. High-soaring swifts fill the air with their shrill whistling, while over the fields, swallows—including the rare, red-rumped variety—abound. At night the bats—Savi's and Kuhl's pipistrelles, as well as greater, lesser and Mediterranean horseshoes—dart about feasting on a multitude of flying insects.

One of the most characteristic sounds of the Languedoc countryside in summer is the monotonous stridulating of the cicada, together with the croaking of frogs and the rasp of crickets. The best-known cicada here is the large *cigale*, which lives on tree branches. Although the *cigale* manages simply on the sap of its host tree, many of the insects here are themselves insectivores. Other notable insect-eaters include the older arthropods from which insects are descended. The scorpion is especially abundant, and often, while returning home along village lanes in late evening, I have seen them climbing over house walls, or during the day, hiding beneath flowerpots or tiles.

Physically, the Languedoc terrain is either flat or undulating, stony, and frequently interrupted by sudden outbreaks of low, rocky hills. For much of the year the climate is extremely dry, with long, hot summers, short winters and prevailing dry, northerly winds—the famous *Mistral* and *Tramontane*—which keep the air fresh and the skies clear. Both summer and autumn bring forceful storms, however, and in late winter, when the moist *Marin* wind drifts off the Mediterranean, there can be lengthy periods of rain. Compared to other Mediterranean regions, Languedoc remains relatively free of tourism, and its old villages of picturesque stone houses have been left much as they have always been. Walking in the *garrigue* can be hot work, however, and heads, arms and legs should be properly protected against the ravages of sunshine, plants and insects. But exploring the area brings great rewards: the heady scent of the air, a view of abundant wildlife and a feeling of peaceful isolation from the modern world.

South of Languedoc the land rises ever higher into the Pyrenees of Catalan-speaking Roussillon, and the *garrigue* of the lower slopes gives way, at higher altitudes, to a woodland flora and fauna of more typically mountainous aspect. As it heads down to reach the Spanish border, the sandy Languedoc coast changes into Roussillon's grander and more rugged shoreline.

Here, as everywhere along the western Mediterranean, hunters and farmers do their usual damage to wildlife and natural habitats. But more than anything else, it is the annual tidal wave of tourists that most endangers what remains of its wilderness. Fortunately, few of these sun-seekers have the persistence to penetrate far into Languedoc's prickly *garrigue* or the wooded Roussillon hills.

GETTING THERE
By air: there are regular scheduled flights from several European cities to the airports of Montpellier and Perpignan; the more frequent flights to Marseille are useful, especially for visiting the Camargue.
By rail: fast and frequent main-line services operate from Paris to all main towns. Other lines come into the region from across the Massif Central. Overnight Motorail trains offer a direct link to Narbonne from Boulogne, Calais, Lille and Paris. There's also a Motorail from Dieppe to Avignon, which leaves just a short drive into Languedoc.
By car: A9 runs from the Spanish border across the Languedoc plain to the Rhône valley. Another *autoroute*, A61, comes into Languedoc from Bordeaux via Toulouse and Carcassonne. N9 and N113 run parallel to the *autoroutes*.

WHEN TO GO
The best time to visit is the late spring and early summer: the summer birds have already arrived, the multitudes of flowering plants are mostly in blossom, and the tourist hordes will not have arrived. If the *vendange* appeals, plan to come in Sept.

WHERE TO STAY
Most larger towns on and around the Languedoc plain are very historic and all have a selection of hotels in every price range. Nîmes and Montpellier are recommended, as are the smaller towns of Béziers and Narbonne. The most attractive coastal towns are Sète and Collioure; both have lots of character. It is possible to find accommodation in the smallest villages or even in the open country; local tourist offices have lists.

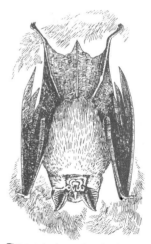

The greater horseshoe bat is one of the larger species that thrive in the western Mediterranean.

ACTIVITIES
Walking: some rewarding long-distance footpaths traverse the *garrigue*-covered

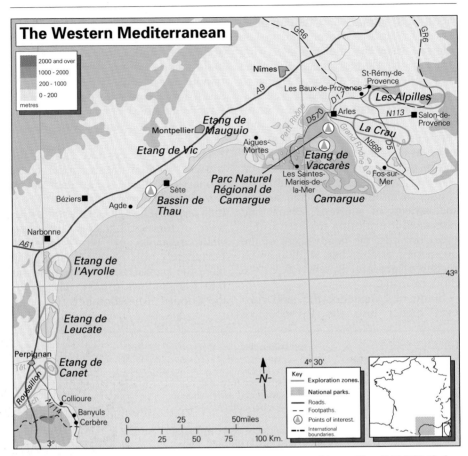

The Western Mediterranean

Key:
- Exploration zones.
- National parks.
- Roads.
- Footpaths.
- Points of interest.
- International boundaries.

slopes rising from the Languedoc plain. GR6 meanders from the Alpilles, across the Rhône and along the valley of the Gard north of Nîmes; GR60, GR74 and GR7 cross the hills north and west of Montpellier; GR77 lies inland from Béziers and Narbonne; GR36 explores the Corbières and climbs into the Pyrenees.

Contact the Association de Tourisme de Randonnée Languedoc-Roussillon, 14 rue des Logis, Loupian, Mèze, T:67 43 82 50.
Riding: guided tours of the Camargue are offered by numerous stables near Les Stes-Maries-de-la-Mer.

194

Contact the Association de Tourisme Equestre en Languedoc-Roussillon (same address as under "Walking", above).
Watersports: sailing schools and clubs are found at La Grande-Motte, Agde, Leucate and Port-Barcarès. Inland, there are similar facilities at Lac du Salagou, 3km (2 miles) from Clermont-l'Hérault.

FURTHER INFORMATION
Tourist information: for regional information on the whole of Languedoc-Roussillon (except Bouches-du-Rhône *département*), contact CRT, 12 rue Foch,

Montpellier, T:67 60 55 42; for Bouches-du-Rhône, 22 rue Louis-Maurel, Marseille, T:91 37 91 22.
For local tourist offices, see individual exploration zones.

FURTHER READING
Polunin and Huxley, *Flowers of the Mediterranean* (Chatto & Windus); H. Harant and D. Jarry, *Guide du Naturaliste dans le Midi de la France*; Andrew Sanger, *Languedoc & Roussillon* (Helm).

Bulls roam through the Languedoc marshlands, grazing on grasses and herbs along the dykes.

La Camargue

Large, flat and marshy delta region of the River Rhône, covering 100,000ha (250,000 acres); much of the region is contained within the Parc Naturel Régional de Camargue

The Camargue has a romance and a haunting appeal matched by few other areas. A flat, windy, barely inhabited land of tall, swaying grasses, this lonely, bewitching region puzzles, astonishes, excites and even alarms the unaccustomed eye. In all its immense area the highest point is an imperceptible "peak" known as the Bois des Rièges, 4.5 metres (15 feet) above sea-level.

Many visitors confine their exploration to the main road (D570) that plunges across the region from Arles to the old coastal town of Les Saintes-Maries-de-la-Mer. While this prevents them from appreciating most of the area's natural habitats, it also serves as a form of protection for the Camargue's abundant wildlife. For while the Camargue attracts tens of thousands of tourists each year, it remains essentially unvisited and unknown. At first sight it reveals nothing of itself: almost everywhere tall, bamboo-like reeds, growing from roadside drainage ditches, act as a curtain drawn across the vista. For a while you sense rather than see the throbbing wildlife that thrives behind this veil.

The Camargue is one of Europe's major wetland regions, with extensive areas of marsh and shallow lakes (*étangs*) providing over much of its surface an unusually salty environment and a haven for wildfowl and sea birds. It is also a major tourist destination, appealing to a dizzying variety of interests. Hundreds of binocular-toting naturalists and birdlovers stalk about the edges of the national reserve, while scores of hunters come here as well—for outside the central protected zone hunting is legal and extremely popular. Other tourists, rid-

ing the native white horses, take guided tours of the Camargue's flat landscapes; tour buses pour into the area on daily excursions; while even larger numbers of people situate themselves on the beach at Les Saintes-Maries-de-la-Mer. Despite all this it's easy enough to escape the crowds. Long, straight backroads and tracks delve deep into the flat, almost eerie, emptiness of this strange land.

The region has a distinctive character. The famous white horses, though nearly all privately owned and branded, are left to live as wild, but don't imagine proud, snow-white herds galloping exuberantly across the salty plains. The horses are small, docile and cautious, and only acquire their handsome white coat when five to seven years old. Even more wary of humans are the herds of *bouvines*, or native black bulls; they, too, live as if completely wild, but are periodically rounded up to perform in bullfights. It was Napoléon III's Spanish wife Empress Eugénie who popularized the idea of the fighting bull. The bullfights of Languedoc and the Camargue, called *courses à la cocarde*, involve trying to pluck coloured ribbons from the animal's horns. For Spanish-style bullfights, also popular here, larger bulls are imported from Spain.

Such local traditions and customs are part of the Camargue's appeal. The herds, whether of bulls or horses, are called *manades*, the ranchers are *manadiers* and the men—Camarguais "cowboys" whose work revolves around herding, branding and keeping an eye on the animals—are known as *gardians*. Traditional *gardian* dwellings, or *cabanes*, dot the landscape: long, low, whitewashed houses, with a cross raised at one end of the roof. But perhaps best known of all the Camargue's attractions is its gypsy population. Swarthy black-haired gypsies—the women clothed in vivid, multicoloured long skirts and adorned with gaudy gilt bangles and bracelets—proliferate in and around the picturesque, though commercialized, lanes of Les Saintes-Maries-de-la-Mer.

In many ways the Camargue is not an ideal area to visit. It's too windy in winter, too shadelessly hot and sunny in summer.

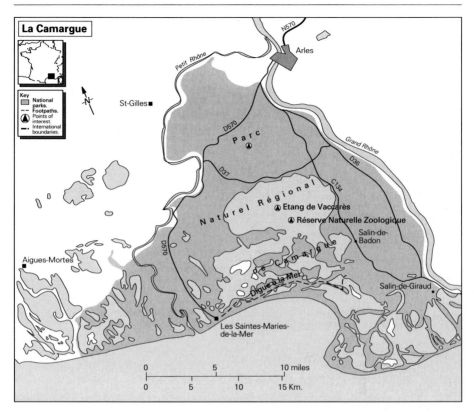

The worst of its disadvantages, especially in summer, is the incredible abundance of mosquitoes, flies, horseflies and other irritating insects. The only really enjoyable time to visit is spring—from say March to mid-May—when tourists and insects are both relatively sparse, temperatures are pleasant, and colourful wildflowers abound in the drying marshes, wild irises adorning the freshwater marshes and ditches.

Certainly it is in wild flora and fauna that the Camargue excels. To experience the wildlife properly, it is essential to get away from the main Arles–Saintes-Maries road (D570). Take any back road, the smaller and narrower the better, really to sense the strange loneliness and stillness that is the very essence of the Camargue. The land is peaceful, but not quiet, for there is an enormous variety of birdsong.

In the past, one of the Camargue's most important features was that seawater extended far inland, mixing with the silt-laden freshwater of the river. Since the late 19th century, however, large tracts of the region have lost their salty character due to construction of a dyke to keep the seawater out, the drainage and reclamation of vast spaces, and the expansion of rice cultivation in the northern Camargue. Nevertheless, the area is still home to numerous bird and animal species.

In the northern part of the Camargue, closest to Arles and St-Gilles, completely drained areas harbour cereal and vegetable crops, while the rice paddies are small, submerged "fields" within high banks. Heading farther south, you find wider areas of flat, uncultivated, marshy terrain. Some is freshwater, and some saline to varying degrees; the unsalty areas are often thronged with poppies and other wild-

The Camargue is famous for wild horses (overleaf).

197

The bulls of the Camargue are fairly small, very robust and capable of living on poor pasture.

flowers in spring. But the most common Camarguais terrain is *sansouire*, formed by saltwater submersion every winter. Here birdlife is profuse: squacco, purple and night heron, marsh harrier, little egret, glossy ibis, coot, bittern, great crested grebe and many other marsh birds are regularly sighted. The night air resounds with the grunting and croaking of frogs and toads.

Another common terrain, the Camargue *pelouses*, are almost-dry expanses of sparse, low vegetation adapted to a salty soil that is not submerged. These areas, dotted with tamarisk and inhabited by wandering bulls and horses, are the haunt of a thrilling variety of birds. In addition to larks and an occasional rare stone curlew, pratincole, bee-eaters and rollers can be sighted.

Everywhere, between fields, beside roads, the land is criss-crossed by drainage channels. Both insects and birds thrive near these ditches, which are several feet wide, sometimes brim-full, extremely soupy and crowded with plantlife and fish. Along them grows a kind of tall, bamboo-like reed (*Arundo donan*), used throughout the region for fences and shed roofs. Water

channels too deep for these reeds support masses of pondweed and water milfoil, and the coypu, a remarkably successful foreign immigrant, is well established among the reedy vegetation. The native otter, becoming rarer and rarer, struggles to survive.

Central southern Camargue—largely taken up by the huge (6,500-hectare/16,600-acre) Etang de Vaccarès—has been designated as a natural zoological and botanical reserve. All development is prohibited and access is restricted. The backroads take you to the *étang* which can be seen from various points on D37 (on the north side) and C134 (on the east). Herring gulls and blackheaded gulls number here in their thousands, and far out in the lake are numerous wading birds, especially huge crowds of pink flamingo. Herons are plentiful, too—all eight western European species, including the rare spoonbill, nest here—while avocets, with their distinctively curved beaks, may also be sighted. Come early in the morning to avoid the cars and buses which stop and disgorge on to the lakeside, leaving their engines running and driving away all signs of the wildlife the tourists have come to see. Around the western and southern edges of the *étang*, footpaths—especially the walkway along the sea dyke—provide much better access.

200

BEFORE YOU GO
Maps: Michelin 1:200,000 No. 83; IGN 1:100,000 No. 66, 1:50,000 No. 303.

GETTING THERE
By air: airports at Montepllier and Marseille give good access to the Camargue on international and internal flights.

By car: head straight down the Rhône valley either on N7 (left bank), the busier N86 (right bank) or the A7. Beyond Avignon, a variety of minor roads continue to Arles and the Camargue.

By rail: there are fast and frequent train services to Avignon and Nîmes, including TGVs direct from Paris, and Motorail services. Nîmes can also be reached on *Le Cévenol*, a train from Paris via the Massif Central—a longer but more scenic ride; change at Nîmes or Tarascon to reach Arles.

WHERE TO STAY
In and around Les Stes-Maries-de-la-Mer is a lot of over-priced and pretentious accommodation, but the town is well situated for an early-morning visit to the *étangs*. A more realistic base is Arles; try the modest Calendal (22 pl Pomme, T:90 96 11 89) or St-Trophime (16 rue Calade, T:90 96 88 38). Nîmes is farther afield, but well within reach.

ACTIVITIES
Bullfights: gaudy posters in Arles and Les Stes-Maries-de-la-Mer give information about forthcoming bullfights, which are held frequently in summer.

Exhibitions: the information centre of the *réserve naturelle* at La Capellière (rte C134; open Mon–Sat 9–12 and 2–5) has a permanent exhibition illustrating the Camargue season by season.

Riding: Domaine de Méjanes (T:90 97 10 51) and several other Camargue ranches and activity centres offer riding holidays; enquire at tourist offices. For organized excursions contact Association Régionale du Tourisme Equestre, Eygalières, T:90 95 90 57.

Walking: Arles tourist office has information on marked walks. The 7-km (5-mile) footway along the Digue de la Mer—the sea dyke from Les Stes-Maries to the Gacholle lighthouse—gives the best views into the *réserve naturelle*.

Watersports: at Les Stes-Maries-de-la-Mer; enquire at tourist office.

FURTHER INFORMATION
Tourist information: Arles, esplanade des Lices, T:90 96 29 35; Les Stes-Maries-de-la-Mer, 1 av de la Plage, T:42 97 83 67. Also Aigues-Mortes, cloître des Capucins, pl St-Louis, T:66 51 95 00; and Nîmes, 6 rue Auguste, T:66 67 29 11.

For wildlife information the best place is the Centre d'Information Nature beside the eastern side of the Etang de Vaccarès at La Capellière, T:90 97 00 97. Or try the main headquarters of the *parc régional*: Mas du Pont de Rousty, on D570, T:90 97 10 93, or Pont de Gau (Etang de Ginès), Les Saintes-Maries-de-la-Mer, T:90 97 86 32.

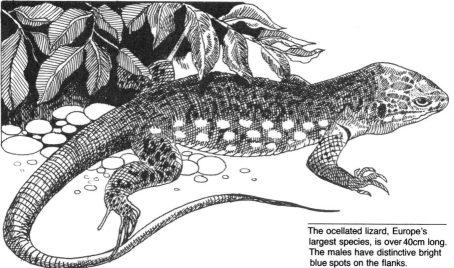

The ocellated lizard, Europe's largest species, is over 40cm long. The males have distinctive bright blue spots on the flanks.

La Crau

A semi-arid desert of stones northeast of the Camargue; one of Europe's most important breeding sites for rare birds

La Crau can hardly be called scenic. Totally flat and waterless, it consists of an immense sea of stones lying on top of a bone-dry silt. Not a single tree relieves the relentless monotony. It is a daunting sight, especially in the burning heat and blinding light of the baking southern sun. Anyone who loves silence and wilderness should come here just to feel the strange atmosphere of this empty expanse. But like many other deserts, La Crau is not as barren as it looks; it has recently been designated the second most important conservation area for rare breeding birds in Europe. The originality of La Crau's wildlife makes it an important

202

outpost of semi-arid Mediterranean steppe, and its conservation is top priority.

Lying northeast of the Camargue and stretching from Salon-de-Provence almost to Arles, then down to Fos on the coast, this curious terrain has become unique in France. In the Middle Ages, far more of the southern French landscape looked like this. Even as recently as the 19th century, La Crau was much larger and more arid. The area was originally formed in prehistoric times, when it was the estuary of the rushing torrent of the Durance, still a turbulent and capricious river, but which abandoned this part of its course and moved farther upstream to join the Rhône. Though the stony landscape it left behind is ecologically important, it has little or no visual charm and offers no facilities. It is also difficult to penetrate, and is therefore little troubled by visitors.

Nevertheless, it is gradually disappearing. Already two-thirds of La Crau is cultivated, and visitors will be astonished by the green

Tall reed grasses are common in the ditches that line the roads and paths of the Camargue.

meadows, olive groves and fields of cereal which enterprising farmers have planted at its edges. In the uncultivated parts, sheep are free to roam, though they find but poor pasture. Only the centre of the area remains largely untouched.

Yet even the sun-baked heart of La Crau harbours a surprising amount of life. Scattered and close-cropped scrubby vegetation emerges from between the stones, and there are tough little thorny bushes of several types, including wild rose, which lends an occasional flash of remarkable beauty. This type of scenery, marked by rough, sparse scrub and stones, is known locally as *coussous*.

On the ground, living among this meagre plantlife, is a large population of insects, including locusts and curious large, wingless crickets (*Prionotopis rhodanica*) moving awkwardly among the stones. Lizards

thrive on the abundant insects. This is one of the principal French strongholds of the large ocellated lizard. Both insects and lizards make it possible for so many birds to find enough to eat in an otherwise unpromising habitat. But where on earth, you might wonder, do they nest in this featureless environment? Sheep pens and old cairns installed during World War II to prevent Allied gliders from landing, together with random piles of stones, apparently provide acceptable nesting sites in the absence of anything better.

The roller, a beautiful, golden-brown bird with a head of almost iridescent turquoise, is merely a day-tripper to La Crau, preferring to nest in the poplars at the perimeter, but ventures into the desert to pick over the stones for food. Even in the midst of the most unfertile-looking parts, there are larks merrily singing. Both Calandra and short-toed larks, together with stone curlew and little bustard, manage to survive here, although La Crau's great

The ancient village of Les Baux, carved into the limestone rock of Les Alpilles, stands sentinel over the dry plains of La Crau.

bustard has recently been hunted to extinction. Black kite are common, too, and there are also a few pairs of red kite. Birdwatchers will appreciate the chance to see a lesser kestrel scanning the ground; the species is not found anywhere else in France.

Another wonderful sight, much more frequent, is of

The distinctive hoopoe is common throughout the Mediterranean.

groups of hoopoe, with lovely crest and black-and-white striped feathers, loping along in their low, undulating flight. And the modest little pintailed sand-grouse chooses this area as its exclusive French nesting site. Spring is the best time to visit, for it is then that the sand-grouse and little bustards are displaying. At other times they are difficult to spot, naturally camouflaged in the hot, stony expanses.

Before you go *Maps:* IGN 1:100,000 No. 66.

Getting there *By road:* N113, from Arles to Salon-de-Provence, is the main road which passes through the village of St-Martin-de-Crau and skirts northern La Crau. A turning to the south, N568, cuts across the southern part. *By rail:* the line from Arles to Miramas gives a good view of the area.

Where to stay: Arles, about 20km (12 miles) away, is the obvious base; see the Camargue section for hotel recommendations. There are a few small inexpensive hotels in the village of St-Martin-de-Crau; try Auberge des Epis, T:90 47 31 17.

Further information *Tourist*
204

information: Arles, esplanade des Lices, T:90 96 29 35; Les Baux-de-Provence, Hôtel de Manville, T:90 97 34 39.

The SNPN at La Capellière (T:90 97 00 97) has material on the wildlife of La Crau.

The Ecomusée de la Crau, near the church at St-Martin-de-Crau, organizes guided tours of the *coussous*.

Les Alpilles

An isolated ridge of craggy limestone crests lying east of the Rhône

Les Alpilles present an extraordinary, beautiful and sometimes disturbing landscape of white rocks weatherworn to bizarre shapes. In truth, both historically and scenically they belong in Provence, and are not part of Languedoc at all; yet their proximity to the Rhône and to the Camargue earns them a place in this chapter. Although the Alpilles chain covers just a small area, it is a captivating and enchanted miniature world which feels lost in time and remote from anywhere.

The entire chain is a narrow strip barely 20km by 4km (12 by 2½ miles) in size, which emerges abruptly from the flat country in the angle between the rivers Durance and Rhône. It rises in a series of hills to central summits of about 400m (1,300ft). In places these hills are barren, in places planted with olive groves, almond, cypress, fruit trees and vineyards, and elsewhere very densely cloaked with wild evergreen Mediterranean vegetation. Typical *garrigue* plants —

especially the kermes oak with its prickly leaves, broom and the local gorse *ajonc de Provence* with its bright yellow pea-like flowers — abound, but pines, too, are abundant, and the air is fragrant with the warm tang of their resin.

The secret to visiting Les Alpilles is to travel the chain (that is, east–west) rather than across (north–south). Drivers and cyclists can discover the area at a sauntering pace on enticing minor roads that thread between fields and forest. My own favourite route is the relatively traffic-free journey along the country lanes from Maussane to Eygalières.

By far the best way to explore Les Alpilles, however, is on foot. Warm, dusty paths criss-cross a peaceful, ever-changing terrain, and the air is alive with the creaky scratchings of insects and the aromatic scent of pine and wild herbs.

The Alpilles are populated with picturesque, characteristically southern villages, and there are several interesting Roman and medieval sites worth seeing. "Capital" of these hills is the lofty fortified town of Les Baux-de-Provence, commanding a superb panorama of the rocky landscape. It has, to its detriment, become a major tourist attraction; all roads to Les Baux from either side of the hills should be avoided during peak holiday weekends. The older, ruined section of town offers excellent views of the landscape. A narrow road climbs from D5 to the summit of La Caume (387m/1,270ft).

Raptors soar above these hills, including Bonelli's eagle and even the spectacular Egyptian vulture.

Before you go *Maps:* IGN 1:100,000 No. 66.

Getting there *By car:* the Alpilles—or at least D5 and D27, the 2 roads that make their way to Les Baux—are almost too easily accessible by car, being just a short drive from Arles (20km/12 miles on D17), Avignon (20km/12 miles on D571) and Nîmes (40km/24 miles on D999). *By rail:* travel by rail to Arles station, where bikes and cars can be rented. *On foot:* by far the best, if the most strenuous, access is the GR6 footpath, which runs laterally all the way across the hills.

Where to stay: this is an area of predominately up-market accommodation, concentrated around Les Baux, Maussane, Eygalières and St-Rémy-de-Provence. Cheaper rooms can be found most readily in St-Rémy, just north of the hills; try the Acacia (T:90 92 13 43), Arts (T:90 92 08 50) or Cheval Blanc (T:90 92 09 28).

Activities *Riding:* for information on organized excursions contact the Association Régionale du Tourisme Equestre, Eygalières, T:90 95 90 57.

Walking: GR6 long-distance path.

Ruins: the ruins of Glanum are the remnants of a Celtic, Greek and then Roman town, which stood just south of today's St-Rémy.

Close to Glanum, off D5, is the C12th priory of St-Paul-de-Mausole, which housed the insane asylum where Van Gogh was a patient.

Further information *Tourist information:* Les Baux-de-Provence, Hôtel de Manville, T:90 97 34 39.

The Coastal Etangs

A string of large, shallow, saline lagoons lying just behind the coast and separated from the sea by a narrow ribbon of sand

The Languedoc coastline extends in a single sandy sweep from the Camargue to the Pyrenees—200 kilometres (125 miles) almost unbroken, except by the rocky outcrops at Agde. This spectacular beach shallows into the warm Mediterranean under skies kept clear and blue by the refreshing *Tramontane* and *Mistral* offshore winds. Looking inland, almost nothing can be seen except grassy dunes and a vast, open sky.

There is astonishingly little development along most of the Languedoc seashore. For long stretches the beach is almost completely deserted, has no facilities at all, and is wonderfully free of the usual cafés, pedalboats and surfboard rentals. In places there are new resort towns, as well as a few older harbour towns with more character, while on the edges of these built-up districts are large campsites.

The most striking feature of the Languedoc seashore is the long, narrow sand barrier running for much of its length. Behind this lie shallow, more-or-less saline, lagoons—or *étangs*—connected to the sea by narrow channels (*graus*). While human visitors stick to the sandy beach, from spring to autumn the *étangs* host an astonishing range of shore and passage birds.

Etangs vary enormously in character. Some are unsavoury, malodorous, highly saline and coated with algae; others are cleaner and fresher, with attractive shorelines and navigable footpaths or tracks. Their history is an interesting one. These distinctive Languedoc waters, rarely more than a metre (three feet) in depth, are separated from the sea by sand bars (*barres* or *lidos*), which have been created by natural Rhône alluvium and sand deposits, mainly since the Roman period.

Between the volcanic, rocky outcrops of Agde and the intriguing Montagne de la Clape (near Narbonne), few *étangs* were formed, as this stretch of coast has been more affected by the estuaries of three of Languedoc's larger rivers—the Hérault, Orb and Aude. These rare *garrigue*-covered coastal uplands offer a foretaste of the vegetation of the Languedoc interior. From Sète to the Rhône, the lagoons are particularly shallow, while south of Sète the *bassins* of Thau and Leucate are deeper, although there are also smaller, shallow *étangs* nearer Roussillon. For many centuries the *étangs* made the seashore an insalubrious environment, largely shunned by man but favoured by myriad insects and birds. Chief among the insects was the unpopular mosquito, which multiplied in huge numbers in the stagnant waters. Today, spraying keeps their numbers down.

The coastal lagoons provide a haven for all sorts of divers, waders and sea birds. Large numbers of gulls squeal and turn above the water, sharing the rich plunder of insects and water creatures with terns, crakes, moorhens, bald coots, stilts, avocets and ducks. The air is filled with numerous small flying beetles and other insects, while the water itself harbours their larvae, together with annelides, leeches, tadpoles, young fish and molluscs, all providing the birds with ample nourishment.

Among the most striking of all the lagoon birds are the pink flamingos and herons. Surprisingly good views are possible from roads passing close to the *étangs*, or by approaching on foot over a shoreline thickly banked with saltworts, marsh samphires and small succulents, which form virtual cushions of vegetation.

Etang de Mauguio, lying north of the busy main road from La Grande-Motte to Carnon, is a particularly good spot to see flamingos, although it is in every other way among the least pleasant of the *étangs*, being highly saline and very marshy in places. Maybe this is why the birds remain here so tranquilly. A much more agreeable spot is the inland village of Villeneuve-lès-Maguelonne (near Palavas), from which small backroads lead down through the vines to the pretty edges of *étangs* of l'Arnel, Moures and Vic.

Right behind Villeneuve is Etang de l'Estagnol, a small, freshwater marsh area designated a nature reserve. Its dense rushes harbour duck and coot nests. Etang d'Ingril, east of Frontignan, best seen from D60 on the south side, and accessible by

The Etang de Vaccarès, is the largest expanse of open water in the Camargue, and is noted for its huge numbers of wildfowl.

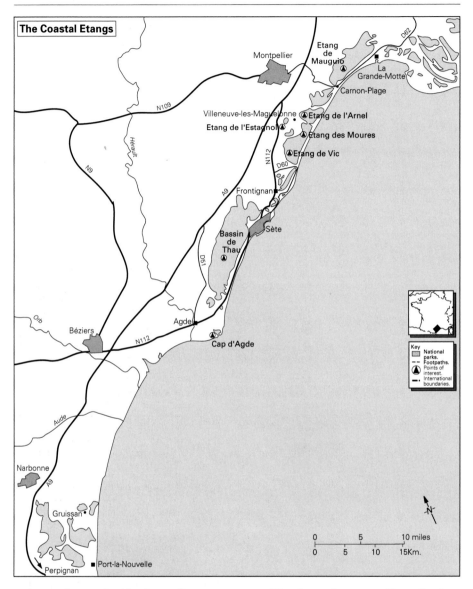

The Coastal Etangs

paths on the north side, is another more marshy area with abundant populations of most of Languedoc's coastal birds and plants.

Largest and deepest of the *étangs* is the Bassin de Thau, a 65-square-kilometre (26-square-mile) lake between the upland ridges of Sète and Agde. Its waters are relatively clear and clean, with large tracts

near Sète devoted to oyster "farms", where hundreds of wooden poles rise up out of the water. On the less interesting southern side, a road runs along the 20-kilometre (12-mile) strip of sand bar separating the *étang* from a fine sandy beach. On the inland side there's a picturesque little port, Mèze, with a small, sandy beach, but other parts of the *étang* are wild and marshy.

BEFORE YOU GO
Maps: Michelin 1:200,000
Nos. 83 and 86. IGN
1:100,000 Nos. 65 and 72.

GETTING THERE
By air: there are international
and internal flights direct to
Montpellier and Perpignan.
By car: the Languedoc coast
and *étangs* are extremely
accessible by car, although
there is no coast road as such.
N112, N113 and N9 cross the
inland plain parallel to the
coast, with numerous turns on
minor roads down to the
étangs.
By rail: a fast and frequent
service runs parallel to the
coast, from Nîmes to
Perpignan.

WHERE TO STAY
Hotels on the coast tend to be
relatively expensive, but there
are exceptions as well as
hundreds of low-priced
campsites. Modern La
Grande-Motte and Cap
d'Agde have plenty of both
kinds of accommodation. Sète
is an interesting and appealing
base; the Grand Hôtel
(T:67 74 71 77) has rooms in a
wide range of prices.

ACTIVITIES
The new resorts, especially
Agde, La Grande-Motte and
Port-Barcarès, have facilities,
with tuition, for an abundance
of leisure pursuits—including
archery, diving, parascending,
riding, sailing, tennis and
windsurfing.

FURTHER INFORMATION
Tourist information: Agde,
rue L.-Bages, T:67 94 29 68;
Aigues-Mortes, cloître des
Capucins, pl St-Louis,
T:66 51 95 00); La Grande-
Motte, pl du 1er-Octobre,
T:67 56 62 62; Port-Barcarès,
on the seafront, T:68 86 16 56;
Sète, 22 quai d'Alger,
T:67 74 73 00.

Flamingos of the saline lagoons of the Camargue.

THE PINK FLAMINGO
By far the most evocative image of the *étangs* of
Camargue and the Languedoc coast is the exotic-looking
flamingo, which gathers in huge flocks in these shallow
waters. The average flamingo population here numbers
from 25,000 to 50,000 individuals. Day and night,
flamingos feed by trawling the bottom of the lagoons, with
their heads held almost completely upside down in search
of vegetation and crustaceans, which they filter out of the
silt. The bulk of their diet is small aquatic invertebrates,
and it's the high level of carotinoids in these tiny creatures
which gives the flamingo its distinctive colour.

During March and April, adults court with balletic
movement of wings, neck and head. Nesting takes place in
large groups, on islands. The nests themselves are raised
platforms of mud, generally about 30 centimetres (12
inches) high, with a hollow on top in which a single egg is
laid. The same nests endure and are used year after year,
the result of constant repairs and rebuilding.

The flamingo is a mainly summer visitor, wintering on
the Spanish coast or (more usually) in North Africa.
However, some pairs do not migrate in autumn; an
estimated 5,000 birds overwinter in the Camargue.

Roussillon

*The eastern Pyrenees where they
descend into the Mediterranean*

As visitors travel south towards Spain through the vineyards and plain of ancient Languedoc, they pass the massive brick defences of the Fort de Salses to enter the land known as Roussillon. Initially the ruddy, sun-bathed coastal lowland seems very like the landscape of Languedoc, though flatter and less fertile. But soon the peaks of the Pyrenees come into view, and the dramatic contrast between the two regions is apparent. High slopes and summits dominate Roussillon's inland horizons while, closer to the coast, green foothills climb into a calmer, wilder, wooded countryside.

Contained entirely within the Pyrénées-Orientales *département* on the Spanish border, the Roussillon region boasts the highest sunshine totals in France. Most of the inhabitants speak Catalan, many as a first language. For Catalans, the name Roussillon applies correctly only to the coastal plain around Perpignan (see Chapter 6, The Pyrenees). South and west of the city the land rises into a magnificent terrain of high ranges separated by broad basins and fertile valleys. The valleys of the rivers Têt and Tech, descending to the balmy coastal plain, are intensively cultivated with lush market gardens and orchards that supply the country with much of its early fresh fruit and winter vegetables. Only close to the coast does the blanket of vineyards reappear.

Along the Spanish frontier, close to the Mediterranean, the Albères hills are perhaps the most pleasing part of French Catalonia, not only visually, but also culturally and even gastronomically. The

The vineyards of the Roussillon plain provide a rich spectrum of autumnal tints contrasting with the drab backdrop of the *garrigue*-covered foothills.

Albères have a cover of *garrigue*, and evergreen forest with dense holm oak and abundant rock-rose and broom, broken up by steep vineyards yielding fine red Côtes de Roussillon wines.

Following the hills inland, the lofty Pic du Canigou (2,784 metres/9,130 feet) comes into sight. Catalans hold this mountain in almost religious regard, and many foreigners have been deeply impressed by it too: Hilaire Belloc described it as "the mountain which many who have never heard the name have been looking for all their lives". Its conical summit stands rocky and spectacular, sometimes shrouded in cloud, soaring far above a tangled landscape of forest and pasture. The view from the top stretches clear across Languedoc and Roussillon to the Cévennes.

The vegetation on the mountain slopes is completely different according to whether it faces north or south. *A la baga*, as locals say ("on the shady side"), pine and fir woods are broken by open pasture. *A la soulane* ("on the sunny side"), the woods are predominantly beech. Crisply cool lakes, enclosed by rushes, cotton grass and sedges, abound. Much more striking are Roussillon's sheltered valleys and open meadows. These large tracts are noted for amazingly luxuriant and colourful meadows of flowers. They can be quite dazzling, with great masses of buttercups and daisies mixed together with gentians, lilies and lupins, while underfoot lies a thick mat of fragrant thyme.

On the lower slopes and on the Roussillon plain, wildlife follows the Languedoc pattern. But towards the higher altitudes there's a chance of seeing—if you're very lucky—a rare golden eagle soaring, a family of *sanglier*, wild boar, pushing through the undergrowth, a genet after dusk, marmot, small groups of izard (the Pyrenean version of the chamois), or a herd of mouflon (the wild forerunner of today's sheep) nervously grazing on a distant slope.

Down on the rocky coast the cliffs are draped with sea fennel, thrift and sea clover. Close to the Spanish border, several scattered colonies of Hermann's tortoise are said to endure, but these have all but vanished because of forest fires and other habitat fragmentation. The area's most distinctive fauna is concealed beneath the waves, however. Most of the coast between Banyuls and Cerbère—from Ile Grosse to Cap Peyrefite—has been designated an aquatic nature reserve and shelters a profusion of warm-water molluscs and corals.

BEFORE YOU GO
Maps: Michelin 1:200,000 No. 86; IGN 1:100,000 No. 72, 1:50,000 Nos. 10 and 11.

GETTING THERE
By air: there are direct flights to Perpignan from provincial French airports and the UK. **By car:** Perpignan is easily reached via N9 and A9 from all points north. From Perpignan 3 main highways penetrate the rest of the region: N114, N116 and D115. **By rail:** frequent main-line trains link Perpignan with

The natural genet has spread throughout France, being particularly numerous in the south-west.

Paris via the Rhône valley. The line continues south through all the towns of the Roussillon coast to Spain. *Le petit train jaune* takes a scenic route up the Tet valley from Perpignan high into the Pyrenees to La Tour-du-Carol.

WHERE TO STAY

The best hotel in Perpignan is the Park (18 blvd J.-Bourrat, T:68 35 14 14); prices are surprisingly moderate and the restaurant is excellent. There are hotels and campsites at Canet, Argelès, Collioure and Banyuls. At Collioure, try the quayside Les Templiers (T:68 82 05 58).

ACTIVITIES

Walking: GR10 and GR36 are the main long-distance footpaths, climbing up from the Roussillon lowlands into the high Pyrenees. There are several shorter footpaths in the Roussillon hills, with several routes up from the Têt valley to the top of the Canigou massif.
Skiing: the higher Roussillon Pyrenees have some unpretentious downhill and cross-country ski centres. Contact the Confédération de la Neige Catalane, Maison du Tourisme, Font-Romeu, T:68 30 02 74.
Skindiving: dive with local club members at Collioure (T:68 82 06 34), Argelès (T:68 81 16 33) and Banyuls (T:68 38 31 66).

FURTHER INFORMATION

Tourist information:
Perpignan's Maison du Tourisme in quai De-Lattre-de-Tassigny (T:68 34 29 94) is well equipped with information about the whole region.

FURTHER READING

Hilaire Belloc, *The Pyrenees* (1909).

MAQUIS AND GARRIGUE

People visiting southern France for the first time will be immediately struck by the dramatic difference between the vegetation of the more temperate northern areas and that of the Mediterranean region. The most characteristic of the naturally growing Mediterranean trees are the evergreen oak and the Aleppo pine. The most common cultivated trees are olive, fig and carob.

Maquis is the name given to the impenetrably dense, rugged evergreen forest and shrubland that covers the region's low, rocky terrain. Principal shrubs include the kermes, holm and cork oaks, the arbutus (strawberry tree) and prickly juniper. Typical *maquis* undergrowth ranges from two to three metres (six to ten feet) in height, with some trees rising to four or five metres (13 to 16 feet). However, true *maquis* has nearly everywhere been replaced by a lower-growing heath and forest which naturalists often refer to as secondary *maquis*. Here trees are generally more scattered and stunted, and bushes and herbs proliferate.

While climate is the overriding influence in the Mediterranean landscape, man's intervention has had a major effect on the region's vegetation. Once fire or deforestation has removed the dense woodland or *maquis*, a more varied community of wild shrubs and flowers can flourish. In areas where the soil has eroded as a result of repeated fires, or where it is naturally shallow and rocky, this more open vegetation becomes fully established as *garrigue*. *Garrigue* is also dominated by tough, tangled, prickly evergreen shrubs such as the kermes and holm oaks. But, interestingly enough, the wild forms of many plant species cultivated in many gardens also grow here: in addition to cistus (rock-rose), juniper and arbutus, plants such as box, flowering viburnum, lentisk and terebinth (turpentine tree), their branches entangled with clematis and honeysuckle vines, thrive in the *garrigue*.

Beneath the taller shrubs pushes a thick undergrowth of thistles, myrtle, fragrant rosemary flourishing as small bushes, and larger bushes of several types of gorse and broom. Occasionally there are small woods and copses of parasol and Aleppo pines, their resin smelling sharply in the hot air.

The single most outstanding feature, however, is the thick carpet of aromatic wild herbs. These include many varieties of thyme, savory, lavender and mint, together with rosemary, garlic and sage. In the Languedoc wilderness, powerful sweet and spicy aromas prevail, and the sense of smell can be as affecting and satisfying as the sense of sight. Wild plants release enticing fragrances at every step.

The *garrigue* type of vegetation bursts out wherever land is not in use, even in small borders between vineyards, or along roadsides, and larger areas of land which can not be cultivated economically are given over entirely to *garrigue*.

USEFUL ADDRESSES

The following organizations provide useful information and assistance for those interested in exploring Wild France and in learning about its flora and fauna. Several of them are mentioned throughout this book, often in abbreviated form.

Amis de la Terre, 72 rue de Château d'Eau, 75010 Paris.

Centre Information Montagne et Sentiers, 7 rue Voltaire, Grenoble.

Club Alpin Français, 9 rue La Boétie, Paris.

Le Conseil Supérieur de la Pêche, 135 av. Malakoff, Paris.

Fédération Française de Cyclotourisme, 8 rue Jean-Marie Jego, Paris.

Fédération Française d'Equitation, 15 rue de Bruxelles, Paris.

Fédération Française de Spéléologie, 130 rue St-Maur, Paris.

Mouvement National de lutte pour l'Environnement, 3 square Watteau, 78830 Fontenay-le-Fleury.

Randonnées Pyrénéennes, 4 rue de Villefranche, St. Girons.

Union Nationale des Associations Ornithologiques (IREPA), Maison Innovation, 2 rue Brûlée, 67000 Strasbourg.

Union Nationale des Centres Sportifs de Plein Air (UCPA), 62 rue de la Glacière, Paris.

Fédération Sportive des Grands Randonneurs (FSGR), 175 rue Blomet, 75015, Paris.

Comité National des Sentiers de Grande Randonnée (CNSGR), 8 av Marceau, 75008, Paris.

FURTHER READING

Guide de la nature en France; (Bordas Paris 1979).

Guide des réserves naturelles de France; A. Reille, Ch. Bonnin Luquot (Delachaux & Niestlé, Paris, 1987).

Où voir les oiseaux en France; Ligue française pour la protection des oiseaux (Nathan, Paris 1989).

France Verte, Claude Marie Vadrot (Editions du May Paris 1987).

Atlas des oiseaux nicheurs de France; Laurent Yeatman (Ministère de la Qualité de la Vie et Société Ornithologique de France (Paris, 1976).

Atlas de Répartition des Amphibiens et Reptiles de France, Société Herpétologique Française (Paris, 1989).

Flowers of the Mediterranean, O Polunin and A Huxley, Chatto and Windus (London 1981).

Flowers of Europe; A field guide. O Polunin, Oxford University Press 1969).

A Guide to the Vegetation of Britain and Europe. O Polunin and M Walters (Oxford University Press 1985).

Important Bird Areas of Europe, International Council for Bird Preservation Technical Publication No 9 (ICBP Cambridge 1989).

La Tortue, Bernard Devaux, Sang de la Terre (Paris 1988).

La Loutre, Christian Bouchardy, Sang de la Terre (Paris 1986).

Conservation of European Reptiles, and Amphibians, Keith Corbett (Ed) (Christopher Helm, London, 1989).

INDEX

PICTURE CREDITS

Front Cover – C. Waite, Landscape Only.
10/11 – C. Guy, Campagne Campagne. 19 –
J. Cornish, Landscape Only. 22 – Stephanie
Pain. 23 – A. Clech, Campagne Campagne.
26/27 – C. Baudu, Campagne Campagne.
30/31 – H. Ouitlier, Campagne Campagne.
38 – A. Chartier, Campagne Campagne. 39
– P. Clatot, Campagne Campagne. 42/43 –
Michael Busselle. 46/47 – A. Dagbert,
Campagne Campagne. 50/51 – Meissonier,
Campagne Campagne. 54/55 – E. Merlen,
Campagne Campagne. 62/63, 66 – A.
Chartier, Campagne Campagne. 67 – F.
Puyplat, Campagne Campagne. 70/71, 74/75
– A. Chartier, Campagne Campagne. 78/79,
83 – Michael Busselle. 86 – C. Guy,
Campagne Campagne. 87 – G. Christian,
Campagne Campagne. 91, 94/95, 98/99 –
Michael Busselle. 103 – C. Siret, Campagne
Campagne. 106 – T. Lamoureux, Campagne
Campagne. 107 – Michael Busselle. 110 – J.
P. Fagard, Campagne Campagne. 111 – J.
F. Girardel, Campagne Campagne. 114/115
– Michael Busselle. 118/119 – A. Chartier,
Campagne Campagne. 123 – C. Waite,
Landscape Only. 126/127 – A. Chartier,
Campagne Campagne. 130/131 –
Christophe, Campagne Campagne. 135 – J.
Y. Uguet, Campagne Campagne. 138/139 –
Gemo, Campagne Campagne. 142/143 – M.
Mouchy, Campagne Campagne. 147 – G.
Rabiller, Campagne Campagne. 150/151 –
F. Puyplat, Campagne Campagne. 154 –
Keith Spence. 159, 162/163 – A. Chartier,
Campagne Campagne. 167 – J. Cornish,
Landscape Only. 170/171, 175 – David
Stubbs. 178/179 – Michael Busselle. 182 – C.
Waite, Landscape Only. 183 – A. Chartier,
Campagne Campagne. 186 – A.G.E.
FotoStock. 187 – Archie Miles. 190/191 – C.
Rouvet, Campagne Campagne. 195 – C.
Rivoire, Campagne Campagne. 198/199 – K.
Graber, Campagne Campagne. 202 – C.
Guy, Campagne Campagne. 203 – David
Stubbs. 206/207, 210/211 – C. Rouvet,
Campagne Campagne.

ACKNOWLEDGEMENTS

The contributors and editors wish to extend
their grateful thanks to the following people
for their assistance:
Dr. Jean–Christophe Balouet, David Black,
Roger Boulanger, Brittany Ferries, Bernard
Devaux, Gerry Dunham, Pauline Hallam of
the French Government Tourist Office,
John Harrison, Judith Harte, Richard
Jones, Jillian Luff, Neville Morgan, Peter
Mills of the French Railways, Susan
Mitchell, Stephanie Pain, Mme. Martine
Renouard, Nina Shandloff, Penny Spence.